FOOD AID

FOOD AID

FOOD AID

*The Challenge and
the Opportunity*

Hans Singer
John Wood
Tony Jennings

CLARENDON PRESS · OXFORD
1987

Oxford University Press, Walton Street, Oxford OX2 6DP

Oxford New York Toronto
Delhi Bombay Calcutta Madras Karachi
Petaling Jaya Singapore Hong Kong Tokyo
Nairobi Dar es Salaam Cape Town
Melbourne Auckland
and associated companies in
Beirut Berlin Ibadan Nicosia

Oxford is a trade mark of Oxford University Press

Published in the United States
by Oxford University Press, New York

British Library Cataloguing in Publication Data
Singer, H. W.
Food aid: the challenge and the opportunity.
1. Economic assistance—Developing countries
I. Title   II. Wood, John, 1924–
III. Jennings, Anthony
338.91'1722'01724   HC60
ISBN 0–19–828519–1
ISBN 0–19–828518–3 Pbk

Library of Congress Cataloging in Publication Data
Singer, Hans Wolfgang, 1910–
Food aid.
Bibliography: p.
Includes index.
1. Food relief. 2. Agricultural assistance.
I. Wood, John B.   II. Jennings, Anthony, MA.   III. Title.
HV696.F6S55 1987   363.8'83   87–5523
ISBN 0–19–828519–1
ISBN 0–19–828518–3 (pbk.)

Set by Promenade Graphics Ltd.
Printed in Great Britain
at the University Printing House, Oxford
by David Stanford
Printer to the University

Foreword

Dianne Spearman

A little more than two years ago, images of widespread famine dominated our TV screens for the first time in a decade. Public reaction was prompt and generous. On both sides of the Atlantic, concerned citizens involved themselves in the funding, delivery, and distribution of food aid in an unprecedented way. In my own country, Canada, public donations outstripped sizeable government allocations for affected countries, and dozens of churches, schools, and organizations mirrored the humanitarian spirit of Bob Geldof and Band-Aid. *Food Aid: The Challenge and the Opportunity* makes a timely appearance during a period of heightened public interest in food aid as a humanitarian response to drought and civil strife.

Public support for food aid in crisis situations has not been matched by a general understanding of the contribution food aid can make to longer term solutions to world hunger. And yet donor countries direct more food aid to long-term developmental objectives than to emergencies. *Food Aid: The Challenge and the Opportunity* will make an important contribution to public awareness and debate by offering the general reader a balanced and comprehensive view of both food aid's developmental potential and its pitfalls. It stands out among recent publications on this subject in being thoughtful rather than polemical, by judging food aid on its own merits rather than portraying it as a second choice alternative to financial aid in the abstract, and by placing it in the context of long-term development assistance rather than famine relief.

Food aid has changed a great deal in the last decade. Once a mechanism for disposal of food surpluses, it is now increasingly considered by development specialists as a resource transfer to promote economic growth and enhance food security in recipient countries. Without demanding specialist knowledge of the reader,

Dianne Spearman is in charge of the Canadian food aid programme within the Canadian International Development Agency.

Professor Singer and Messrs. Wood and Jennings, all specialists in this field, share their views and experience on the use of food aid as a tool for development. In doing so, they draw not only upon academic analysis of development but also upon the practical insights gained as they and their colleagues at the Institute of Development Studies have offered guidance to decision-makers in food aid donor agencies.

One of the lasting contributions the authors and their colleagues have made is to shift debate away from fruitless discussion of whether or not food aid is 'good' aid, to a more sophisticated and analytical consideration of what it can achieve, in what circumstances, and what must be done to ensure that it is effective. Food aid is a resource which, like all others, can be used either well or unwisely. Much of this book explains for the general reader what is involved in using it well.

The effective use of food aid to address longstanding structural food problems can mean many different things. The proceeds from its sale in recipient countries may be used to invest in increased agricultural production, or food aid may provide direct assistance to the very poor who lack the income to buy the food needed to meet their nutritional requirements. In other cases, it may support policy reform or contribute to secure food supplies and stable prices. By showing the reader the various ways in which food aid can contribute to lasting food security, the authors have underlined its enormous developmental potential. By explaining that each type of food aid has its own requirements for effectiveness, they also reveal something of its complexity.

The obvious conclusion is that food aid must be carefully managed. The large and growing needs of developing countries for imported food mean that food aid will be an important component of development assistance for years to come, and it is essential that recipient countries derive maximum long-term benefit from such massive resource transfers. It is also important to heed the cautionary note of Chapter 11 concerning disincentive effects and the potential dangers of dependency.

Like other kinds of development assistance, food aid can have negative as well as positive results. But negative effects are by no means inevitable. This book provides concerned citizens and government decision-makers with an explanation of how potential problems may be avoided, so that food aid will not substitute for local production but rather stimulate agricultural growth while alleviating chronic hunger.

These are concerns which we in Canada hear constantly expressed by parliamentarians, the press, and the public. The same interest in the long-term impact of food aid is voiced in other donor countries. Continued public support for large food aid programmes will therefore depend on its development effectiveness. Food surpluses will not make the case for food aid. It will have to be clear that food aid is a good investment in future food security, a development transfer which is at least as efficient and effective as competing claims on limited development assistance budgets. Donor agencies will be called upon to demonstrate that food aid is not a disincentive to local farmers, that it supports and complements agricultural development activities, that it helps to prevent recurring 'emergencies', and that it assists and encourages recipient governments to invest in their rural areas and maintain policy frameworks which stimulate productivity.

Food Aid: The Challenge and the Opportunity shows clearly that food aid can make an important contribution to long-term food security in all of these ways. It explains what this means in practical terms and draws attention to the careful planning and management needed to realize its full developmental potential. Food aid will be with us through the rest of this century, and it will only be as effective as donors and recipients together choose to make it. This is the challenge and the opportunity.

Preface

The importance of the subject of our book needs no emphasis. Food aid, whether we like it or not, is with us—not only to stay but also very probably to increase. It is a vital element in the welfare and indeed the survival of many millions of people in the poorer countries of the world, particularly in Africa. It is also a very controversial subject: as has been said of other matters 'you cannot live with it and you cannot live without it'. I think most reasonable people would, however, agree that food aid, if improperly handled, can do more harm than good, and there are plenty of horror tales to testify to that. Yet equally, when properly handled food aid can do a great deal of good and can be a vital instrument of development—and there are plenty of success stories to testify to *that*. That at least is the line which we pursue here.

We hope this book will be useful to any reasonably educated person who wants to inform himself about such an important instrument of policy and development. At the same time we hope that, for the more academically-minded, this book may also be an introduction to, and a guide through, the formidable and quite exhaustive literature which has grown up around the subject.

All the three authors, in their various ways, are people who have had considerable administrative and field experience in handling and studying food aid in a variety of circumstances. This includes food aid given bilaterally on a national basis, multilaterally through UN organizations (particularly the UN World Food Programme in Rome) and through voluntary non-governmental organizations (NGOs). We hope these experiences are reflected in our book. It is hardly necessary to say that none of the organizations with which we are connected has any responsibility for the contents of this book. This responsibility is entirely ours.

The book was written at the Institute of Development Studies at the University of Sussex. This has been of great benefit to us since we were able to draw on the excellent library and other facilities of the Institute; in particular, we had the benefit of exchanges of views with other colleagues who have equally specialized on food aid questions. The existence of a food aid 'cluster' of economists

involved in food aid questions is indeed one of the features of the
IDS. Among the colleagues to whom we are thus indebted are E. J.
Clay, Tony Leeks, Simon Maxwell, and John Saunders. We are also
indebted to John Shaw of the World Food Programme. Once again
it is needless to say that none of the above should be held accoun-
table for any errors or omissions on our part.

We are also grateful to all those, at the IDS and elsewhere, who
helped with the typing and other preparation of the manuscript,
and to the Oxford University Press for their efficient editing and for
suggesting many improvements and amendments to our original
manuscript.

H. W. S.

J. B. W.

A. J.

Contents

Abbreviations

AFBF	American Farm Bureau Federation
CAP	Common Agricultural Policy (of the EEC)
CARE	Co-operative for American Remittance to Europe
	Co-operative for American Relief Everywhere (from 1949)
CCC	Commodity Credit Corporation
CCP	Committee on Commodity Problems
CFA	Committee on Food Aid Policies and Programmes
CFS	FAO Committee on World Food Security
CIDA	Canadian International Development Agency
CNAE	Companha Nacional de Alimentacão Escolar
Comecon	Economic Association of Communist Countries
CRS	Catholic Relief Services
CSD	Committee on Surplus Disposal
DSM	Dried skimmed milk
DWM	Dried whole milk
EC	European Community
EEC	European Economic Community
ECOSOC	Economic and Social Council (of the UN)
EDF	European Development Fund
EGS	Employment Guarantee Scheme
ETU	Emergency Transport Unit
FAC	Food Aid Convention
FAO	Food and Agriculture Organization (of the UN)
FAS	Foreign Agriculture Service
GATT	General Agreement on Tariffs and Trade
GDP	Gross Domestic Product
GNP	Gross National Product
IAC	Intergovernmental Advisory Committee
IBAP	Intervention Board for Agricultural Produce
IBRD	International Bank for Reconstruction and Development (also known as the 'World Bank')
ICARA	International Conference for Assistance to Refugees in Africa
ICCH	International Commodity Clearing House

ICRC	International Committee of the Red Cross
IDA	International Development Association
IDS	Institute of Development Studies (at the University of Sussex)
IEFR	International Emergency Food Reserve
IFAD	International Fund for Agricultural Development
IFPRI	International Food Policy Research Institute
IGCR	Intergovernmental Committee on Refugees
ILO	International Labour Office
IMF	International Monetary Fund
IWA	International Wheat Agreement
IWC	International Wheat Council
LDC	Less developed countries
LWF	Lutheran World Federation
MCH	Mother and Child Health (Centres)
MSA	Most severely affected areas
NFDM	Non-fat dried milk
NFIU	Non-food items unit of WFP
NGO	Non-governmental Organization
ODA	Overseas Development Administration
OECD	Organization for Economic Co-operation and Development
OSRO	FAO's Office of Special Relief Operations
UBR	Uncommitted budgetary resources
UMR	Usual marketing requirements
UNBRO	United Nations Border Region Operation
UNDP	United Nations Development Programme
UNDRO	United Nations Disaster Relief Organization
UNHCR	United Nations High Commission for Refugees
Unicef	United Nations International Children's Emergency Fund
UNRRA	United Nations Relief and Rehabilitation Administration
USAID	United States Agency for International Development
WFP	World Food Programme

Note on 'tons', 'tonnes', and 'metric tons'

- A metric ton = 1000 kg and is the same as a 'tonne'. Conventional forms of writing this are either 'tonne' or 'MT'.
- A US ton is 2000 lb due to their 'hundredweight' being 100 lb rather than the UK 112 lb which give a ton of 2240 lb, known in US parlance as a 'long ton'.
- The difference between the UK or long ton and the metric ton is therefore negligible but amounts to over 10 per cent in the case of the US ton.
- In this text US figures are quoted in US tons whereas international and European data are cited in 'tonnes', i.e. 1000 kg or 2246 lb.

INTRODUCTION

The need for food aid to relieve appalling conditions in many parts of the globe is patent. Modern communication systems, television, and vivid reporting have brought human disaster right into millions of living rooms. The response to harrowing scenes of malnutrition, starvation, and deaths continues to be remarkably generous on the part of a multitude of individuals touched by the sufferings of fellow humans, cutting across the barriers of distance and race.

This concern attests to the development of an international conscience with a sense of personal involvement on the part of ordinary people. It has not always been so. At the beginning of this century the death of a few tens of thousands of people in, say, floods in Bengal or famine in Africa would hardly rate more than a couple of lines in a European or North American newspaper. Even the great potato famine in Ireland in the middle of the last century did not raise any international response. Those who despair of humanity ever making any moral progress should take heart from these recent developments.

Adverse economic trends in many of the traditional donor nations do not appear to have diminished the generous responses to human suffering so far as the individual is concerned, so that a regression into a state of unconcern is unlikely. These responses, though, have their limitation as they are mostly related to emergencies and disasters of one kind or another, but disasters such as starvation, famine, and drought are but the visible tip of a network of deeper and more complex problems. If the scenes of hunger and infant mortality are to stop appearing with their now almost monotonous regularity, taxing the new-found generosity of individuals, attention will need to be focused, with equally meaningful responses, on these deep-rooted problems and not just on the tip of the problem each time it breaks surface. This is a far more exacting task for which there are many theories, but we must find effective ways to pass the baton from food aid to long-term development.

The ultimate mission of food aid is much more than just a

palliative to salvage a limited number of disaster-stricken people; its challenge is to work itself out of the need to provide food aid at all, by making those aided self-reliant as producers or buyers of food.

1 FOOD AID:
What is it? Who needs it?

Taken in its widest sense, every infant and young child in this world
is a recipient of food aid and depends upon it for survival. The fact
is, though, that food given to an infant or young child by its mother
and from the earnings or other resources of its parents is not generally looked upon as being a form of food aid, since the care of children is regarded as being part of family life and family obligations.
Yet if this food was not provided from a source external to the
infant recipient, it would not survive. Looked at in this way, then, it
can be said that any individual who is unable, for any of a variety of
reasons, to provide for his own sustenance through his own
resources is in need of food aid. The establishment of a need for
food aid or entitlement to it, does not of course mean that the individual will necessarily receive it, since that will depend on a whole
range of economic and social factors. However, when viewed from
this angle the need for food aid will reveal a range of potential
recipients who depend, or might have to depend, on food aid (that
is, food from an external source) for survival. This approach will
thus be found to provide a better insight into the great potential as
well as the considerable complexities of food aid as a concept, and
is more meaningful than looking upon it merely as an *ad hoc* hand-
out to certain distressed sections of humanity whose plight may
have been temporarily highlighted by the media.

If one moves beyond the immediate family responsibilities of
providing for young children, it will be found that in many societies
the concept of responsibility extends to a much wider family circle,
to include more distant relatives who might for one reason or
another be unable to provide for their own sustenance from their
own resources through age, illness, displacement, loss of a parent or
of employment, crop failures, and so forth. In most industrialized
countries this concept has now been taken considerably further, to
include all members of the society within a network of social
arrangements, leading to the creation of the Welfare State.

Although most citizens now take this state of affairs as a natural right, it should not be forgotten that its generalization is of quite recent historical date—as readers of Dickens will be aware. In fact, the development of social security systems was a long and frequently discontinuous process, linked not only to the arousing of social conscience but also to the ability of the economy to provide the necessary services and finance. *Zakat* or almsgiving for the sustenance of the poor is one of the pillars of the Islamic faith as it is of Christianity. The tradition survived in Britain in the Middle Ages as the distribution of Maundy money by the Crown and in the construction and running of almshouses. Various professional associations or guilds in many European countries also set up schemes to care for their elderly or incapacitated members. A number of religious and charitable organizations would provide health care and communal kitchens to certain deprived groups. It was not until the beginning of this century, however, with a growing social conscience, the development of trade unions, and the establishment of efficient revenue collection methods in the larger nation states, that nation-wide systems such as we now know, began to be developed.

This generalization of the sustenance concept naturally brought with it all the necessary depersonalized procedures designed to ensure proper accountability for the use of tax-payers' monies and national resources. A state could not undertake such a custodial role without laying down various eligibility criteria for food aid as well as other indirect means of providing sustenance such as health services, extended credit facilities, relocation grants, housing subsidies, retraining programmes, and so on: basically any facility that would enable an individual to restore his or her productive capacity. If no conditions were imposed on access to such aid, human nature being what it is, a total initiative-stripping dependency would result.

The Concept of International Responsibility

Much of the current discussion of the pros and cons of food aid stems from the fact that the international community of nations is groping its way towards the establishment of some kind of international social security system, and the state of the art as well as much of the argumentation in favour or against is rather similar to that relating to the development of national schemes in industrialized countries four or five decades ago. Some regard the whole process of providing any form of charity or social security as a brake on personal or collective initiative and therefore a disincentive to development and productivity, while others maintain that deprivation, wherever it might occur, must be remedied in view of the increasing interdependence of all states in the modern world and the development of what might be termed an international social conscience. The essential difference between established social security systems and the current thinking about questions of food aid, is that the former takes care of the deprived, temporarily or otherwise, in reasonably affluent and developed societies, while the latter has to take into consideration not only the deprived in other parts of the world, but also the need to help those other states to develop their economies and their productivity to a point where they would be able to organize their own systems of social and food security. In the short run it is the former 'bailing out' actions that predominate and make the news headlines, but in the long run it is the latter developmental considerations that alone can solve the problem satisfactorily. In industrialized countries as well as in regional groupings such as the European Economic Community (EEC) there are areas of relative deprivation or poverty which need to be more heavily subsidized or underpinned than others; the same factors are obviously also operative in respect of developing countries of the so-called 'Third World'.

A measure of the development of an international social conscience is provided by a comparison of the objectives and the membership of the League of Nations which was set up following the Treaty of Versailles after the 1914 war, and those of the United Nations established in connection with the 1945 peace. Two other major milestones in this process, not initially having any apparent connection with food aid, were the Bretton Woods agreement signed in 1944 and the launching of the Marshall Plan for the reconstruction of war-torn Europe in 1947. The former provided the framework for international financial stability among the principal countries with free market economies, thus enabling development and reconstruction to take place by this means while the latter provided for various forms of assistance to Europe. Once in operation it was found that almost half of the Marshall Plan expenditures were on food aid; the needs for this gradually decreased as national productivity was built up through the other components of the aid package such as equipment, transport, and loans. Many of the principles and objectives of the Marshall Plan were subsequently applied to the developing countries, especially in the 1950s and 1960s when a large number of former dependent territories were granted or obtained their independence and needed considerable support in the initial development of their economies. These initiatives were started under what came to be known as the PL 480 programmes described in detail in later chapters. This symbol refers to Public Law No. 480 which was adopted by the US Congress in 1946 to permit the free disposal of surplus grain and certain other agricultural products and/or their sale at less than the going commercial rates to designated countries.

It is popularly assumed that food aid is only concerned with the physical transfer of donated food to recipient mouth. This certainly happens in the case of emergencies such as refugee influx or, perhaps, natural disasters where large numbers of people have to be collected and fed in camps or settlements, but these do not, in fact, represent more than about 20 per cent of the total amount of food aid donated by the industrialized countries. The other 80 per cent consists of concessional sales or food donated for purposes of budget support. Any country that is not able to reach self-sufficiency in food production from its own resources must either purchase food on the commercial market or rely on some form of food aid—or perhaps both. Under the conditions of general economic stringency that generally prevail in developing economies, any money spent on the purchase of food means that some other development programme or even recurrent expenditure will have to be sacrificed. Much of the 80 per cent food aid transfers mentioned are in fact designed to meet this kind of situation. The food aid provides import substitution, that is to say it replaces the foreign exchange expenditure that would have had to be made and thus becomes an aspect of budgetary support to the recipient country. In the case of concessional sales, the food aid is generally channelled into national distribution outlets, usually at subsidized prices, the revenue in local currency being used to support national infrastructure or other developmental programmes or projects. This also becomes an indirect financial support. The importance of this is that the distinction between food aid and financial aid is removed. Although many references will be found in food aid literature and in the media to the relative merits of food aid or financial aid, the discussion is largely irrelevant, not only in the light of the practice mentioned above, but also since in the majority of cases, developing countries in need of aid would have to spend a considerable amount of money on the purchase of food on the commercial international market, if the aid were given only in terms of financial assistance.

Establishing Needs

Although it is relatively easy to list various categories of people who, under differing sets of circumstances, should theoretically be eligible for food aid on the basis of established needs, the question of who actually gets it, and under what circumstances, and in what form, opens up a whole range of complex issues, all of which enliven the debate about food aid.

Needs, in respect of communities or even of nations, can be established in rather the same way as individual needs; as a structural or temporary inability to provide one's own sustenance from one's own resources. Structural need may arise from the application of too rigid economic or political formulae, insufficient availability of arable or otherwise productive land, human and/or animal over-population leading to ecological degradation, a land-locked or otherwise geographically unfavourable position, lack of natural resources, and so on. Temporary inability may be due to drought, crop failures, fall in producer prices or other disincentives to production, civil strife, or natural disaster. There is also a range of needs that cover part of both these categories, such as the problems related to peri-urban unemployment, malnutrition due to inappropriate utilization of available resources, epidemics with longer-term complications, a seasonal or other temporary rise in food prices placing even staples beyond the means of the low income groups, and so forth.

Increasing Awareness of Needs

Judging by the media reports from various parts of the world covering urgent food needs in all the above categories, it might be assumed that these are all recent and arise from increasingly deteriorating conditions in different parts of the globe. This may be part of the truth but not all of it. Much of the apparent increase in need is due to our increasing awareness of the problems, the development of a kind of international social conscience moved to do something about these problems. Both these factors have been accentuated by the very rapid progress made in recent years by all forms of communications, whether in the form of road/rail/air links or as telephone/telex/satellite systems, together with the use of computerized data. Half a century ago a typhoon, say, in the Bay of Bengal would hardly have rated more than a few lines on an inside page of a major newspaper in Europe or North America, and probably even less in the African or Latin-American press. Today, however, television brings these things, starkly visible, right into millions of living rooms. What was once 'far away' and therefore capable of being swept under the carpet in terms of having to do anything about it, now leaps into immediacy in a much more compelling fashion and has sufficient impact to arouse a degree of self-sacrifice to remedy the situation in terms of money or services. National boundaries, ethnic considerations, distance, are all swept away in the face of such immediacy. One of the most striking recent examples of this has been the success of the collaborative effort of the many 'pop' music stars in raising funds for famine relief in Africa under their 'Band-Aid' and 'Live-Aid' programmes in the United Kingdom and the USA respectively. However, the remedies to such disaster situations in themselves are relatively simple: it is a matter of getting food and other emergency supplies of medicines, blankets, etc. to the right place in sufficient quantity and of course, at the right time. These are post-fact actions, that is to say the aid only becomes available once the disaster has occurred and been officially acknowledged by a government statement or request for assistance. Consequently the funds derived from popular appeals, together with those provided on a more consistent basis by international organizations such as the United Nations High Commission for Refugees (UNHCR), the World Food Programme of the United Nations (WFP) as well as major bilateral agencies, can do much to alleviate the distress caused by the group of temporary problems mentioned earlier. But unless something is done to tackle some of the structural group of problems mentioned, then the temporary ones are liable to keep on recurring and even escalating, since many of their causes lie in the structural area. Regrettably, there are no simple solutions to these structural problems and many of the remedies necessary are frequently unpalatable or politically inexpedient. As a consequence there is often, on the one hand, little enthusiasm for assistance in these areas on the part of potential recipients and on the other, they have little donor appeal since results are likely to be quite a long time in forthcoming.

Towards Clearer Definition of Needs

Part of the problem lies in the fact that the various reasons behind lack of food availability, crop failures, inability to cope with droughts, and so forth are insufficiently explained to the general public in donor as well as in recipient countries. Since these reasons are not explained the role of food aid in contributing to their solutions is unspecific and often uncorrelated. The lack of clear direction often leads to a resurgence of negative views, maintaining for instance that irreversible climatic changes are taking place, that there is nothing that can be done about ecological damage, desertification and so forth, and people begin to question the whole concept of aid including food aid. Such views are unwarranted, for the simple reason that most of the industrialized countries do not merely allocate funds for aid and food aid out of self-interest, but also because they have come to consider it as a moral obligation. Not only have North America and Europe built up large agricultural surpluses which can be made available as food aid, but perhaps even more importantly, they now hold the keys to technological development and know-how.

The question 'why food aid?' which might have been asked with some relevance 40 or so years ago, has in the meantime been answered by the increasing use of food aid as an instrument for relief as well as for development. In 1974, in consultation with groups of donors and third world countries the United Nations set a target of 10 million tons of cereals. Pledges amounting to 7.6 million were made and this target has now been exceeded. Twenty years ago India was a country with a large food deficit and thus a recipient of considerable amounts of food aid to the extent that some pessimistic forecasters doubted her ability ever to emerge from a total dependence on food aid, yet by the early 1980s India had become an exporter of cereals. The food aid had contributed to the 'bailing out' aspect by permitting India to break out of the vicious circle of malnutrition, intermittent famine, crop failures, post-harvest losses, and lack of adequate logistics capacity in rural areas, while the technological know-how assisted her in developing new crop varieties with high yields and drought resistance; improved marketing and storage facilities; expanded veterinary services; milk bottling and processing; capital for fertilizer plants; dams and irrigation schemes, along with the requisite managerial skills. If such results can be obtained in a country with around twice the population of Europe, the USA or the Soviet Union they should logically also be achievable elsewhere. The reasons for despair are hardly justified, however daunting the short-run difficulties might appear to be. Media coverage and articles available to the general reading public provide quite extensive coverage of the various things that go wrong. During the serious droughts in the Sahel region of Africa in the 1970s there were scenes of dying cattle, parched earth, and the misuse of food aid; and the same occurred in the cases of Somalia in the early 1980s and more recently in Ethiopia, Chad, and the Sudan. But how much coverage was given to massive reforestation schemes in Algeria designed to stop the encroachment of the desert northwards, the development of the Niger river basin, range-management and reforestation in Somalia, irrigation and soil conservation schemes in Ethiopia, road-building, housing, and school construction, school and hospital feeding programmes in many of these affected countries as well as in Latin-America, and the Middle and Far East? For in all of these activities food aid has played and continues to play a part. Droughts, crop failures, natural disasters of all kinds also strike developed countries but it does not mean that a drought causes a famine, or that a natural disaster requires massive external assistance. Pastoralists in many parts of the world inhabiting some of the driest and least productive areas of their countries are able to survive droughts much better than their well sheltered urban counterparts, and it is generally the urbanites who launch the pleas for help, not the pastoralists. The explanations of these apparent contradictions are rarely given other than in specialized or academic literature.

Complexities of Development

There is also little explanation of how all the various technological advances can be brought together to focus, along with food aid and other forms of aid, on the many structural problems of development. Although food aid may be desperately needed by the many who find themselves caught up in one or other form of disaster or conditions of deprivation, its long-term purpose is to do away with the need for food aid by developing productive capacity to a state where a relative immunity to adverse conditions can be built up, as has been done in most of the industrialized countries. Technological advances have now reached a point where theoretical remedies and solutions can be found, even to structural problems. In fact the range of proven and available technological know-how—together with capital availability to implement it—is such that one begins to wonder why there should any longer be a need for food aid, that is to say why it has not already worked itself out of a job. There are in reality no set formulae for development. Despite the many pretenders to the place of honour in the search for a panacea, none has as yet been found. Development is at once a complex and also a mobile evolving concept. Communities and states tend to react to external stimuli and challenges rather in the same way that a person does. Personalities often react in quite different ways to identical stimuli or challenges and the development of personality cannot be programmed, despite many ideological attempts to do so. One community might, for instance, gladly accept food aid so as to free some of its members to undertake infrastructure development or other capital works that would increase their productive capacity in subsequent years; another might treat it with contempt as being beneath its dignity to receive charity; while yet another may become so addicted to getting food without effort that it is unlikely to want to take up any productive work.

Absorptive Capacity

There are also limits to what a community or a state can absorb in the way of external inputs; there is no benefit to be gained from sending large shipments of cereals to replenish national grain stocks if there is no available storage at the port, or if the transport system becomes so clogged trying to move it out that all other users are kept away. Even bringing about greatly improved crop yields in a district without ensuring suitable storage, marketing, and transport back-up may only cause a local glut and depress the prices for everyone in the region so that other farmers are forced out of business; expensive equipment can quickly become useless if there is no one to maintain it or instruct people in its operation. Again there are often problems of uneven development, even within one region or area: statistics might indicate that agricultural production is sufficient to provide for all the persons in the area, while the government may have needed the crop for export, or the producers may have decided that better returns could be had by turning the cereals into alcohol; malnutrition may exist almost alongside an area of abundance, either because there is no transport to get it where it is needed, or because there are regulations in force prohibiting the moving of agricultural products from one zone to another, with the result that the impoverished zone may be forced to have recourse to food aid exempt from such restrictions, and so forth. In general agricultural production data only give gross figures and do not take into account the quantities normally put aside for seed stock, for reserves, buffer stocks for price stabilization etc., some of which may have to be compensated for out of food aid.

Productive Capacity

In addition to the range of technological assets available to development, there are various forms of financial assistance designed to increase or maintain food production. Agricultural credit and loan facilities are becoming increasingly available and have been instrumental in many parts of the world in enabling farmers to break the financial stranglehold of usurers. Funds for these types of operation are frequently derived from the sale in local currency of donated food aid bulk shipments, delivered to and commercialized by government grain monopolies or importers.

However impressive the range of technological and financial aids that are available to accelerate the development process, it is the fit and able-bodied who benefit the most from them. In North America it is reckoned that meeting the cereal needs of the population and the accumulation of large yearly surpluses are brought about by a mere 9 per cent of the labour force engaged in agriculture. In many developing countries the labour force in agriculture may go up to 80 per cent of the total and still not meet national production requirements. Part of the problem is that much of that labour force—in which in many areas women predominate—is suffering from one form or another of malnutrition. This may be directly attributable to insufficiency of energy intake in the form of food; it can also arise from debilitating illnesses such as a range of intestinal parasites, bilharzia, malaria, measles, and so on. These are prima facie medical questions but lack of resistance to these plagues is also frequently due to prolonged periods of undernourishment from early childhood. It is precisely in this area of human needs that food aid can play a significant and long-term remedial role beginning with assistance to Mother and Child Health Centres where food with high nutritional value is designed to meet the needs of both mothers and infants showing indications of undernourishment. The provision of the food element brings to such centres (where medical assistance such as immunization and anti-parasitic treatment is given) a number of people who, in the absence of food, would probably not come until a child or the mother became seriously ill, by which time it is frequently too late for any treatment. Undernourishment can also occur in apparently well-organized and prosperous communities simply because people cannot gain access to the required food. This may be because the monetary income does not provide enough to purchase what is needed, or because of the large size of a family with only a single income earner, or because of ineligibility to gain access to fixed-price shops or other rationing system. Any one of such constraints can put a person or a whole family into a position where it can no longer sustain itself without external assistance and will eventually suffer from lowered physical and mental capability. Food aid also assists the improvement of nutritional standards through school and institutional feeding and, in the longer term through assistance to schools and institutes training nurses, nutritionists, and nutrition educators.

Response to Government Requests

The view taken so far in this summary has been an external one, that is to say, external to the societies or communities for which food aid is intended or supplied, and is one taken by a large number of reviews on questions of food aid. It is, however, an essentially distorted view and tends to overlook the real needs of the populations concerned, or at least not to identify them adequately.

Obviously it is quite irrelevant to those suffering from deprivation
to know whether it is due to some remote structural cause or just
lack of rain or something else: what they require is food.

In the first place food aid is not only provided by external
agencies. A number of governments run their own food aid programmes such as hospital and school feeding, and support to certain incapacitated or underprivileged groups, all from national
resources. It is, perhaps, even more important, in the second place,
to realize that what are generally believed to be externally con-
ceived programmes are not really so. They are merely programmes
that have been created in response to a national or regional need,
whether long- or short-term. Media coverage of many emergency
situations, where attention is focused on the expatriate administrators and organizers of assistance programmes, with national
operators keeping a low profile, adds to the impression that external operators are in charge. This point of view can lead to serious
misunderstanding of the development process and of development
needs, including food aid needs or food needs in general.

Aid programmes, including food aid programmes of any size, are
in fact, only embarked upon at the express request of a government.
Small ones run, say, by voluntary organizations can operate in con-
juction with communites or individual institutions but even then
only upon invitation. Naturally, in practice there is always a dialogue between potential donor and potential recipient before any
formal steps are taken, but nevertheless the ultimate decision lies
with the recipient government, community, or institution.
Although the necessary tools and supplies required to solve a particular problem may be well known, they may not necessarily be
available from the intended donor and the recipient may consider
that what the donor has to offer is not likely to be adaptable to
local conditions. Although such processes of dialogue are
considered by some as an impediment to effective long-term and
systematized assistance with development problems, it means in
general that a recipient will only accept what he thinks he can make
best use of; the amount he is in a position to handle. A problem for
recipient countries that is often overlooked is that free gifts of aid,
such as grants of either food or capital, can increase the recurrent
cost budget. That is to say any extra activity that requires more
staff, more transport, more storage, more maintenance, or more
training will have to be met by extra funds provided from the

national budget. When that budget is already over-stretched and in deficit, as is so often the case in developing countries, governments will hesitate to assume new burdens unless they see some fairly rapid benefits, since the added deficit might have to be covered by further loans and further national indebtedness. Until quite recently most donors have steered away from supporting recurrent expenditures, regarding this as a government responsibility, but without providing any clues as to how the government could be expected to meet the extra costs. Food aid through concessional sales arrangements has often helped to solve this type of problem.

The onus on the recipient government to make final decisions on food aid or aid in general is important in another way, namely that the recipient government or institution is in a far better position to know how much external assistance it can absorb than the donor. Imposed structures and imposed models, like exotic plant species, do not take root unless the ground is well prepared. A number of developing countries will look upon the technological achievements of the industrialized countries as a form of arrogance and would prefer to work out their own methods even at the risk of slower rates of development. This merely proves the earlier point that there are really no simple solutions to the development process and none of the models, however successful in the country of origin, is infallible. Attempted imposition of external models is certainly likely to lead to symptoms of rejection.

Additional impediments to longer-term solutions have been created by the way in which many donor and corresponding recipient government institutions have been built up. There is little available experience or policy covering the largely uncharted territory between relief and development, despite many years of operation in each of these sectors. Much of the reason for this is that historically, different organizations, agencies, and constituencies have handled relief and emergency operations on the one hand and development on the other. This dichotomy is frequently reflected in the recipient countries where disasters and emergencies often become the responsibility of special commissions staffed by personnel temporarily seconded from other departments or ministries (and what ministry would give away its best people!), whereas development action would be carried out by the permanent staffs of ministries or institutions in corresponding technical or professional fields. The obvious disadvantage of this situation is that funds raised for emergencies are not usually available for development purposes and consequently only have a palliative effect without addressing themselves to root causes. The gap between relief and development needs to be bridged in the mandates of the various donor agencies as much as between ministries and commissions in recipient countries.

The intention of the following chapters of this book is to set out in plain language the various ways in which food aid can and does work, the various obstacles and constraints that it is likely to run up against, and how these and other challenges might be met. It is also the intention to maintain the perspective of the conditions at the receiving end since it is the impact of food aid and the actual results obtained from it that are most likely to influence future donor policies. There is already an extensive specialized literature on all aspects of food aid and the book does not aim to add anything new to this. Nor does it pretend to be an academic treatise but rather hopes to explain some of the many aspects of food aid in development that tend not to reach the general reading public due to their dispersion among a number of specialized journals and publications. In so doing it may help to bring a number of apparently disconnected strands together and to make the events and activities related to food aid in development somewhat clearer.

2 FOOD AID:
How did it start?

A look at the history of food aid shows how perception of the challenge, and response to the opportunity, of food aid has changed over time. Our understanding of the problem of hunger has changed dramatically, and our response has been much more complex than simply a humanitarian desire to feed hungry people. By seeing food aid in its historical perspective we may, hopefully, learn lessons from the past and avoid repeating the more obvious mistakes!

Food aid can be said to have existed in one form or another for almost as long as society itself. Communities have provided succour to their members in times of emergency, war, or other disaster. The first well-documented food aid gesture was that of the USA in providing emergency aid to earthquake victims in Venezuela in 1812, for which Congress passed the Act for the Relief of the Citizens of Venezuela authorizing the President to purchase goods to the value of $US50,000. Although some people hoped that this would create a precedent, later proposals to formalize overseas assistance were turned down on the grounds that the US Constitution did not give Congress power to use public funds for foreign relief. As a result it was not until near the end of the First World War that the President, under exceptional wartime powers, established the precedent. Before that time there had been a number of private donations of food to foreign areas or communities in distress. Beginning in 1896 the US Department of Agriculture, sidestepping the Congressional veto on relief actions, began shipping out cereal surpluses through its Foreign Agriculture Service with the avowed intention of developing new markets for US cereals, and presidential prerogative was used to provide relief operations for earthquake victims in Martinique (1902) and Sicily (1908). But again these remained low profile operations and did not develop into a structured food aid programme.

Britain was also one of the pioneers in giving food aid. This was primarily as a means of colonial famine relief, and supplies of wheat were purchased for distribution in the Indian famine of the 1890s, and also for British Somaliland and the Sudan in the early 1900s. The bitter misery of the Irish famine, vividly described by C. Woodham Smith in *The Great Hunger*, led to Britain providing £100,000 of Indian meal for distribution in Ireland in 1846 and in 1847, approximately another 100,000 tons were ordered.[1]

Earlier Long-term Food Aid Programmes

The first major long-term food aid operations evolved from the special post-war relief credits voted by the US Congress first for the period between the signing of the Armistice in 1918 and the signing of the Treaty of Versailles in 1919, and second, in a so-called reconstruction period running from 1919 to 1926. A total of 6.23 million tons of food was shipped under these programmes. The principal areas of distribution were the various dismembered parts of the Austro-Hungarian Empire and of Germany, since the blockade was still applied to them during the armistice period and they were unable to trade. Some of the relief also went to Finland, the Balkan States, and the war-ravaged parts of Belgium and France. Relief credits were also made available by Britain under rather similar conditions to the USA grants, some of which were used for the purchase of food. Food aid was also provided to the Ukraine in 1921–2, but this was through the Red Cross and did not directly involve public funds. The importance of this American initiative lay not only in the quantity of relief provided, but also in establishing the precedent for operations of this type, involving prominent personalities in the operation of food aid, the most significant of these being President Herbert Hoover, and bringing a general realization of the value of food aid as a politically stabilizing factor.

With the end of the special credits in 1926, and with the USA still producing considerable surpluses of cereals, moves were made to formalize the type of arrangement started in 1896 by the Department of Agriculture. The first bill to this effect was presented by Congressman Norris in 1929, but was defeated. By 1933 a different approach allowing American surplus foodstuffs to be sold at concessional prices was more successful. In 1933 President Roosevelt proposed an Agricultural Adjustment Act initiating agricultural price support and production controls, that was duly passed by Congress. Under an amendment to this Act the Grain Stabilization Board was created to provide direct subsidies for agricultural exports. In order to implement these decisions, it was necessary to create an instrument for paying out the subsidies to the farmers and to keep some control over the funds: an Executive Order of 16 October 1933 created the Commodity Credit Corporation (CCC) which was authorized to buy, sell, and make loans to farmers in agricultural commodities. This organization continued to function through various changes in US food aid policy and received approval from the US Congress in 1939, authorizing the sale of stocks of agricultural produce to foreign governments to establish food reserves against possible outbreak of war. It became the vehicle for managing agricultural surpluses and the basis for the first structured food aid programmes. The original scope of the CCC was widened by an amendment to the Agricultural Adjustment Act in 1935 (PL 74-320) which authorized its use of customs revenues to subsidize agricultural exports and encourage domestic production. The outbreak of the war in 1939 led eventually to the passing of the Lend–Lease Act of 1941 signed before US entry into the war in December of that year. Under this Act some $US6 billion of agricultural products (though not all food items) were shipped to the Allied powers. After the end of the Second World War US policy makers found no difficulty in providing rehabilitation assistance to Europe, since the successful precedent had been established by Herbert Hoover and Congressional action after the end of the First World War. The Marshall Plan and all subsequent US food policy and actions derived from this period.

The fact that so much attention is paid to US surplus disposal and food aid does not mean that there were no similar developments elsewhere in the industrialized countries before World War II. The others attracted little attention because they operated within a network of associated states or communities, such as the British Commonwealth, the French Community, Portuguese overseas territories, the Italian, Belgian, and German empires, and so forth.

The Post-war Period

Food aid programmes developed considerably over the post-war period. In 1955 US food aid amounted to $US385 million and in

1980 peaked at $US1,307 million. Rapid population growth, increasing urbanization, and the poor performance of agricultural production, particularly in Africa, led to a rising demand for food aid. Some countries, for example South Korea, rapidly increased their exports to earn foreign exchange for raw material imports, and food aid was seen as a stop-gap measure. The early momentum in the growth of food aid was not maintained after the sixties. Its share in total aid fell steadily until at the start of the eighties food aid accounted for 10 per cent of total aid, and was worth less in real terms than it was 20 years earlier. Significant structural changes have occurred over the post-war period in the organization and distribution of food aid. The share of multilateral agencies grew from only 1 per cent of food aid in 1960–62 to more than 20 per cent in 1979–81. This growth in multilateral food aid was due primarily to the emergence of the World Food Programme (WFP) as the second largest source of assistance, in dollar terms, after the World Bank, within the UN system. Many recipients objected to being tied to bilateral food aid relationships and welcomed the means of escape through multilateral food aid.

The European Recovery Programme, more popularly known as the Marshall Plan, was the largest transfer of bilateral aid in world history. The disruption of harvests by the diversion of men and machines to war, and poor harvests in 1945 and 1947, led to a desperate food shortage in Europe. Britain was forced to introduce bread rationing, an exigency avoided throughout the war. It was estimated that, whereas Americans were living on about 3,300 kcal per day by 1946, 125 million Europeans had only 2,000 kcal per day, and in some areas daily rations were reduced to 1,000 kcal. Of the total aid package of $13.5 billion, 25 per cent was committed to food, feed, and fertilizer.

Humanitarianism was important, but it was not the only factor in encouraging countries to make such heavy commodity commitments under the Marshall Plan—80 per cent of which came from the US and Canada. Strategic considerations were seen by some in the US as of paramount importance in deciding where the aid should go. Political motives were also important. Communism was seen as a threat due not only to Soviet military expansion, but also to national communist movements.

Just as the Brandt Commission in the eighties argued for

increased support of the poor 'south' by the rich 'north' to ensure mutual survival, so an important motive in Marshall Plan aid from the US was the recognition that a strong Europe was essential for US foreign trade, jobs, and incomes. The memory of the 1930s global recession was still vivid, and by creating links through the aid it was hoped that new markets for American goods would be opened up.

The Marshall Plan was a precedent for the programme-type food aid later evolved under the Agricultural Trade Development and Assistance Act. Commodities supplied by the US to Europe were allocated directly to individual governments, which sold the food for their own local currency through regular market channels. This had the advantage of quickly rehabilitating food marketing systems, and was one of the earliest examples of using food aid to overcome foreign exchange shortages. The food aid received released for European governments hard currency which would otherwise have had to be spent on food imports. Normal commercial sales to traditional US trade partners were blocked by their lack of foreign exchange. The aid programme was seen as an opportunity to remove surpluses of certain commodities, the price of which, and producer incomes, would otherwise have fallen to clear the market.

The Marshall Plan thus had advantages both for recipients and for key interest groups in the donor countries. This harmony of vested interests proved to be a major feature of the growth of food aid. The undoubted success of the Marshall Plan owed much to the massive size of the programme, and to the ability of the recipients to use the aid well. The US maintained overall control, but recipient countries had a lot of freedom in deciding the direction of the aid. There have been many calls for a Marshall Plan-type programme to be repeated for the Third World. Unfortunately the parallel between contemporary North–South and US–Europe Marshall Plan should not be drawn too closely. Much of the physical and institutional infrastructure and expertise of the European economies remained intact. The aid was used to rehabilitate industries, rather than create new industries, so that food aid was necessary for only a short time. Nevertheless, the experience of the Marshall Plan may be seen as an important advance in the evolution of food aid, and many parts of the programme were incorporated in later food aid programmes.

Current American Food Aid Legislation

The legal basis of modern American food aid was laid with the
enactment in 1954 of Public Law 480, known as the Agricultural
Trade Development and Assistance Act. Building on his earlier food
aid experience, Hubert Humphrey's leadership was a major factor
in the successful passage of the Act (see Appendix 1). Public Law
480 embodied all the different motives which had led to the growth
of food aid. However it was ultimately the support of the US
farmers—represented by their principal lobbying group, the American Farm Bureau Federation (AFBF)—that assured the eventual
passage of PL 480. The early 1950s saw bumper harvests in North
America, and their surplus wheat stocks rose from about 13 million
tons in 1952–3 to over 42 million tons by the end of 1953–4. The
stocks held by the US, at 25 million tons, were equal to the then
level of world trade in wheat. The danger to US agricultural prices
and producer incomes was obvious. PL 480 provided the legislative
basis for the US Government to buy the surplus wheat from farmers
and disburse it on appropriate terms to developing countries who
needed to import wheat as cheaply as possible.

The use of food aid under PL 480 as a surplus disposal instrument was paramount but the humanitarian motive was also evident. John F. Kennedy in a pre-election campaign speech stated:

I don't regard the existence of . . . agricultural surpluses as a problem. I
regard it as an opportunity . . . I think the farmers can bring more credit,
more lasting goodwill, more chance of peace, than almost any other group
of Americans in the next ten years, if we recognise that food is strength,
and food is peace and food is freedom, and food is a helping hand to people
around the world whose goodwill and friendship we want.[2]

The strategic and political value was also recognized. Senator
Hubert Humphrey observed:

Our values are different from the totalitarians. If it is a world-wide
struggle, it would seem to me we would want to mobilise all the resources
we possibly can in order to win it. And in a world of want and hunger what
is more powerful than food and fibre?[3]

PL 480 was recognition that food aid had become a permanent
feature of American government and policy. Between 1955 and
1966 some 30 per cent of US agricultural exports were government
financed. A new emphasis in food aid policy was introduced in

1961 with the appointment by J. F. Kennedy of George McGovern to head the office of Food For Peace, within the Executive Office of the President. The emphasis on surplus in the food aid programme was to be changed into the use of food as a 'long range investment in progress'. This concept of food aid was in accordance with Kennedy's New Frontier image, and the optimistic belief that all problems could be solved with the appropriate combination of money and technology.

In fact American food surpluses began to decline in the mid-sixties. American wheat stocks probably peaked in 1961–2 at about 38 million tons, and by 1967 had declined to 11 million tons, partly because of increased demand from China, the Soviet Union, and Eastern Europe, and partly as a result of government subsidies to farmers for not growing cereals. To counter the run-down in the surplus from 1966 the US put land back into production so that crops produced could be used for food aid. Despite this measure surplus disposal continued to be the major determinant of food aid from the US over the post-war period.[4]

Further amendments to PL 480 focused food aid more on development objectives. Dissatisfaction with the 'bottomless-pit' characteristic of the Food For Peace programme led, in 1966, to revisions in PL 480 which required that food aid and other economic assistance were to be tied together, and made them conditional upon recipients providing evidence of their commitment to increase food production and other self-help measures. Food aid was to be shifted gradually away from sales for 'useless' local currency, under Title I, to long-term dollar repayable loans. A new Title was created to allow PL 480 funds to be used to support technical assistance and research in agriculture in developing countries.

In the early seventies the war in South-East Asia resulted in a massive programming of food aid to South Vietnam and Cambodia. During 1974 over 66 per cent of Title I commodities went to these two countries and led to the charge against the Nixon administration of conducting a 'Food for War' campaign. The US was then faced with a food scarcity situation and the Administration decided to give preference to Title I, over Title II commitments. Whereas Title II provided for the use of food aid on a strictly grant basis, Title I was on commercial and concessional credit terms, so the switch was seen as a significant hardening of the terms of US food aid. The resulting Congressional uproar led to a full-scale review of the Food for Peace programme, and a significant shift towards humanitarian and development objectives. The International Development and Food Assistance Act of 1975 aimed at shifting PL 480 towards the poorer developing countries by stipulating that 75 per cent of Title I aid should be allocated to countries having a per capita income of less than $300. Title III (see Appendix 1) was amended to create a new 'Food For Development' programme which made use of local (Title I) counterpart funds for agricultural and rural development projects, conditional upon self-help measures. Another amendment required the government to cut food aid to any country violating human rights.

Over the three decades of operation of PL 480 the values and priorities of the US Congress have changed significantly, and this has been reflected in the implementation of the food aid programme. The emphasis on the vested interests of surplus disposal and development of markets for US firms and products, and the use of food aid as a political strategic instrument, while still evident, became less dominant. United States concern with meeting the challenge of world hunger, and promoting developing countries' agricultural potential came more to the fore, even though the programme has become smaller in real terms.

The dominant position of America in the early post-war growth of food aid is shown by the fact that total food aid commitments of all non-American donors from the early 1950s to the mid-1960s amounted to only 1.5 per cent of the value of PL 480 shipments.[5] By the eighties, although the share of the US had fallen to under half, the food aid 'burden' was still concentrated, with five donors accounting for over 90 per cent of food aid transfers—the USA, the EEC (including member countries), Australia, Canada and Japan.

It was not until the signing of the Food Aid Convention (FAC) in 1967 (for details see Chapter 4), that the situation was created in which countries had a significant inducement, other than altruism, to expand their food aid. For the first time a range of donors accepted a binding commitment to participate in a food aid programme. The risks of instability in the supply of food aid were reduced and, to the relief of the US, international burden-sharing was widened. The aim of the first FAC was 'to carry out a food aid programme with the help of contributions for the benefit of developing countries'.[6] The start was not very auspicious since the total food aid commitment agreed on by the convention was 4.5 million tons of wheat a year, less than half the original US proposal. Nevertheless it spread the burden of food aid from three to twelve countries (and more if all the member states of the EEC are included). The formal commitment under the FAC ensured that there would be a good aid programme in the medium term irrespective of the short-run domestic agricultural situation, and any policy programming temptation to shift resources around, between commodity and other assistance, on a year-to-year basis. Attempts to increase the overall FAC commitment were successful only in the 1980 negotiations, when most signatories agreed to higher levels of minimum contribution, to a total of 7.6 million tonnes.

European Community Aid

Over the last decade the European Community has emerged as the second largest source of food aid. Trying to identify the growth of EC food aid is complicated, since both national programmes and EC community programme resources have been channelled bilaterally, multilaterally and via non-governmental organizations (NGOs). At the end of the sixties about one-third of the EC food aid programme was organized as 'Community action', and administered by the EC Commission; the remainder was programmed bilaterally as 'National action'. By the mid-eighties the position had been reversed with two-thirds of the EC food aid programme organized as 'Community action'. Taking into account bilateral food aid of members prior to their accession to the Treaty of Rome, in real terms allocations have not risen significantly from the early 1970s to the mid-eighties.[7]

At first the EC was reluctant to become involved in sharing the costs of food aid. Its attitude shifted as big surpluses grew with subsidies to EC farmers from the Common Agricultural Policy. A large part of the EC food aid programme involved grants of surplus dairy products such as dried skimmed milk (DSM), butter-oil, and butter. Increasing criticism of the EC programme has, however, led to a more developmental orientation, as with US food aid. For example, there has been a deliberate cut-back in dairy aid because of reservations about possible adverse nutritional effects in countries unaccustomed to cow's milk. The management of EC food aid has been reorganized to place more emphasis on food strategies and increased self-reliance in food production in recipient countries. There has also been a commitment to multi-annual programming in the context of policy dialogues with recipients and other aid agencies. All of these changes have improved EEC food aid as a development, rather than a surplus disposal tool. But there is still much criticism of EC food aid, including delays in procurement and shipment as well as lack of monitoring.[8]

Multilateral Food Aid

The creation of an effective system of mutilateral food aid proved more difficult and slower than the growth of a framework of bilateral food aid. This is not surprising given the natural unwillingness of nation states to relinquish control over such a useful instrument of domestic and foreign policy.

The origin of modern multilateral food aid was rooted in two meetings which took place in 1943. The meeting in May at Hot Springs, Virginia, convened by President Franklin D. Roosevelt, laid the foundation for the creation of the Food and Agriculture Organization (FAO). In November of the same year an agreement was signed in Washington, DC, which established the United Nations Relief and Rehabilitation Administration (UNRRA).

The United Nations Relief and Rehabilitation Administration (UNRRA) was the first significant 'experiment' of a multilateral agency to deal with food aid, and to attempt international co-operation to prevent a famine. The objectives of UNRRA were set out in a speech by President Roosevelt: ' . . . first to assure a fair distribution of available supplies among all the liberated peoples, and second, to ward off death by starvation or exposure among these peoples'.

Between 1943 and 1948 UNRRA distributed about $3.7 billion of aid, about half in the form of food. The distribution of the aid was based on a means test and most went to countries which had been occupied by the Axis powers. As an experiment it was regarded as only partly a success. Not having authority to stockpile food, UNRRA was hampered in its planning. Distribution was generally left to recipient governments and much of the food was sold through the black market.

The termination of UNRRA in 1949 marked the end of operational multilateral food aid until the foundation of the World Food Programme in 1963. Despite this setback, important new programme initiatives continued. The conference held in May 1943 at Hot Springs with the participation of 44 governments had agreed on establishing a permanent organization in the field of food and agriculture. The Food and Agriculture Organization sprang to life in 1945 following agreement by the five big powers on a constitution prepared over two years by a UN Interim Commission on Food and Agriculture chaired by Lester Pearson of Canada. The first Director-General of FAO, Sir John Boyd Orr, adopted a radical stand for an interventionist role for FAO since 'food is more than a trade commodity; it is an essential of life.' He advocated 'a world food policy based on human needs', reconciling the interests of producers and consumers of agriculture and trade. While accepting the objectives of Boyd Orr's proposals, the delegates were not prepared to support his institutional proposals, in particular the creation of a World Food Board, which could distribute food according to need. The power of sovereignty and self-interest was too great for such a vision of humanitarianism and idealism.

Following the disappointing response to Boyd Orr's radical proposals, in the fifties new initiatives and concepts advanced by FAO were more limited in scope and objectives, and were pursued at different times. For example in 1954 the FAO Committee on Commodity Problems drew up Guiding Lines and Principles of Surplus Disposal in response to the reappearance of surpluses. They have been used almost daily by food aid programmes for more than thirty years as a code of international behaviour. Indeed, a critical stage in the evolution of multilateral food aid for development was the staff work and discussions at expert and intergovernmental levels in FAO during 1954, and field surveys carried out in Egypt and India. Ezekiel, in his brilliant case study of India,[9] showed convincingly how food aid could make it possible to increase the size of the development effort above what would otherwise be possible without running into inflation or balance-of-payments deficit. The intellectual basis was laid for an operational multilateral food aid agency to play a key role in changing surpluses from burden to asset by their use in support of projects and programmes to achieve development.

Little real progress was made towards establishing an operational multilateral approach to food aid until the 'conversion' of the US administration in favour of the idea. This conversion came about in 1960, motivated by the wish to share the burden for meeting the food needs of the developing world, and to create an additional outlet for surplus commodities. Within the US, domestic interests opposed to policies creating permanent surpluses (and subsidies to farmers) were gathering strength, raising fears about the reliability of food aid. Following a US sponsored resolution, in October 1960 the UN General Assembly invited FAO to study possible multilateral arrangements for 'the mobilization of available surplus foodstuffs, and their distribution in areas of greatest need'.

The then Director-General of FAO, B. R. Sen, was authorized to undertake the study. The recommendations for multilateral action, based on the work of an expert group chaired by H. W. Singer, and a thirteen-member advisory committee, evolved into a joint decision by the UN and FAO to establish the World Food Programme on an experimental basis, for an initial period of three years from 1962. The programme was judged successful, and its continued operation was approved in 1965.

A burst of institutional development had taken place towards the end of the fifties, and as usual there was fierce competition amongst those already established to expand their own empires. One such battle was between the World Bank and the United Nations for a proposed soft financing agency. The World Bank won and the International Development Association (IDA) was created within the World Bank. It is suggested that the creation of a multilateral food agency was a consolation prize for the UN system.[10] This historical 'accident' leading to the separation of financial aid and food aid was to cause problems in the future.

The World Food Programme

A similar 'historical accident', important in the evolution of multilateral food aid, was the leading role played in the setting up of WFP by George McGovern as US delegate to the Intergovernmental Advisory Committee, and also as President Kennedy's Food For Peace Commissioner. An important quid pro quo in getting US support for launching WFP was that its activities should be complementary to America's PL 480. This led to a social rather than an economic emphasis in the original conception of WFP and McGovern referred to emergencies and malnutrition, and to 'other fields such as school-lunch, or labour-intensive projects as pilot activities whose purpose would be to develop some diversified experience'. Also, to keep the WFP small and to prevent it from competing with the major Title I operations of PL 480, the WFP was restricted to a project basis. The danger of a narrowly focused agency was compounded when the initial response of recipients and donors proved lukewarm. India and Pakistan, for example, were suspicious of WFP aid, fearing that the US would use it as an excuse for reducing PL 480. At the second pledging conference the response of donors was disappointing. The US pledged $130 million, but restricted its contribution to no more than 50 per cent of the total commodities available to WFP, or more than 40 per cent of the total cash resources up to a level of $6 million. The response of other donors was very poor and only 60 per cent of the target of $275 million was achieved.

Overcoming these early problems WFP went from strength to strength, and pledges for the 1969–70 period exceeded the target by 42 per cent. In twenty-two years of operation WFP has provided about $6.8 billion of food aid to 1,300 development projects in 120 countries and $US1.6 billion to emergency operations in 96 countries.

In practice, the concern over competing with PL 480 did not restrict the role of WFP, and it went on to become a pioneer in the structural evolution of food aid. It was among the first agencies to give primacy to development objectives, and to the careful evaluation of results achieved. By the beginning of the seventies requests to WFP for food aid were far greater than the resources available to it and new criteria for allocation were adopted, leading to an increased emphasis on the poorest countries, and on the poorest people in those countries. By 1984, 86 per cent of its development assistance went to low income, food-deficit countries. The World Food Programme established the feasibility and special advantages of a multilateral food aid programme, including improved co-ordination, reduced administrative costs, fewer political pressures, the chance to provide more coherent programme assistance, a wider and more appropriate choice of foodstuffs to recipients, and the ability to engage in multi-year programming.

From is earliest days WFP has made a key contribution in responding to food emergency needs, although its programme was geared primarily to development. A fixed amount of resources was reserved each year for emergency use by the Director-General of FAO, on the recommendation of the Executive Director of WFP. Concern grew about the adequacy of resources to cope with even limited emergencies, and the food crisis of 1973–4 was convincing proof that more provision was needed for emergency aid. As back-up for WFP in times of acute shortage a proposal to create an emergency reserve of 500,000 tonnes of cereal was submitted to the 1974 World Food Conference. It was rejected, but a similar proposal was accepted by the UN General Assembly the following year, thereby creating the International Emergency Food Reserve (IEFR), administered by WFP.

The resolution agreed by the General Assembly specified that the IEFR was a transitional measure, until the establishment of a world food grain reserve. Slow progress was made with contributions, and by 1976–7 only 115,000 tonnes, as against the target of 500,000 tonnes, had been pledged. In 1978, however, the General Assembly agreed that the IEFR should be maintained on a continuing basis with annual replenishments. Thereafter the IEFR target, although criticized as inadequate, was regularly attained. There are now proposals to increase the IEFR to 2,000,000 tonnes.

The World Food Programme was the only UN agency given a mandate to use food aid specifically as a development tool. Other UN agencies have occasionally become involved in food relief as part of their general responsibility, for example the UN Disaster Relief Office (UNDRO), as part of a short-term response to dire hunger and malnutrition, caused by natural phenomena.

In the case of some agencies food aid has helped in carrying out their primary task. A good example is the United Nations International Children's Emergency Fund (Unicef). Soon after the end of World War II Unicef provided food relief to vulnerable groups. The operation of WFP after 1963 removed the burden of child-feeding, and after 1968 Unicef concentrated its food aid on emergency situations. The US was the largest donor of food to Unicef, providing half a million tonnes between 1959 and 1976. In 1976 Unicef and WFP agreed on a memorandum of understanding which set out the areas of responsibility for each agency, whereby Unicef's limited food aid operations would continue to supplement assistance through WFP as the main multilateral channel.

More recently, since the recent world recession of 1980–3 and the subsequent and continuing debt crisis affecting many developing countries today, Unicef has become especially concerned with the impact on the condition of children of the world recession and of the adjustment policies forced upon developing countries to cope with the recession and debt crisis. There is ample evidence that the impact of such adjustment policies— often under the pressure of IMF conditionality—on the condition of children (and other vulnerable groups) has been disproportionately heavy and resulted in a deterioration of their nutritional and overall living standards.[11] The combating of such dangerous and possibly irreversible damage to the human resources of developing countries creates a new need for food aid and the opportunity for its constructive use. A programme for such intensified use of food aid, and for the intensified co-operation between Unicef and WFP required to cope with this new dimension of food aid, was hammered out at a recent (November 1985) conference in New York. The IMF has agreed that the necessary austerity for debtor and balance-of-payments deficit countries should not result in a pointless counter-productive deprivation of children, pregnant and lactating women, and other vulnerable sections of the community.

Non-governmental Organizations

A striking feature of the history of food aid relationship in the post-war period has been the growth of the contribution of non-governmental organizations. Their evolution has in many ways mirrored the changes in the objectives and experience of bilateral and multilateral food aid agencies. Just as official food aid received a major impetus from the reconstruction needs of war, so the impetus for post-war reconstruction led to the start of NGOs, for example, Christian aid. Even earlier, the Save the Children Fund, the oldest of the large foreign aid charities, had been founded in 1919 from the Fight the Famine Council, which opposed the Allied blockade of Germany. President Herbert Hoover, who co-ordinated food aid efforts during and after World War I, called together representatives from twenty-seven American voluntary groups to assist in European recovery after World War II. These civic, religious, charitable and farm groups formed the Co-operative for American Remittance to Europe (CARE).

The role played by individuals was often critical in shaping the nature of the NGO. For example Oxfam's two initial godparents were the widely different talents of the Revd T. R. Milford, Master of the Temple and a Canon of Lincoln, and Jackson-Cole, an energetic, successful, self-made shop-owner from the East End of London:

without his vision, business ability and use of his own firm's resources Oxfam would never have gone outside Oxford . . . With the end of the war and with the tremendous needs arising, he realised that the traditional approach to charitable work would be inadequate. Charities would have to be run on businesslike lines.[12]

With the end of the period of post-war reconstruction NGOs broadened their objectives. In 1949 the Charity Commissioners approved the widening of Oxfam's registered objectives to 'the relief of suffering arising as a result of war or any other cause in any part of the world'. In the US, CARE changed its name and objectives, to the Co-operative for American Relief Everywhere, and was the first of American voluntary agencies to take principal responsibility for lobbying for, and distributing, the grant-type food commodities later to become Title II of PL 480.

Some NGOs co-operated with governments for political ends— for example, the US Government used the NGOs as 'neutral conduits' for aid to countries (mostly Communist) such as Poland and Yugoslavia with which they wished to improve relations but for domestic reasons had to keep the contact discreet. As with the official agencies, gradually their emphasis turned from immediate relief to development. It was decided by an increasing number of NGOs to try to implement the maxim inspired by the UN Freedom From Hunger Campaign—'Give a man a fish and you feed him for a day; teach him to fish, and you feed him for a lifetime.' At the end of the sixties Oxfam was spending less than 10 per cent of its grant budget on disasters, more than half on medical and welfare projects in non-emergency areas, and 40 per cent on agricultural development and technical training.

The change in roles resulted in tensions and often heated debates within many NGOs. To respond to charity for those in blatant distress requires merely Yes or No. . . . To respond to an interest in world development is a very different matter, with many uncertainties and confusing tracks. Honest differences of view existed on such issues as family planning, and unlike the official agencies the NGOs had no statutory requirements to fall back on. Indeed, the debate on the usefulness of food aid has raged most fiercely amongst NGOs. A strong, though largely anecdotal attack on food aid led to the downgrading of food aid in the programmes of Oxfam, albeit temporarily.[13] Such difficulties were exacerbated as the educative and conscience-raising roles of the NGOs became more important in the seventies. Some NGOs have extended the traditional role of voluntary organizations from relieving the suffering caused by poverty, to encouraging participation of the poor in the political process to demand their just, basic human rights, and more permanently reduce the biases against them in the development process. As a result, the NGOs have increased the risks of causing disillusion amongst their grass-roots contributors, who have been accustomed to see tangible, quick results from their giving, such as responding to appeals for Cambodia and Ethiopia; and (in the case of UK NGOs) running foul of the Charity Law Commissioners.

Over the last two to three decades the development activities of NGOs have mushroomed. Almost 2,000 NGOs are now mobilizing private financial and human resources in Western countries. These resources are channelled through some 6,000 to 8,000 NGOs in more than 110 developing countries. Development grants from privately contributed funds in Western countries are estimated at about $2.4 billion annually, supplemented by over $1 billion in government funds.[14]

Despite the sustained growth in NGOs, the size of their food aid contribution in value and physical terms is generally dwarfed by the official agencies. Availability of data on the use of NGOs by bilateral and multilateral agencies is limited but, by way of illustration, in the US fiscal year 1981 the two main US voluntary agencies CARE and CRS were responsible for distributing 52 per cent of US grant food aid (Title II) or approximately 1 million tons.

It is only since 1978 that the European Community has made significant use of NGOs for distributing food aid, especially for dairy products. The history of NGOs indicates that their real contribution must be seen in qualitative terms—namely, their flexibility and speed of response, their ability to influence governments and to educate people in rich countries, and to implement, at a grass-roots level, projects which reach the poorest in developing countries.[15] The official agencies have increasingly used the NGOs because of their advantages in implementing food aid projects, both for emergency relief and development. The delicate balance which the NGOs have sought to achieve, between large size of impact and small-scale grass-roots operation, is difficult, but their history indicates a successful response to the increased opportunities.

Conference Diplomacy

'Conference diplomacy' has made an important contribution to the history of food aid by providing a mechanism to ensure that as a country (and especially the US) moved from surplus producer it would still participate in food aid. Secondly, it was used to 'encourage' all nations to share the burden of food aid. In 1967 the signing of the Food Aid Convention as part of the International Grains Agreement meant that food aid could become part of the conference diplomacy 'horse-trading', whereby a country's food aid commitment could be negotiated as part of a bargain package including other aid, trade, and tariff issues. If some net food importing countries lost out on the 'swings' of having to give food aid, they could gain on the 'roundabouts' of more favourable tariff treatment elsewhere, or the benefits of membership of a club as in the case of the EEC members.

The major example of conference diplomacy in the evolution of food aid post World War II was the convening by the UN of the World Food Conference in November 1974. It was the first UN sponsored intergovernmental meeting at ministerial level since the Hot Springs Conference of 1943 and was attended by 130 countries. The Conference was initiated by Henry Kissinger, then US Secretary of State, to tackle the threat of world-wide malnutrition, as the price of wheat on the world market was rocketing, and stocks were severely depleted.

In retrospect, the Conference enjoyed many of the preconditions necessary for successful multilateral development diplomacy.[16,17] There was much goodwill on the specific issue of food, and there was some willingness to compromise. The sterile confrontation which has largely characterized North–South negotiations was to some extent broken by flexible coalitions based on interests, rather than ideology. Thus a major achievement of the Conference was agreement on a resolution to establish the International Fund for Agricultural Development (IFAD). This resulted from a new alliance of the West and OPEC, which together account for the two-thirds of the votes required for project approval by IFAD.

A further achievement of the Conference was to agree on a commitment to provide minimum target levels of food aid including 10,000,000 tonnes of cereals per annum, and proposals on food aid for emergencies. To achieve the objectives, institutions were created or re-formed. In practice the councils and committees had no 'teeth' either to intervene through purchases, or to bring wayward governments back into line in their market activities. Similarly, the World Food Council had no real power, but had to depend on the basic goodwill and vested interests of member governments. The progress which was achieved in reaching the food aid target levels, and making improved provision for emergency needs, may in fact be attributable to better weather and improved harvests, rather than the conference diplomacy!

The Conference did succeed in focusing publicity on the issue of food aid, and placed it in a wider context of food and development. Its proposals must be judged as excessively optimistic—again the challenge had been underestimated, the response muted, and the opportunity only partly grasped.

The history of food aid reveals the emergence of a diversified and highly structured system, based on a complex web of bilateral and multilateral agencies and NGOs, making use of food aid as a development tool. The transition has been one of emphasis, since it would be naïve not to recognize the continuing significance of strategic, political, and vested interests of individual states, and pressure groups within those states. In particular, the use of food aid as a tool for surplus disposal, and the need to maintain farmers' jobs and incomes, has remained important. The United States has lost its pre-eminent position as other bilateral and multilateral agencies have responded to the challenge of food aid.

The transition has also been gradual over decades. Occasionally it is possible to identify a major breakthrough, or an inspired individual, for example, the Marshall Plan, the creation of PL 480 and WFP, a Hubert Humphrey, a Boyd Orr. More characteristically the emergence of a food aid system has been a long, hard slog, the product of a myriad of day-to-day bureaucratic decisions, creating a general philosophy, where food aid has been brought within the context of an overall development strategy, which emphasizes the needs of the poorest, and the overall requirements for food policy.

References

1. Smith, C. W., *The Great Hunger* (London, 1975).
2. *New York Times* (30 January 1979).
3. Lappe, F. M., and Collins, J., *Food First: Beyond the Myth of Scarcity* (Boston, 1977), p. 328.
4. Hopkins, R., *Food Aid and Development: the Evolution of the Food Aid Regime*, in WFP/Government of the Netherlands Seminar on Food Aid, The Hague, 1983.
5. Wightman, D., *Food Aid and Economic Development* (New York, 1968).
6. *Food Aid Convention* (HMSO 1967) Cmnd. 3840, (London, 1967).
7. Clay, E., *Review of Food Aid Policy Changes Since 1978*, WFP Occasional Paper No. 1 (Rome, 1985).
8. Africa Bureau Cologne/IDS, *An Evaluation of the EEC Food Aid Programme* (Brighton, 1982).
9. Ezekiel, M., 'Uses of agricultural surpluses to finance economic development in under-developed countries—a pilot study in India' in *Food for Development*, FAO (Rome, 1985).
10. Meier, G. M., and Seers, D. (eds), *Pioneers in Development* (New York and Oxford, 1984).
11. Jolly, R., and Cornie, G. A. (eds), *The Impact of World Recession on Children—a Study prepared for Unicef* (Oxford, 1984). (For both general evidence and a series of country studies.)
12. Whitaker, B., *A Bridge of People. A Personal View of Oxfam's First Forty Years* (London, 1983), p. 17.
13. Jackson, T., with Eade, D., *Against the Grain—the Dilemma of Project Food Aid* (Oxford, 1982).
14. Development Assistance Committee, OECD, *Aid Agency Co-operation with Non-Governmental Organisations* (Paris, 1985).
15. Minear, L., 'The role of NGOs in development', in Clay E. J. and Shaw J. (eds), *Poverty, Development and Food*, Festschrift for Hans Singer (London, 1987).
16. Berridge, G., and Jennings, A. (eds), *Diplomacy at the UN* (London, 1985).
17. Weiss, T. G., and Jordan, R. S., *The World Food Conference and Global Problem Solving* (New York, 1976).

3 FOOD AID:
Why not write a cheque instead?

Even the most passionate advocates of food aid would accept that there are occasions when a cheque would have been better. The unfortunate, bemused, and blundering aid official in John Updikes' novel *The Coup*, would doubtless have preferred his aid agency masters to have sent a cheque, rather than the mound of unwanted breakfast cereals and savouries which became his funeral pyre! The 'double-tied' nature of food aid—tied by both types of aid—namely by food, and by source—for example, to American PL 480—may appear to have major disadvantages compared with the flexibility of cash. A cheque could take the form of freely usable foreign exchange, to be spent on any type of import from anywhere, or of local currency, to be spent on any type of local goods or service.

In practice, the distinction between food aid and a cheque is not nearly so clear-cut as might appear, just as we have seen that the role of food aid is more complicated than simply feeding hungry people. Food aid seen as an international resource transfer may make a key contribution to a country's balance of payments, or may provide a budgetary resource for hard-pressed governments, or be a significant income transfer to selected target populations. Unfortunately for many recipients, if they did not get food aid, there is little likelihood that they would receive cash instead. The implications and possibility, in fact rather than theory, of additional cash or food aid will, in part, depend upon the use to which the aid would be put—namely programme, project, or emergency aid. The problem is further complicated because the distinction between these three categories has become increasingly blurred.[1] In some countries 'emergency' aid is not a one-off event, but because of repeated man-made or natural disasters it becomes semi-continous, and resembles programme aid. Increasingly stricter conditions attached to programme aid, and its provision on a multi-year basis, are also blurring the distinction between project and programme aid. In practice, if food aid is to be effective in whatever role, some cash as a complement is essential. After all, someone has to pay to ship it. Furthermore, the use of food aid may generate cash—which again blurs the distinction between financial aid and food aid.

Surplus Disposal

A major historical cause behind the growth of food aid was the pressure to dispose of food surpluses generated in developed countries by an agricultural sector often enjoying protection from foreign competitors. Although the importance of surplus disposal as a factor behind US food aid diminished as the need for aid to identified groups of recipients grew, surplus disposal has remained important for the US, and is illustrated by the continuing legal requirement in PL 480 that there must be a determination of availability by the US Secretary of State for Agriculture before any shipment of specific commodities can be made under the Act. Again, recent official evaluation of the Canadian food aid programme states:

to the extent compatible with our development and humanitarian objectives, food aid policy should continue to take account of *Canada's economic interest* in increasing the value-added portion of agricultural commodities and in reducing the high inventory costs that arise from occasional domestic over-supply of agricultural commodities.[2]

In the case of the European Community, behind the protective barriers of the Common Agricultural Policy food aid has assumed rising importance. In so far as surplus disposal was a factor, food aid would be additional to financial aid. The case should not be overstated, since it is estimated that about half of Title I PL 480 long-term credits would anyway have been provided via other US programmes. The fact that major food aid donors agreed to provide food aid as a multi-annual commitment under the Food Aid Conventions also reduces the strength of the assumption of 'additionality'. Some countries, for example the UK, which have not had food surpluses, have still given cash for food aid from their aid budget, and this may be seen as a straight trade-off between financial aid and food aid, both of which are provided out of the same aid budget. Even the increases in emergency aid to Ethiopia, Somalia etc. in the 1980s were largely resources shifted from elsewhere in the UK development budget. There is a movement towards 'full-costing' of food aid resources, and each EEC member state puts its support for Community food aid within its national aid ceiling. Commonsense appraisal of major donor aid policies indicates that despite these arguments food aid must in part be 'additional' to financial aid. If the EEC and the US were to reach for their cheque books to substitute for food aid, it would mean monetary increases of 40 per cent and 25 per cent respectively. This seems very unlikely when in fact in the 1980s the value of total aid flows in real terms has fallen.

Targets, Flows, and Safeguards

Furthermore, the fulfilment of food aid international targets compares favourably with financial aid targets. For example, the current commitment for cereals food aid under the Food Aid Convention, of 76 per cent of the 1975 World Food Conference target of 10 million tonnes of cereals, surpasses the typically poor performance in reaching financial aid targets. Underlying this better target fulfilment of food aid than of financial aid, and the case for food aid being 'additional', may be not so much the superiority of food as aid, but rather the 'muscle' of the supporting interest-groups, such as the farmers, and the vested interests of politicians. The bureaucratic setting in which total aid budgets are fixed, and within this sum, how budgeting practices determine the allocation between financial and food aid, is an important, but as yet largely unknown, factor in the debate on whether food aid is additional to other forms of aid. What is certain, however, is that over time, distinct food aid management, procedures, practices, and institutions have emerged, which now constitute a separate and in a sense, additional channel for aid. Food aid donors have national policies, and bureaucracies exist with vested interests which provide a momentum for food aid, separate from a decision on whether or not to give a cheque. Bilateral food aid co-ordinating mechanisms have been agreed, for example the Food Aid Convention, and multilateral food aid channels, especially the World Food Programme, ensure continuity of food aid and burden sharing. The follow-up to the world food crisis of 1972–4, and the 1975 World Food Conference, may be seen as a critical step in establishing food

aid as a major additional source of aid. Channelling food aid multilaterally has had the advantage of enabling smaller donors to derive
greater benefit from the inputs than they would have been able to
obtain individually. It also provides opportunities for triangular
transactions involving food exporters from developing countries,
and results in savings on overhead administrative costs. Triangular
transactions would involve a cheque being signed which would
finance the export of food from the food surplus to the food deficit
developing country. An example is the transfer of maize from
Zimbabwe in 1982 to cover food deficits in neighbouring countries,
and facilitated by the WFP/IEFR. Triangular transactions illustrate
the danger of over-simplification, that is of presenting the issue as a
straight choice between a 'cheque' and food aid.

In a simple and direct way food aid, by supplying imports which
a poor nation has neither the creditworthiness nor the foreign
exchange to import, makes more food available to that nation. If,
on the other hand, food aid replaces what would otherwise have
been imported commercially, the recipient country enjoys an
almost equivalent gift of foreign exchange, or a reduction in what
its indebtedness would otherwise have been.

Most donors make a condition in granting food aid that it shall
not replace normal commercial imports. The USPL480 legislation,
for instance, requires the President to 'take reasonable precautions
to safeguard usual marketings of the United States . . . '
(Sec. 103(c)) in implementing the Act. The motivation behind the
restriction on food aid (to be given only if it exceeded 'usual marketing requirements' (UMR)), was unashamedly to protect the
interests of the donors from unfair competition, and not necessarily
to further the development of the recipients. In practice the implementation of the legislation has been flexible, although occasionally, even for low income countries, a hard line is taken. For
example, donors to Tanzania have specified balance-of-payments
support as the purpose of their assistance and donor evaluations
have commented on how difficult it is to apply 'usual marketing
requirements'. (A more detailed description of the UMR device
appears in Chapter 4.) Some donors have concluded that Tanzania
has violated the usual marketing requirements, substituting food
aid for commercial imports. Canadian food aid was halted in
1982–3 to penalize UMR violation, but was resumed in 1983–4
even though Tanzania had not met its UMR commitment that year

due to lack of foreign exchange, so that the food aid, in substituting for non-existent national cash, became financial aid.

Since 1979–80 wheat aid has represented about 60 per cent of Tanzania's total marketed supplies. Though food aid has formed a part of the import structure, it should not be assumed that additional imports would or could exactly replace food aid. Tanzania's foreign exchange situation worsened after 1978, but its food import requirements were also high and rose sharply in the late 1970s and the early 1980s. If the food aid received in 1981–2 had actually been bought commercially, in addition to the amount spent on commercial imports, the total cost would have represented 30 per cent of the aggregate non-oil foreign exchange availability in that year, and would have been equivalent to the combined value of that year's exports of sisal and cotton.

Balance-of-Payments Support

A similar picture exists for many other low income countries. Their balance of payments has been squeezed by deteriorating terms of trade and mounting indebtedness. In the ten-year period 1973 to 1983, World Bank estimates show that Africa's debt increased by 22 per cent a year, greatly exceeding the growth of output or exports. The 'debt/service ratio' is one indicator of the state of health of a country's balance of payments. It measures the share of export earnings that have to be used to make the contractual debt payments of interest and repayments of principal before foreign exchange can purchase imports. For sub-Saharan Africa, the debt/ service ratio rose from 4.6 per cent in 1974 to 20.3 per cent in 1983, and the debt position is expected to worsen over the eighties. Measures to ease the low income countries' balance of payments will take on increasing importance. Case study evidence from Asia indicates that for a number of large importing countries such as South Korea and Sri Lanka, food aid did substitute to a considerable degree for commercial food imports. By contrast, in India, for over 20 years the largest recipient, less than a quarter of cereals food aid substituted for commercial imports.

Judging the development impact of the financial support to the recipient government generated by the value of food aid through balance-of-payments support, is very difficult. The impact will depend upon how the freed foreign exchange is in fact used. It may be that the use is concentrated on capital imports and raw materials vital for development. But it may also be that the foreign exchange set free by the food aid is spent on buying the latest and most sophisticated foreign military hardware—of little or no use to development. Any evaluation involves assessing a country's entire development efforts and the impact of aid, and what would have happened without food aid. One extreme scenario is that the government could decide to allocate all the freed foreign exchange to purchasing more food. Some critics suggest that the foreign exchange generated by the food aid simply allows governments to avoid or delay politically unpalatable policy decisions relating to more realistic agricultural policies, exchange rates, and economic policies.[3] If a government lacks the political will to undertake economic reforms that would benefit the agricultural sector but antagonize the local elites presumably they would still be inclined to postpone the reforms irrespective of whether they received a cheque or food aid. Others argue that 'there is a remarkable measure of agreement on the economic policy and institutional measures required to address the long-term food problems'.[4] Food aid in providing balance-of-payments support associated with World Bank and International Monetary Funds (IMF) structural adjustment programmes has a crucial contribution to make. Large-scale programme food aid for balance-of-payments support provides an opportunity of maintaining incentives for local food producers, since there need not be an automatic rise in food imports that would depress prices. The balance-of-payments relief by food aid leads to faster development, which should eventually lead to a higher level of commercial imports and higher demand for local food, so developed country exporters and the developing countries would both gain. Against this there is, however, a threat of increasing dependency on commercial imports. Imports of wheat and rice into Africa have risen sharply in the last decade to around 10 million tonnes per annum by the early 1980s, equivalent to the cereal consumption of one in five Africans, or the whole urban population of that Continent. To ensure that the most is made of the opportunities afforded by the balance-of-payments support generated from programme food aid, donors have been pressing for dialogue, and agreement on food aid to be conditional on economic reforms, sometimes as part of a national food strategy. There is also nothing intrinsically 'wrong' with graduating from food aid to commercial food imports—this may be in accord with the market development as determined by a country's comparative advantage. Taiwan and South Korea are both examples of successful merging of food aid development objectives and market development.

Counterpart Funds for Budgetary Support

Food aid may also have a 'cheque effect' when the sale of food aid by governments for local currency generates revenue, or counterpart funds, to be used in budgetary support. Low per capita income, low (and in some cases, negative) growth, and high dependency ratios within families, result in low savings ratios in the poorest countries. Their gross domestic savings have averaged only 3 per cent of GDP compared with 22 per cent for the middle income countries. Large subsistence sectors and weak trading sectors further limit taxable capacity, and most of the least developed countries have tax/GDP ratios below 10 per cent. Higher ratios could be counter-productive through an unfavourable impact on producer incentives. Taxation of farmers is relatively high, and levies of 40 to 50 per cent are commonly imposed on export crops. The fiscal systems of these poorest countries usually fail to capture inflationary gains and the profits derived from speculative trade and investment: yields from direct taxes remain nominal and tax evasion is widespread. Access to credit through borrowing via the Central Bank is limited by the threat of inflation (and in certain cases further restrained by IMF conditions for loans). For some developing countries which do not fully control their monetary policy, to raise additional local resources can be as difficult as earning additional foreign exchange.

In this situation the 'uncommitted budgetary resouces' (UBRs) which the sale of food aid generates may make a vital contribution to development. Even if food aid is freely distributed, for example as meals or take-home food in schools where government would otherwise have made provision, this also provides budgetary support. As in the case of freed foreign exchange, the additional budgetary support from food aid offers an *opportunity* for development, not a *guarantee* of development. It depends upon what the government does with the resources, either independently or in joint programming with donors. If the additional budgetary resources are simply used to import luxury goods or military equipment, the development impact is not likely to be significant! It is, however, possible simultaneously to lower food prices to consumers, pay higher prices to producers, undertake agricultural investment, and provide extension services to cut producer costs.

As in the case of balance-of-payments support, budgetary support is also 'fungible', that is, available for any purpose, whether for development, or non-developmental; it is therefore extremely difficult to tie its effects down with any accuracy. Nevertheless, as with balance-of-payments support, donors have attempted to monitor the use of budgetary support, and to ensure that most is made of the opportunities afforded by it.

On the whole the United States has had the strictest programming procedures for counterpart funds and generally they are deposited into special accounts. In Tanzania's case Title I and Title II counterpart funds were deposited in special accounts in Tanzania's National Bank of Commerce and the Co-operative and Rural Development Bank. Proposals for the usage of counterpart funds had to be approved by both the US and Tanzanian Governments. Canada requires that 'the funds generated by the sale of the food would be used for development projects within the country as mutually agreed to by the two governments'.[5]

In its Foreign Policy Review in 1970, the Canadian Cabinet emphasized that Canada should require counterpart funds to be established by recipients of food aid and other commodity aid. However, an evaluation of food aid undertaken by the Canadian Government in 1983 indicated that counterpart funds not allocated to specific projects or programmes within a reasonable time might be released to provide support for the recipient's general development programme.

A 'selective requirement' approach has been recommended following a policy review of Canadian food aid in 1982. The review also argued that greater consideration should be given to the administrative costs involved in the management and control of counterpart funds.

Canada and Australia have usually had easier requirements for counterpart funds usage. Canada has required only 20 per cent of the funds to be spent on projects agreed to beforehand by the two governments, while the other 80 per cent was to be contributed to the development budget of the Government of Tanzania. However, the expenditure items in the development budget were required to be identified on an annual basis. A CIDA evaluation describes one such case when this condition was not met: 'Agreement with Canada that proceeds from the sale of Canadian food would be used to finance rural road construction was not honoured by the Government of Tanzania. Instead, the funds were used by the consignee, a state corporation, to subsidize farmers to stimulate agricultural production. It would buy local products at a high price and sell them at a low price to consumers. The deficit was covered by sales proceeds of food aid.'

Counterpart funds generated by sales of Australian food aid have not been stringently programmed. Again in the case of Tanzania it was not until 1981–2 that there were any specifications for the use of the sales proceeds. Australian food aid counterpart funds seem to have been used in water supply improvement and livestock development. Counterpart funds generated from sales of US PL 480 aid have been used to support crop storage, food crop production and processing, agricultural research, agricultural training, rural infrastructure works, and agricultural credit. The programmed portion of Canadian food aid counterpart funds has been used in support of the Canadian Wheat Project, the Spare Part Project, and the Railway Programme, all aimed at achieving the Canadian objective of improving food production and distribution.

The proceeds generated from programme food aid in Senegal, in particular PL 480 Title I, and the Economic Support Fund, have been used to provide budgetary support and encouragement of a policy dialogue in conjunction with the IMF, World Bank, and France, aimed at accelerating a structural reform programme. Some PL 480 Title III proceeds have provided local currencies for internal budget and local fund shortages.

In Kenya also the proceeds from PL 480 have played an important role in the evaluation of a policy dialogue which has increased reliance on the private sector and community self-help:

The point of policy dialogue and AID programme assistance is to encourage the Government of Kenya (GOK) to adopt economic growth policies which will lead to an improved standard of living for all Kenyans in terms of increased employment and income. These macro policies will benefit all Kenyans, but particularly those in rural areas. The requirement for balance-of-payments and budget support has increased both the necessity for reform and the opportunity for policy dialogue and policy implementation, particularly with regard to improved control of GOK expenditures, interest and exchange rate and adjustments, improved export incentives and import administration, freer importation of required agricultural inputs, improved prices for farmers, and a larger role for the private sector in agricultural marketing.[6]

Whether a transfer takes the form of a cheque, or food aid which generates finance for balance-of-payments, or budgetary support, the impact on development depends critically on the type, efficiency, and equity of the activities financed with these funds. Will the government have the ability and political will to allocate the resources to development, or will they be frittered away? Will the additional resources generated by food aid be used as an excuse to delay necessary adjustment measures? Will the donors have the ability and the political will to co-operate as aid partners in a dialogue which translates into realistic and appropriate conditions to assist development? The indications are that harsh lessons of inefficient economic policies, especially those which harm local farmers such as depressed farm-gate prices, over-valued exchange rates, and inefficient or even corrupt state marketing boards, inadequate aid co-ordination, and harmful conditions imposed on aid partners, are being learnt, albeit slowly.

A Cheque or Food Aid for Projects?

To say that it is necessary to choose between a cheque and food aid is misleading at the project level, as well as at the level of the economy as a whole. Public works, in which food-for-work is provided, in part or whole payment to project workers, are the most important use of project food aid. They offer the opportunity of improving nutrition, creating long-term employment, supplementing below subsistence incomes (for example, of landless householders and small farmers), and creating and maintaining infrastructure vital for development, such as feeder roads and irrigation schemes. Additional employment leads to increased demand for wage goods, and for the poor and largely rural households most of the additional demand would be for food. Food aid in meeting this generated demand prevents inflationary pressure from building up, and enables expansion to continue to pay for them. The generation of demand also means that the produce of local farmers should be in greater demand, not less. Little evidence has been found of localized disincentive effects in major food-for-work programmes in Ethiopia and Bangladesh.[7]

In recent years both recipients and donors have increasingly treated food aid as another source of cash. The 'monetization' of food aid has resulted in much greater flexibility in its use, and made it easier to avoid the problems that arise when food is regarded as part of a narrow package of food-for-work. The Executive Director of WFP in his 1983 annual report drew attention to WFP assistance releasing financial resources for development:

In about one-third of the projects assisted by WFP, food replaces expenditures which would otherwise have had to be made by the project authority, and thereby releases what are in effect additional resources, which can be used for development purposes. Classical examples of this function of food aid are dairy development or food reserve projects—although the same thing happens in food-for-work projects, in which a certain portion of the worker's wage is paid in food, or in school feeding projects, in which the money that the school authorities would have had to spend on food can be used for other purposes, such as the construction of additional schools or the provision of teaching materials. In designing this type of project, particular attention is paid to the programming of the use of the savings or, if sales are involved, of the sales proceeds.

The more flexible use of food aid through monetization etc. has enabled food aid to play a major role in tackling the growing problem of finding maintenance and recurrent expenditures for keeping projects going. Hard won gains in development have been lost as projects have not been maintained. Water-supply projects using diesel pumps have collapsed with no money to buy spare parts, or food. Transport has been particularly badly hit with large investment in bitumen roads wasted as they revert to little more than rough tracks through bush. Vehicle fleets have been immobilized without spare parts, and government officials desk-bound hoping that at least they will get paid, even if there is no money left to effectively do their job!

The cost of key complementary inputs for food aid projects has escalated rapidly, and many projects have slowed down or halted because of the lack of complementary inputs. One such example is a WFP project for the construction of access roads and maintenance of secondary roads in the Comoro Islands:

234 kilometres of road have been maintained or constructed during the period from January 1981 to December 1982. Depending on the damage caused by rains, road maintenance works were carried out four, five or more times a year but their efficiency is hampered by a lack of tools, equipment and materials. Also, a proper drainage system does not exist and this lack renders access to the villages difficult during the rainy season. Secondary roads are vitally important because in most cases they represent the only link between villages.

Rising oil prices and greater calls on local resources for transport, storage, and handling of project inputs and outputs, have caused difficulties for some food aid projects. To ensure implementation and continued operation, a proportion of the aid commodities have been sold to finance the cost of essential complementary inputs. In Ethiopia and Bangladesh the WFP has agreed, on an experimental basis, to the sale of grain by the state food trading agency to defray local transport and handling costs. The founders of the WFP foresaw that contributions would need in the aggregate to be in the ratio of about two-thirds commodities and one-third cash and acceptable services, the latter being essential for the payment of ocean freight. This ratio has not recently been achieved, with the non-commodity ratio reaching only 16 per cent in 1984. There is a Non-Food Items Unit (NFIU) within WFP, that works in close collaboration with field staff in identifying non-food items. The requests are listed in a catalogue published twice yearly, and distributed to all potential donors. In 1983 the resources available to the Non-Food Items Unit enabled them to meet less than one-third of requests. The shortage of complementary inputs meant that execution of many food aid projects in the field was badly hampered. Operation and maintenance of on-going projects were neglected and the expected benefits failed to materialize.

Lessons from recent experience with food aid projects are that the food input should be seen as one complementary element and that a sharp distinction between 'cheque' and 'food' is harmful. Co-operation between 'food' and 'financial' aid agencies has become more necessary and is growing. At the seventeenth session of the WFP Committee for Food Aid it was announced that the World Bank was granting a 'cheque' for two million dollars to WFP to fund complementary inputs for selected projects in Africa. Canada in 1983 provided half a million dollars to purchase equipment as essential inputs for a WFP project to improve and maintain roads in

Bolivia. An evaluation of PL 480 Title II supported non-government organization food-for-work and nutrition projects in Indonesia recommended allowing 10 per cent of the project commodities per year 'for monetization to meet other programme costs'.[8] Improved inter-agency co-operation and seeing more clearly the complex linkages which characterize food aid projects, would facilitate a change in image for the food aid—away from what some would see as an inferior form of assistance. This 'poor relation' image of food in the aid scene has led in some instances to inadequate planning and provision for complementary resources. A more self-confident, but realistic assertion of the contribution of food aid could lead to its integration into projects having substantial levels of capital investment finance, with better design and operational management.

Relative Merits of Cash and Food

The case study evidence does not present a clear picture on the relative merits of cash and food at the project level. The type of remuneration seems to be secondary in determining success, compared with a host of factors at the local level, including the ability and integrity of officials. A study of the employment guarantee scheme (EGS) in Maharashtra (funded by India's own resources), found that the food element was the greatest attraction. Other instances for Angola and Mozambique showed that the cash component was irrelevant as nothing could be bought with it. The food was all that mattered.

The EGS and Bangladesh programmes show that the weakest and most disadvantaged can benefit from food aid projects. But there is evidence that the economically and politically powerful still find ways of capturing a bigger share of benefits, for example as the public investments increase land productivity, and the assets held by the rich obtain windfall gains. Food has the advantage of being highly visible, expecially if it is exotic or distinctively packaged, but evidence for larger programmes shows leakages of about a third of resources up to site level from a range of malpractices. Whether a cheque would be any better than food is disputable—some leakage seems to be inevitable given a bureaucratized allocation of resources, whether in poor or rich countries! The example of a WFP food-for-work project in Ghana shows that while funds may be released via whole- or part-payment of wages they may not reach their intended purpose. This situation was well set out in a WFP evaluation report on the project in 1983:

Deductions have always been made from workers' wages. In September 1983, savings generated at the assisted farms amounted to about 4.8 million cedis. While the state farms sent most of their savings regularly to the Treasury, the EEC-assisted farms kept the funds in their own accounts, and the World Bank-assisted GOPDC plantation sent part of the savings to the Treasury and kept part in its own accounts. State farms have recently kept their savings in their own accounts, mainly because the government failed to provide the required funds for transporting commodities.

So far no funds have been spent for the purposes stipulated in the plan of operation. In a period of budgetary constraints, the Government considered the transfer of savings as an additional source of income and did not allocate the corresponding amount to the Ministry of Agriculture for improvement in the extension service. Expenditure has been made from savings not transferred to the Treasury (768,052 cedis), but, mainly to meet handling and transport costs for WFP commodities that the Government was unable to cover.

The report to the government consequently recommended that:

beginning immediately, savings generated by project 2258 (Phase II) should no longer be sent to the Treasury, but to the counterpart funds account at the Bank of Ghana, and from there to a special account in the Ministry of Agriculture, for utilisation. The Government should release the funds sent so far to the Treasury. Past and future savings should be utilised internationally to purchase inputs (seeds, fertiliser, tools) for the plantations' future food production programme.

A key factor in determining project performance in food-for-work type projects has been the motivation of the workforce. If incentives—whether of food or cash—are inadequate, productivity and the quality of work falls. Experience from Bangladesh and Ethiopia shows that work performed reflects the motivation of those who gain from it. On reforestation projects in Ethiopia in the early seventies, the workers felt they were gaining nothing from their labour, and the gains were all going to large landowners: they were planting a high proportion of the trees upside down!

Alpha-value

Food aid has a cost to the donor and a value for the recipient. In some cases the value to the recipient is higher than the cost to the donor, in others the opposite. The operation of those factors further tends to blur the distinction between financial and food aid. A simple formula used for measuring the income transfer efficiency of food aid commodities is the 'alpha-value'; that is, the ratio of the value of the commodity to the food aid recipients compared with its acquisition and delivery cost.[9] The value to the recipients depends on what substitutes exist for the food aid in their diet, or if they are producers, whether they are net sellers and if so at what price. If a kilogram of wheat for food aid costs 20 cents to buy, 20 cents to ship, and 10 cents to distribute at the receiving end—making a total cost of 50 cents, and the substitute for the food aid for an individual in the target group is to buy sorghum at 15 cents per kilogram—the alpha-value would be 0.3, i.e. 15/50. In this example, the individual recipient would be better off receiving a cheque for 30 cents (the 'saving' in shipping and distribution costs), if local food supplies were available, rather than the kilogram of food aid wheat. The higher the 'alpha-value' the more effective food aid becomes. If it is low, as in this example, the food aid may still be valuable, but it may be that a cheque would be better, or another type of food aid commodity, say sugar or oil, with a better 'income transfer efficiency'. Similar studies of EEC dairy-food aid suggest that other forms of transfer, for example, financial transfers or export credits, could provide the same value to many recipient countries at a lower cost to the European Community budget.[10]

In fact the true value of food aid for the recipient should be measured by the income transfer rather than the cost of providing the food. The income supplement concept is based on the idea that food aid represents income. It may be measured by comparing the value of the beneficiaries' diet with and without food aid and/or adding any income derived from the sale of food by the beneficiaries.

There is an important sense in which the developed countries have in practice made their food aid commitment to the developing countries in a 'cheque' form, and as a result the food security of developing countries has been reduced. The objective of food security interventions is usually to boost food consumption and real incomes of a group, region, country, or even globally, when there is a danger of shortfall below acceptable levels. During the 1972–4 world food crisis the overall impact of food aid, as experienced in countries such as Sri Lanka and Bangladesh, as well as the food supply system as a whole, was to make matters worse. This happened because the food aid programmes of major donors, especially the US and Canada, were budgeted on an annual basis in financial terms, and individual country programmes were also organized on an annual financial basis rather than in volume terms as commodity commitments. As world market food prices rose the real value of the cheque committed by the donors fell. So in the crisis, just when food flows should have risen, in fact they were reduced to a third of the levels in the late 1960s! Lessons were learnt from the world food crisis, as illustrated by the Food Aid Convention's quantity commitment of 7.6 million tonnes, and the IEFR provision of 500,000 tonnes, rather than a 'cheque' for a fixed financial sum. Nevertheless it is suggested that there is still scope for improvement of food security by donors establishing a network of reserves to provide adequate back-up for commitments, especially in times of international food crisis. Locally placed and controlled food security stockpiles would be likely to be more acceptable to recipient governments, as well as reducing costs, and providing commodities more suited to local tastes.

One situation when a 'cheque' would appear to be best, is when food is available, but poverty and famine occur because individuals and households do not have the purchasing power to acquire the food. A complex of factors, for example employment, forms of socio-economic transactions in villages, such as credit and charity, and own production and prices, influences real income, referred to by Sen as 'exchange entitlement'.[11] Experience of major famines such as Bangladesh (1973–74) and Ethiopia (1972–74), shows that it is not just the supply of food but the 'exchange entitlement' that determines which households can finance food purchases out of income, and which go hungry, and when. Special rural credit programmes and tax relief have long been established as measures to sustain the assets and employment of farmers and dependents worst affected by emergencies. International aid agencies are able to participate in rural works programmes, for example in Ethiopia and Bangladesh, as effective responses to emergency situations, illustrating again the interdependence between a 'cheque' and 'food'.

When 'emergency assistance' has to be provided year after year it is more likely that food will be available for assistance than a 'cheque'. Aid agency practice is to earmark resources as a reserve for emergency use, but in a 'continuing emergency' which has characterized many sub-Saharan countries, there is a danger that emergency aid may doom certain kinds of development food aid to failure (see Chapter 11). The transition from relief to development, whether at country level or for groups within a country, has yet to be satisfactorily resolved.

In so far as the choice exists between food and a 'cheque' for funding a particular project, some evidence shows that it is the food that is disbursed much more quickly. Estimates for Bangladesh show generally between 75 per cent and as much as 88 per cent of the cumulative commitment of food aid disbursed in a year, which is considerably more satisfactory than disbursement of financial aid in Bangladesh. In practice the stages in the project cycle of identification, design, and appraisal, for most projects take much longer than sorting out the specifics of a food aid flow—for emergency relief this may mean the difference between life and death.

References

1. Clay, E. J., and Singer, H. W., *Food Aid and Development: Issues and Evidence*, WFP Occasional Paper No. 3 (Rome, September 1985).
2. CIDA, *Evaluation Assessment of the Canadian Food Aid Programme* (Ottawa, 1983) pp. 16–17.
3. Pym, F., Speech to the Royal Commonwealth Society on Britain's Contribution to Development (London, December 1983).
4. OECD, *Development Co-operation* (1984 Review) p. 22. Paris, 1984.
5. CIDA, *Evaluation Assessment, of the Canadian Food Aid Programme* (1983) p. 9. Ottawa.
6. United States Congressional Annex (1985) p. 209.
7. WFP/CFA, *Sales of Grain to help meet the Internal Costs in Least Developed Countries* (Rome, 1983).
8. Bryson, J. and others, *Assessment/Redesign of the CRS PL 480 Title II Programme in Indonesia* (Washington, DC, 1984).
9. Reutlinger, S., *Project Food Aid and Equitable Growth: Income Transfer Efficiency First*, in WFP/Government of the Netherlands Seminar on Food Aid, The Hague, 1983.
10. Clay, E. J., and Mitchell, M., 'Is European Community food aid in

dairy products cost effective?', *European Review of Agricultural Economics*, vol. 10 (Amsterdam, 1983).

11. Sen, A. K., *Poverty and Famines: an Essay on Entitlement and Deprivation* (Oxford, 1981).

4 FOOD AID:
Who controls it and who can get it?

With food aid now averaging about 9 per cent of all overseas development aid from all donors—or the equivalent of $US2.5 billion in round figures—it is evident that there will be questions arising as to how this large cake should be sliced, by whom and for whom. Furthermore, the slicing has to be carried out with care and consideration since, despite its size, there is still not enough for everyone. It is interesting to note that the first World Food Conference called under the auspices of the United Nations in 1974 to mobilize some international action to begin to tackle the apparently increasing level of hunger and malnutrition in the world, set a yearly target of 10 million tonnes of food aid. At the time this was considered Utopian but a decade later the target was met and in 1985 it was exceeded. This was due to increasing international awareness of the problems of the food-deficit countries of the developing world and the correspondingly positive public and private responses from the better-off countries, which the World Food Conference also doubtless helped to bring into sharper focus. There have been particularly significant increases in the amount of food aid given in response to the recent series of emergencies and crises in Africa.

The total amount of aid available to the developing countries is generally dicussed as though it were a single cake, as this is handy for conceptual and planning purposes. The reality is, naturally, rather different: ingredients are dispersed among a number of donor bins; others with no produce to give have put some vouchers in the till to be used for groceries. In addition, the ingredients in the bins are usually cut up into small lots earmarked for special customers or for special purposes. Some ingredients are put into a good mix through international or regional organizations but this accounts for less than a quarter of the total cake.

Cutting the hypothetical cake would be an easier task if the size of the slices could be pro-rata'd against some convenient and reasonably predictable denominator such as population growth or

Gross National Product (GNP), but one of the problems with food aid planning is that it has to deal with such a wide range of variables. Some of the needs may arise from what are known as structural problems, that is to say there may be a food shortage because there is simply not enough land to support the population and there is not enough income generated to buy it commercially, as may be the case in some of the small island economies; in other cases shortage may be due to economic policies that concentrate on urban and/or industrial development and low food prices for the urban population, to the detriment of agriculture and so forth. In other cases the need for food aid may only be seasonal, perhaps to make up for a crop failure, or a temporary lack of foreign exchange that resulted in a cut-back in commercial food imports, or perhaps covering a two- or three-year drought cycle. Again, sudden and large requirements may result from outbreaks of civil war or political repression resulting in crises of mass exodus. Setting aside too much of the total cake for the last two categories, which contain the greatest number of variables, could perhaps deprive some of the steadier 'customers' of their supply which they may be using in a long-term process of infrastructure development and agricultural improvement with a view to working themselves out of the need for food aid—as, for example, India did in the 1960s and 1970s. In recent years an increasing amount of food aid has, in fact, had to be used for emergencies, both natural and man-made ones; to earmark too much of the cake for these essentially humanitarian, but none the less palliative actions, could detract from a number of more truly development-oriented programmes; alternatively to earmark too little—a quantity that is not even predictable—would mean perhaps mass starvation of innocent population groups.

The international community has been struggling with these various questions since the emergence of the concept of food aid as an international aid and development instrument toward the end of the Second World War and since no perfect solution has been found, the process is still going on.

The process began with US entry into the War in 1941 and discussions were held with Britain on the question of stockpiling and utilizing the large cereal surpluses that were likely to be created in the USA, Canada, and Australia, due to the curtailment of many of their traditional markets as a result of the wartime naval blockade and other restrictions. The first concrete results of the discussions came in August 1942 with the creation of an international wheat pool to be administered by an International Wheat Council with headquarters in Washington, DC. This council superseded the Wheat Advisory Committee that was originally established in London in 1933.

Although the original intention of the Council was simply to act as an instrument for inter-governmental relief in war-stricken areas, it soon became involved in the more complex negotiations surrounding an International Wheat Agreement when it became clear that almost none of the earlier traditional customers in Europe would have the necessary funds to make commercial purchases; this, and the ending of the need to supply large armies, could together cause a massive fall in prices, leading to a crisis of agricultural production. There was at that time, still an all-too-painful memory of the depression of the 1930s, when farmers were compelled to let their land go out of production and even to destroy crops because millions of people did not have the money to buy the food they needed, while industry stagnated because of the drop in farm incomes.

The Drive for Marketing Agreements

Wheat producing and importing countries had been struggling for years to arrive at a mechanism that would set floor and ceiling prices and export quotas in order to achieve some market (and thereby production) stability. The first International Wheat Conference was held in Rome in March 1931. It was not until eighteen years and six conferences later, that the Seventh International Wheat Conference held in Washington, DC successfully completed negotiations for a multilateral contract-type agreement with price ranges and guaranteed sales. The agreement was ratified by the four exporting and 37 importing countries (including the USA that had failed to ratify a similar proposal in 1948) and came into force in August 1949. Although this was a modestly positive achievement in the international arena, it was conducted outside the international machinery within the UN Food and Agriculture Organization, that had proposed the creation of a wider-ranging International Food Board in 1946. This failed to materialize as it was considered too ambitious: the difficulties experienced in getting agreement on a single commodity during the Wheat Conferences certainly confirmed this. In the light of the success of the Wheat Agreement negotiations, the FAO at its General Conference in the autumn of 1949 launched a proposal for an International Commodity Clearing House (ICCH) to build up a world food reserve and to provide an outlet for various commodity surpluses. Although this was turned down a less ambitious advisory committee on Commodity Problems (CCP) was approved. This committee still exists, but it was its sub-committee, the Consultative Committee on Surplus Disposal (CSD) that played the more important role in resolving some of the conflicts of interest between commercial considerations and surplus disposal. One of the devices evolved by this group was the adoption by the international community of a kind of indexing known as Usual Marketing Requirements (UMRs). The original purpose was to draw up a list of commercial food imports by commodity and country over a period of years. If food aid in the form of surplus disposal was only given after that level had been reached, then it could be shown that the surplus disposal was not having an adverse effect on the commercial market interests. Although this provided a useful formula that is still applicable to middle income countries, its applicability to low income countries is marginal since they generally do not have the foreign exchange for commercial purchase. Furthermore, food aid is now often used as a means of budget support and in that sense acts as a replacement for commercial imports. Nevertheless, the CSD and the UMRs still exist and their usefulness lies in the fact that all food aid transactions from any donor are reported to the CSD and given a serial number, with the donation or loan, as the case may be, reviewed in relation to the UMR of the country concerned. The CSD now meets on a monthly basis in Washington, DC and provides a forum through which donors not only notify food aid but are also able to consult with each other.

The UMR device thus comes into play whenever a country requests food aid. The calculations are based principally on the average commercial imports over the preceding five years, but a number of other variants enter into the calculations such as:

(a) a substantial change in production in relation to consumption of the commodity concerned in the recipient country;

(b) evidence of a significant trend during the reference period in the commercial imports of the commodity concerned by the recipient country;

(c)   a substantial trend in the balance of payments or general economic position;

(d)   any exceptional features affecting the representativeness of the reference period;

(e)   any other considerations that the government may raise in its request.

Once these various calculations have been agreed upon between donor and recipient, the amount of concessional or grant aid is decided upon so as not to displace normal commercial transactions, and yet provide the food aid. Although this UMR system has its drawbacks and seems unnecessarily complex, it was effective in getting around the principal road-block in the way of developing effective food aid programmes, namely the caveat relating to commercial displacement. Had it been possible to devise this formula earlier, much of the controversy that surrounded the use of food as aid in the early post-war years could have been avoided.

As it happens, historical trends in food aid have justified the UMR approach rather than detracting from it. In the earlier years of its development food aid tended to go mainly to what are known as middle-income countries, partly because of the donor's greater confidence in getting repayment if the food aid was in the form of a loan, and partly because the middle income countries had the administrative and logistics capacity to absorb greater quantities of food aid with fewer snags than the less developed ones. The policies of donors since the 1970s have however, been to give priority to the low income, less developed countries where the needs are greatest. The UMR principle has provided economic justification for this since, as indicated earlier, the commercial imports of these countries had never been high, so that the likelihood, or the scope, of displacement through food aid was considerably less than would be the case with higher income countries.

When discussing food aid, in particular that coming in the form of cereals, it is easy to lose sight of the importance of the proportional relationship between it and commercial imports, which explains to a large extent the continuation of the CSD and UMR systems. A review of ten years of food aid operations, undertaken by J. W. Mellor on behalf of the FAO,[1] showed that although total

Table 1. Per capita volume of total cereal imports and food aid in developing countries by region and income group

Region or income group	Year	Food aid per capita (kg)	Total cereal imports per capita (kg)
Asia	1961–1963	3.82	11.54
	1976–1978	2.06	12.98
	1981	1.13	16.13
Latin America	1961–1963	8.31	25.00
	1976–1978	1.17	43.26
	1981		
North Africa/Middle East	1961–1963	24.13	35.81
	1976–1978	2.89	16.21
	1981	9.77	111.34
Sub-Saharan Africa	1961–1963	0.62	7.87
	1976–1978	2.89	16.21
	1981		
High income developing countries	1961–1963	3.27	12.89
	1976–1978	2.60	58.73
	1981	1.18	96.45
Middle income developing countries	1961–1963	3.27	12.89
	1976–1978	2.04	22.10
	1981	2.26	31.13
Low income developing countries	1961–1963	6.34	10.41
	1976–1978	3.56	9.19
	1981	2.94	7.42
Total developing countries	1961–1963	5.59	14.49
	1976–1978	2.74	21.59
	1981	2.36	30.19

food aid to developing countries had dropped with the exception of sub-Saharan Africa, total cereals imports had risen steeply in the two decades from 1961 to 1981. This is evident from Table 1.

The adoption of the UMRs worked in favour of the recipient country as well as the donor, since it was a means of acting against uncontrolled dumping of agricultural products that might have a depressive effect on local prices and thus on local production. As will be shown in Chapter 11 the possible disincentive effect of food aid on production continues to be the subject of considerable polemic.

The USA was by far the largest world producer of cereals; it is thus not surprising that her actions played a determinant role in the development of food aid—initially as a bilateral instrument, particularly after the frustrations over UNRRA as described in Chapter 2—and then again as an international tool after the success of the Marshall Plan. In a certain sense the operation of the Marshall Plan was relatively plain sailing; a large proportion of the aid went to wartime allies of the USA, with whose psychology and operational procedures they were already familiar, and furthermore, it was food aid closely linked to financial and relief aid. It was found that dealing with less familiar countries, often with different world outlooks and administrative procedures, raised a whole range of new questions. This led to an increasing move toward international solutions, which took a definite upturn with the election of J. F. Kennedy as President of the USA. The PL 480 legislation, passed in 1954 and described in Chapter 2, provided the framework for utilizing the available resources. However, with the increasing number of formerly colonial territories gaining independence, there was a parallel resistance on their part to 'tied' aid, that is to say, aid that was subject to one or other type of restriction on its availability or its use, or receipt of which could be interpreted as dependence on the donor country and its policies. Multilateralism provided a solution to such questions, though only as a supplement to, and not as a substitute for, the US and other major bilateral programmes.

The first formal approach in line with this new trend, was taken by Senator George McGovern addressing FAO's Intergovernmental Advisory Committee on Food Policy on 10 April 1961 when he stated that the US Government favoured a multilateral approach for the use of agricultural commodities as a supplement to bilateral arrangements and that a multilateral programme should be developed with the widest possible contribution by member countries. The USA was willing to initiate a fund for this purpose amounting to $US100 million over a three-year period. As a result of these proposals an international expert group under the aegis of the FAO was called to consider ways and means of using an expanded programme of surplus food utilization. This report was published both by the UN and FAO in 1961 under the title *Development Through Food: A Strategy for Surplus Utilization*. This report formed the basis for the creation of the International Development Association in 1959 as the 'soft' loan arm of the World Bank and of the UN Special Fund which provided a considerable boost to international technical assistance programmes, in all of which the USA also played a key role.

For the record, it should be noted that Unicef had been providing food aid, mostly milk products targeted on children, some time before these events.

The advantage of all these arrangements was that they gave the developing countries access, not merely to more funds and food but also to a wider range of choice, thus lessening the risk of domination by, or dependence on, any one donor. It also provided a means of escaping from the rigid annual budgeting of bilateral programmes. These processes continued to develop favourably until the growing demand for food aid, coupled to decreasing supplies due to adverse climatic and financial conditions in many of the donor countries, raised all the questions associated with scarcity, that is of slicing the cake rather than handing it out liberally.

The first effect of this change was for the principal food aid donors, mainly the USA, Canada, and Australia, to try and interest other high-income countries in contributing more, especially countries in western Europe and Japan. This approach was not unsuccessful but the main problems remained, i.e., that all the contributions to multilateral as well as to bilateral actions were on a voluntary basis and allocations were only made on a year-to-year basis in accordance with national budgeting cycles; and although legislation such as the PL 480 Act in the USA provided a ceiling, it did not, over a longer period, provide a floor. An important step to overcome this was taken in 1967 with the creation of a Food Aid Convention (FAC) by which a number of governments for the first time legally bound themselves to provide minimum specific quantities of food aid in cereals. This move was made in the context of wider issues leading to the signing of a Wheat Trade Convention and an international grains agreement which had been proposed several times in earlier years but never ratified. The specific quantities to be provided by each member country under the FAC had been worked out within the framework of the Kennedy round of GATT Trade negotiations. Scarcity in relation to demand had another lasting effect on food aid, namely, far greater attention being paid to utilization, methods of channelling, designation of beneficiaries, and general accountability. It also meant, as a further consequence, that potential recipient countries had to prepare their requests in much more detail and with much greater care and data than before.

On the donor side this need for tighter programming led to individual countries or groups of donor countries selecting preferred areas for their food aid, either in geographical or in functional terms. Consultations among a number of bilateral donors led in this way to a useful complementarity and avoidance of duplication of effort. However, a concomitant disadvantage from the recipient side was that this trend also led to donors becoming choosier about whom they would assist and for what reasons. This became known as the concept of conditionality of food aid which was resisted by many recipients and led them to push for a larger slice of the cake as multilateral aid. These concerns, together with the continuing relative scarcity of food resources as aid in relation to growing needs—particularly in the field of emergencies—were aired at the World Food Conference held in 1974 under the joint auspices of the UN secretariat and the FAO.

Of the various actions arising from the World Food Conference described in Chapter 2, three were designed to widen the scope of multilateral food aid. The first was the creation of the International Emergency Food Reserve (IEFR) with its 500,000 tonnes of yearly replenishable 'capital'. The second was the replacement of the Intergovernmental Council (IGC), the governing board of the World Food Programme, by the Committee on Food Aid Policies and Programmes (CFA), for the co-ordination of all food aid, not just WFP, including the operation of IEFR. The third was the creation of the FAO Committee on World Food Security (CFS). Since the IEFR contained international commitments it had to be approved by the UN General Assembly and this was done in September 1975.

The objective of replacing the IGC as the WFP governing body by the CFA was to involve greater participation in food policy and programming from the donor and recipient communities. As a first step in that direction, it drew up a set of Guidelines and Criteria which were brought out at the CFA meeting in Rome in May 1979. These are shown in Appendix 2. Although these are not in any way binding commitments like the Food Aid Convention, it is interesting to note that soon thereafter the US Agricultural Act of 1980 was brought into force under Public Law 96–494. Title III of this law, called the Food Security Wheat Reserve Act, sets up a reserve of four million tons to meet emergency humanitarian needs in developing countries.

Criteria for Poverty Threshold

The tighter programming and relative scarcity of funds for development after the early 1970s led to a concentration of food aid on the low income poorer countries as indicated in the CFA Guidelines and Criteria. The practical problem that arose was, however, to decide upon the yardstick that would determine such poverty and its threshold. Within the food aid donor/recipient group there was an obvious tendency for donors to shorten the list and lower the threshold and for recipients or potential recipients to do the opposite. For this reason there was need for a *deus ex machina*, which came in the form of the World Bank. The Bank's 'soft' loan division, the International Development Association (IDA), is empowered to make loans at a minimal or zero interest charge to countries whose GNP does not exceed a certain figure. A footnote added to the CFA's Guidelines and Criteria confirmed that the term 'low income' covered countries eligible for concessional assistance by the IDA—adding that the poorest countries within this group should receive special attention. The GNP of a country represents the total value of goods and services produced within an economy, including government and private spending, fixed capital investment, net inventory charges, net exports. Real GNP growth describes the increase in the volume of national output after allowing for inflation.[2] The World Bank produces annual data covering all economic aspects of the countries, subdivided into income groups and categories ranging from low income, lower middle, upper middle, oil producing, etc. In terms of food aid the first category is the most relevant although some of the middle income groups are recipients of food aid, while some in the low income group are not.

Since the GNP of a country can vary in terms of its production in relation to population growth, terms of trade, and so on, the threshold is not a fixed one. In 1983, for example, it was $US810, in 1984 $US790. The figure is naturally affected by the $US exchange rate against other currencies as well as by the country's actual GNP differential from year to year. The erosion of this apparently hard and fast standard led to other criteria being established. The United Nations Conference on the Least Developed Countries held in Paris from 1 to 14 September 1981 identified 31 countries in that category while the General Assembly in New York some weeks later added another five to the list. The criteria were not only GNP but also included such factors as low literacy rates and low contribution of manufacturing industries to the economy. The World Bank had a list of 34 low income countries with a note to the effect that in the case of six of them the GNP could not be accurately calculated. The Committee on World Food Security of the FAO then took a hand in the matter and produced a list of 47 food deficit countries plus another seventeen who were regarded as the 'most seriously affected' ones, declared to be below the level used for eligibility for IDA assistance, which in the year in question was $US805 per capita.

It can be seen from the foregoing that there are some semantic differences in the designation of low income poor countries. It will be found that by taking the World Bank's listing of countries by ascending schedule of GNP, the IDA threshold covers all the low income group of countries and comes about half-way up the list of lower middle income ones. Consequently the World Bank definition of low income should not be confused with the IDA eligibility threshold, which for the year in question was $US805, while the upper limit of the World Bank low income group was $US410. The FAO listing, on the other hand, intended showing only the food deficit countries within the IDA limit, since there are countries in this group who are not necessarily food deficit, such as Burma. A list of the low income food deficit countries according to the FAO formula and a listing of the World Bank's low and lower-middle income countries at the time of going to press are shown in Appendix 3.

Even the listing of food deficit countries, which would appear the most logical from the point of view of food aid, does not necessarily represent reality, for the reason that food aid may be given to countries which may not have a food deficit when measured in overall terms, but may well have groups of people who, by reason of low income or perhaps of ration systems from which they are excluded, cannot get access to the available food. Food deficit then is one of the principal criteria for eligibility to food aid, but not the only one. Furthermore, this type of listing reflects the status of a country over a longer term and cannot therefore take into account sudden emergencies, whether natural disasters or man-made.

These questions are mentioned, not only to show the difficulties that arise in trying to determine basic criteria for aid eligibility according to guidelines, and the evident pressures on those trying to decide how the cake should be sliced, but (perhaps more importantly) to show that they arise largely because food aid is such a flexible instrument of development and of assistance.

Eligibility for Food Aid

The first step in eligibility for food aid is, of course, a government or an institutional request for it. In the case of voluntary organizations it may be simply an agreement to operate in the country in question for some specified purpose, with food aid coming as a component later. Donors are not in the habit of putting up notices of food availability nor of the particular restrictions or conditions that might apply to its being granted. Particularly since the end of the era of pure surplus disposal in the early years of food aid operations, and since the period of scarcity that arose in the early 1970s, almost all donors have some kind of restrictions or provisos covering the use of food aid in the recipient country. The scarcity situation also led to greater donor insistence on various kinds of accountability, whether in the form of financial accountability or impact assessment. This is not out of zest for bureaucracy but because the public and the private donors to voluntary organizations want to be reassured that their efforts are not being wasted or used for some non-humanitarian or non-developmental purpose. The recipient country, for its part, will also need food aid for some specific purpose, be it budget support, famine relief, agricultural development, or other need. Eligibility will then become a question of marrying up this requirement with one or other of the donor programmes that appears to fit that requirement. In this process a potential recipient country may make enquiries with a number of possible donors and if it is a large request there may be consultation and sharing among donors. Alternatively, a country may merely ask an international organization to help it sort the problem out. Bilateral agencies of the donor countries and international organizations have offices in most of the developing countries, so that, many of the problems can be discussed and sorted out between donors and recipients well before a formal request is made. This will contain all the necessary justifications for the assistance and will fit in with the conditions or restrictions of the chosen donor. In such a process there is often a lot of give and take on both sides.

As a result of a number of years' experience in food aid programming certain donors have developed preferred geographical or functional areas in which they feel the kind of aid they can offer will be best applied. In other cases there may be enabling legislation on the donor side that restricts them to certain areas or situations in which food aid may be provided, or lays down categories of aid and limits the total or the proportional amounts that may be allocated to each category.

In the case of the USA, for instance, the Title I programme of concessional sales 'provides for the concessional sale of agricultural commodities to friendly countries', implying that if the recipients turn nasty they will be cut off. Title II grant programmes aim to alleviate hunger and malnutrition of peoples in the poorest countries in the world, through US voluntary agencies, inter-governmental organization, or directly with recipient governments. Title III is a food for development programme giving special emphasis to improving the access of poor people to food and to enhancing in other ways the quality of their lives. Commitments up to five years' duration may be made under Title III. (Title III entitlements were added to the PL 480 legislation by virtue of the International Development and Food Assistance Acts of 1977. Not less than 15 per cent of the aggregate value of Title I agreements shall be allocated to Title III programmes and projects under this Act, though provision is made for various exceptions.) It was not until 1980 for instance that any transfer of food aid from one title to another was allowed. This was done in the interests of flexibility and in view of the rapid fluctuations in the requirements, but these transfers were limited to 15 per cent of the funds available for programming in any fiscal year. Various elements of conditionality enter into each of these types of programme.

Title I allocations, for example, are credits repayable either in dollars over 20 years, or in convertible local currency over 40 years. The maximum grace period before starting repayment in the case of the dollar credits is two years, while for convertible local currency credits this may go up to ten years. There is also a minimum interest rate of 2 per cent during the grace period and 3 per cent thereafter. In certain cases also a specific down payment may be required before the agreement is signed. Other clauses in such agreements may stipulate that the recipient country must use the local currency which they derive from the sale of food aid on the local market (known as counterpart funds) for some specified purpose, such as expansion of food storage facilities, tropical soil use, diversification of the economy and so forth. These activities would all be in the interests of national development, but constitute none the less an element of conditionality. The Title III programmes have the advantage of being multi-year programmes and certain repayment conditions are waived if the funds generated from local sales are applied to agricultural development, nutrition, health services, or population planning. Recipients, however, still have to satisfy the Title I requirement of ensuring that adequate storage is available prior to shipment of the food aid and also that the shipment will not result in disincentives to agricultural production.

The Title II programme covers humanitarian as well as development needs. This means that it is the source of all US PL 480 emergency food aid for refugees and other disasters. The development aid is generally in the form of assistance to projects and a large proportion of the Title II programme is handled through voluntary organizations such as CARE and Catholic Relief Services (CRS).

Since its inception in 1970–1 the food aid programme of the EC has been growing steadily and now comes next to that of the USA in magnitude. In the 1986 programme, the EC is to provide 1.6 million tonnes of cereals, the same quantity as was provided in the 1985 programme, while the USA programme, that runs from July/June rather than a calender year, 4.6 million tons were provided in the 1985/6 programme. The EC also earmarked an additional 386,700 tonnes of cereals for emergency use, which could be raised to 0.5 million if the necessity arises. The European Community has also become a major provider of milk products (skimmed milk powder, butter-oil, and butter) with a total of 137,300 tons in 1985 as against 153,472 tons provided by the US in their 1984–5 programme.

Although the EC acts as an international organization it is not referred to as such nor as a multilateral one. So as to avoid confusion with the various international agencies under the UN, the EC is generally categorized as a regional programme.

The EC also has its eligibility and allocation criteria for its food aid. These differ somewhat from those of the US and international organizations. The EC criteria are based upon the following elements:

(a) GDP per capita based on World Bank data;
(b) satisfaction of nutritional requirements, based on FAO's calorie data;
(c) capacity to import commercially using export revenue, based on IMF data;
(d) foreign exchange reserve position, also based on IMF data.

The GDP carries the most weight since poverty is considered the most important cause of hunger and malnutrition. The IDA eligibility cut-off point is accepted as the primary pre-requisite for eligibility and the country with the lowest GDP receives the maximum share of EC food aid allocations. Details of the mathematical calculations of the weighting, covering the cereals component for the 1986 programme, are shown in Appendix 4. The wider policy implications and trends of the EC programme are mainly determined within the framework of the Third Lomé (Lomé III) guidelines, aiming at an improved integration of food aid with the development process and in conjunction with the elaboration of food strategies within the low-income food deficit countries. The EC is well placed to do this since it also administers capital assistance through the European Development Fund (EDF) and many of its members have quite large technical assistance programmes. The elaboration of these food strategies is intended to ensure that food aid for recipient, or potentially recipient, countries is optimally integrated with other inputs and with the long-term development plans of the respective recipient governments. Many of the EC's policies and procedures are still in the process of elaboration and refinement as the Community is a relative newcomer to the field of food aid.

An interesting feature of the EC food aid programme is that a clear distinction is drawn between, on the one hand, that provided to a government, either to generate counterpart funds through sales, or for distribution to specified groups, and that provided to international or voluntary organizations on the other. These are referred to in EC documentation as the 'direct' and 'indirect' programmes respectively. There is also a welcome degree of flexibility in the programmes since supplementary allocations can be made in the course of a year to respond to special requirements (including emergencies). The pooling of resources within the Community also adds to its effectiveness in terms of availability of commodities. Unlike many bilateral donors, however, the EC does not have a shipping fleet or line of its own and shipment is carried out through tendering within the member states which tends to introduce delays or irregular deliveries.

EC Member States' Programmes

There is, naturally, a close association between the EC's own programme, known as 'Community Action' to which 56 per cent of total resources are allocated, and the programmes of the individual member states, known as 'National Action', which account for the remaining 44 per cent. The latter are funded from the national food aid or aid budgets of the various contributing member states, rather than from the intervention stocks through the Intervention Board for Agricultural Produce (IBAP)—that is, surplus resulting from the Common Agricultural Policy as in the case of the EC's own programmes.

In the case of the UK the 'National Action' programme has been used for the purchase of her share of obligations under the Food Aid Convention which amounts to 110,734 tonnes of cereals out of the 7.6 million tonnes due from all signatories under the latest 1983 extension of the FAC. Although costs fluctuate, this currently represents an expenditure of around £15 million. The remainder of the total UK food aid budget, averaging recently about £100 million, is provided to the EC for the Community action programme some of which is used for the EC's contribution to the FAC commitment and some for other commodities such as milk products and vegetable oil, etc. The policy objective of the UK food aid programme is succinctly stated as the relief of hunger, with some priority for famine relief in Africa.

Other member states of the EC act in a similar manner. The four largest contributors have been Germany, the UK, France, and Italy, since the EC food aid began in 1970–1. The contributions have varied somewhat over years, but the ranking and order of magnitude

Table 2. Contributions to EC food aid by member countries, 1984–1985

Country	'000 tonnes grain equivalent*
Federal Republic of Germany	347.4
France	262.5
Italy	173.7
Netherlands	150.9
United Kingdom	137.6
Belgium and Luxemburg	96.7
Denmark	25.0
Greece	9.0
Ireland	6.0

* A number of data on food aid give tonnages 'grain equivalent'. This was done to simplify value calculations and also calculations of nutrition/energy requirements. Wheat and maize are reckoned at par (100) while 100 tons of rice would be shown as 330 tons of grain equivalent and edible oil about 900 tons.

of these national actions for 1984–5 was as shown in Table 2. In the case of all the EC member states, with the exception of France, food aid is an integral part of the national aid budget, so that any increase in food aid—say, for emergencies—would generally result in compensatory cuts elsewhere in the other components of aid.

Other Donors' Programmes

The Scandinavian Countries

Though not bound by treaty obligations like the EC, the Scandinavian group of countries (Norway, Sweden, Finland) generally act in concert so as to make optimum use of their resources. Since there are no particular climatic differences that would ensure availability of a variety of commodities, this co-operative action is reflected in the selection of specific geographic or functional areas in which these donor countries operate; these are known as their 'programme countries'.

Canada, Australia, and Japan

Outside the USA and the EC group, the next largest contributors are Canada and Australia, and more recently Japan. These all show different preferences and have different criteria.

The first shipments of Canadian food aid were made in 1951 coinciding with the beginning of Canada's official aid programme under the Colombo Plan. There is still some preference for Commonwealth countries and more recently for French-speaking territories. The main rationale was a humanitarian one, though some consideration also had to be given to domestic as well as to external interests. Thus, the main objectives have been summarized as follows:[3] (i) to alleviate human suffering; (ii) to assist in increasing food production through the use of food as development capital; (iii) to enhance Canada's role as a major food exporter to the extent compatible with the other objectives for food aid.

Within the last category considerable attention is paid to the FAO Surplus Disposal procedures and the UMRs, and more recently there has been an emphasis on using cash resources for the purchase of food in developing countries for distribution as food aid in the area, rather than direct shipment of commodities from Canada. The bilateral component has consisted largely of commodities for sale for the generation of counterpart funds and the multilateral component for targeted programmes. In recent years Canada's food aid has accounted for around 10 per cent of the total world food aid.

While the commodities available in the Canadian programme are predominantly wheat and maize, Australia has an availability of rice and sugar. Japan is likewise able to supply quite large quantities of rice and has also been using cash resources for the purchase of other cereals from Asian countries for its food aid programme. A list of current contributors to food aid programmes world-wide is shown in Appendix 5.

Switzerland

Some of the smaller donors have special functions, such as Switzerland which provides funds for food aid through the International Committee of the Red Cross whose headquarters are in Geneva, and the Swiss Disaster Relief Organization with head offices in Bern.

Multilateral Aid

In general there is a growing tendency for the smaller donors to provide a higher proportion of their contribution multilaterally.

This trend is also taking place with some of the larger donors such as Australia and the Scandinavian group. The World Food Programme, through its field representation in all the food deficit countries, is in a position to provide programme management and supervision that it would be extremely costly for a smaller donor to set up independently. Furthermore, commercial and political considerations tend to play a smaller part in the case of these donors. The larger food aid programmes are in a position to command a wider range of commodities on a scale sufficient to satisfy the main nutritional requirements of the programmes they have selected. They may also have a sufficient availability of cereals, say, to make a noticeable economic impact on a recipient country over a period of time. Smaller donors do not have this capability on their own, other than through small selected targeted programmes which are expensive to adminsister and monitor. These considerations have led to a much higher proportion of the smaller programme contributions being channelled multilaterally than of the larger ones.

When considering the mutilateral aspect of food aid it is useful to compare its status with that of the various member states *vis-à-vis* UN organizations. Membership of the principal UN organizations is linked to an assessed contribution in cash, based on a combination of factors such as population, GNP, etc. Non-payment can mean expulsion; alternatively one year's notice of intention to withdraw and cease payments has to be given as was recently the case with US and UK and Singapore's withdrawal from Unesco. Membership of some UN organizations such as the UN Development Programme and Unicef, is on the basis of voluntary contributions. In this context the signing of the Food Aid Convention was a milestone in international food aid, since for the first time, it represented an assessed contribution, to be honoured by the signatories. Up to that time all contributions—including those to WFP—were voluntary, that is to say, made at annual pledging conferences by governments who wished to contribute. Furthermore, all of the contributions to the FAC were to be used as grant aid, and not as credits or loans. The creation of the FAC removed one of the principal obstacles to long-term programming on an assured basis.

The Food Aid Convention is subject to periodic revision, the current commitments under the 1980 revision and its 1983 extension run through to 30 June 1986. To date, each periodic revision has been upward. A proportion of the commodities derived from the

FAC are earmarked to fuel the International Emergency Food Reserve which was initially set up under the control of the WFP at 500,000 tonnes of cereal equivalent. This reserve figure has also been exceeded, with total contributions in 1984 amounting to 620,638 tonnes and in 1985 to 769,528 tonnes. The range of commodities available and the number of contributing countries is revealing (see Appendix 6).[4]

Voluntary and Independent Institutions

In addition to these government-to-government food aid programmes there are a number of voluntary agencies and independent institutions that have their own food aid programmes. In recent years their importance has been growing, particularly in the light of the increasing number of natural and man-made disasters that have been given prominence by television and press reports. The recent success of Band-Aid/Live-Aid is perhaps the most representative of this trend.

Some of these institutions, such as the League of Red Cross Societies, the International Committee of the Red Cross, derive their funding from both public and private sources. Other voluntary organizations such as Oxfam are sustained entirely by private donations. They are predominantly directed toward the alleviation of emergencies and disasters through relief, rehabilitation, and health services. More recently some, such as Band-Aid and Oxfam, have endeavoured to use funds derived from emergency appeals to undertake remedial rather than palliative actions to ensure that some of the causes of such disasters (famine and so on) do not recur, or can at least be detected and tackled at an earlier stage. In the case of these organizations, food aid is only a facet of their overall operation: the Save The Children Fund and Médecins sans Frontières, for instance, have emergency relief and rehabilitation in the medical field as their first priority, but medical rehabilitation of severely undernourished children is of little avail without accompanying supplementary feeding. Some of these organizations have been able to raise quite large sums: the League of Red Cross Societies distributed, in food aid alone, just under $US50 million to 28 countries in 1985. The most publicized activities of these organizations are in connection with disaster relief work, but access to their food and other aid can often be obtained in more normal times in connection with health questions (immunizations, etc.), children's welfare, care for the aged, or via church groups. Due to their relatively limited resources, however, they prefer actions of a limited scope within a district or community in which some impact can be assessed.

The Recipient's View

From the recipient point of view, one of the most important considerations is whether the food aid is provided as a grant—that is, a free donation—or whether it comes in the form of a loan or a credit. Although such credits and loans are easier to negotiate than financial ones, the repayment obligation remains, as well as settlement of service charges, all of which represent a charge either against foreign exchange or against recurrent expenditure in local currency. The International Monetary Fund recently decided to make available lines of credit for food purchase in certain food deficit developing countries, but the largest availability of food aid as credits or loan comes from the US Title I programme, as indicated earlier.

Grants of food aid are given bilaterally in the event of emergencies or for some specific 'target' purposes and all the multilateral food aid is in the form of grants. Multilateral food aid has the additional attraction from the recipient point of view that it is apolitical and the conditionality is the same for all recipients and consists essentially of using the food aid for mutually agreed purposes over an agreed period to provide reports/accounts and permit periodic evaluation of progress. Before the creation of the Food Aid Convention and the US Title III programmes, multilateral assistance was the only form of multi-year food aid available. Although, in practice, most bilateral programmes were continued from one budget year to the next, there was no legal basis for anything more than yearly allocations. This provision was of course designed, in the case of a bilateral donor, to protect him from complications arising from an inability to supply over a longer period due, say, to adverse climatic conditions, changes in the terms of trade, and so on.

At the same time recipients were reluctant to embark on longer-term plans based on supply from annual allocations from a single donor, due to the risk of curtailment or change in supply. A government may have integrated a food aid component into a five-year development and would need to be assured that it does not suddenly dry up half-way through the plan, leaving the country to purchase the remainder from its own resources.

In the shorter term, say where food aid has been used as a component of a development project of limited duration, the recipient's concern is not so much with annual programming, but rather with timing and timely arrival of supplies. In terms of the time it takes to get a request for developmental food aid approved there is little to choose between the bilateral and the multilateral bureaucracies. Timing is naturally of even greater importance in the case of crises where food shortages arise and famine threatens—that is not something that can wait or be shelved like the building of a new bridge. Hungry people have proved to be one of the most efficient destabilizers of all shades of regimes, and constitute one of the more persuasive arguments in favour of the various proposals that have recently been formulated for national food security schemes.

Apart from the time it takes to get a project approved, and continuity of supply, there is also the question of the timing of deliveries, for instance so as not to arrive in a rainy season when roads are impassable, or when ports are congested with seasonal exports. These questions are discussed in greater detail in Chapters 7 and 8.

From the recipient's point of view, longer-term programming, especially for development projects, is very desirable, but negotiations can take quite a long time and where the problems cannot wait, there has been a tendency to dress up requests as emergencies, with the knowledge that donor response is much more rapid and frequently much more generous in such cases. At the other end of the time-scale, on the other hand, there is often a tendency to dress up as a development project a requirement that is in fact a social service. This can arise in the case of institutional feeding programmes in schools or hospitals. As long as the schools or hospitals covered by such a project continue to operate, there will be a requirement to keep on feeding the people in those institutions. The only question is to guess who is going to give way first—the donor who feels he has been locked into an unending commitment, or the government or institution that figures it has finally solved its recurrent cost problems? In theory the recipient authorities are supposed to take over full responsibility for the continued operation of these types of project once the duration specified in the project agreement comes to an end. In practice, however, these agreements are far more frequently renewed than cancelled, because the donor cannot face the agonizing accusation of letting a number of children or patients starve. From the recipient side, financial authorities too often find it easier to let the children or patients suffer than make the necessary financial adjustments and foreign exchange allocations that might start a chain reaction from other institutions requesting equal treatment. A recipient, faced with the possibility of donor curtailment of supplies, can of course always shop around for another donor, but it is in this way that dependency on food aid can be built up.

Dependency

The unsolved question then is: at what stage do requests for extensions of food aid projects or programmes begin to reflect actual or incipient dependency? This is not only a question for donors who may shy away from getting entangled in an unending commitment, but is also relevant for recipient governments who may have become locked into a cheap food or food subsidy policy they cannot remove without risk of discontent or riot.

Paradoxically, it is not usually those who are really hungry who protest most, but those who have been relatively well off and suddenly find themselves either with less food or having to pay more for the same amount. Against all this, it has to be remembered that the most successful food aid programmes, in terms of working themselves out of a job, are those where there has been a massive food input over a long period of time, as was the case with India, South Korea and Taiwan—yet in none of those cases did dependency on food aid occur.

References

1. Food and Agriculture Organization, *Food and Nutrition*, vol. 10, No. 1 (Rome, 1984), pp. 91 ff.

Food aid:

2. *Reuters Glossary of International Economic and Financial Terms* (London, 1982).
3. Government of Canada, *Official Development Assistance Strategic Overview* (Ottawa, 1981).
4. Food and Agriculture Organization, *Food Aid in Figures*, 1985.

5 FOOD AID:
For what purposes?

In defining the setting in which a global attack on hunger was to operate, the 'founding fathers' of the present international machinery provided a formulation that is still valid today. At the United Nations Preparatory Conference on Food and Agriculture, held at the invitation of US President Roosevelt at Hot Springs, Virginia, in 1943, the 44 participating states in the final Act of the Conference recognized that freedom from want means a secure, adequate, and suitable supply of food for everyone and that poverty is the first cause of malnutrition and hunger. The Act went on to say that special measures for raising nutritional standards would be of little value unless progress was made on a much wider front, through national and international action to raise general prosperity levels, particularly where such levels were low. It also pointed out that the interests of the producers of food, who represented two-thirds of the world's population, needed to be safeguarded to ensure an adequate livelihood for them.

Regrettably, despite more than 40 years of capital, food, and technical assistance inputs on a scale far larger than those founders would have thought possible, and although recently efforts have concentrated on those areas where prosperity is low—prosperity levels in these very areas have continued to sink even lower, particularly in Africa. Fortunately there has been compensation in Asia where many countries have seen a marked increase in prosperity. It is evident, then, that some analysis of the purposes of food aid in differing contexts is required.

In previous chapters allusion has been made to food aid operations of a palliative nature and to others of a developmental nature. It is useful to consider this first cell division, so to speak, as it puts some of the subsequent, more complex, sets of purposes in better perspective. The basic purpose of food aid remains the satisfaction of hunger as outlined at Hot Springs, but there are levels of intensity, urgency, and locations that have to be taken into account.

The most urgent categories are those in which famine is deemed to have set in, and deaths from starvation have been reported already. This situation is likely to result in an international response, calling for rapid and generally large deliveries of food aid to the affected localities. There is little point, under those circumstances, in embarking on an academic debate about the possible causes of the emergency, before undertaking any action. Something has to be done urgently; this is generally demanded not only by the affected country, but also by the media and public opinion in the more affluent and unaffected countries.

Provided that the right kind of food aid is supplied at the right time to the right people—three big 'ifs'—responses of this kind are capable of solving most of the immediate problems, but in the longer term cannot hope to have anything more than a palliative effect. What happens once hunger has been satisfied and infant and other mortality rates brought down? Should there be a change of objective in the course of such a palliative operation to find out what really caused it and what might be done about preventing a repetition—and if so, at what stage of the operation? Again, will those who sponsored the rescue operation go along with using their resources for something evidently less immediate and less directly humanitarian? Furthermore, some 'emergencies' have been known to drag on for several years—particularly refugee-related emergencies. This can create a host of new problems: is the food merely acting as a magnet creating a self-perpetuating situation; how great is the burden on the economy of the host country, or damage to the ecology? The implication is that the food aid might well have been used for a more constructive purpose.

To those who see food aid as a development tool for the relief, in association with other forms of development aid, of hunger and deprivation on a lasting basis rather than as a hand-out, it is distressing to note that a growing proportion of the available food aid resources has to be spent on such emergencies, the majority of which are man-made and thus theoretically preventable.

It is important to note, however, that it is in these emergency actions that food aid, together with the means to get it to the right place in sufficient quantity, plays the key role. As soon as one moves out of these palliative types of operation into developmental ones, the element of urgency decreases. This allows time for a review of the appropriateness of the food aid, giving rise to questions of selectivity, targeting, evaluation and so forth. In addition, the role of food aid and its supporting logistics undergoes a relative decrease in importance since other components may enter into the calculation such as government supporting actions, external technical or capital assistance, etc. Furthermore, there is a longer timeframe in which to solve logistics problems with less danger of overloading existing national infrastructures.

In practice the purposes and objectives of various categories of food aid may be summarized as follows.

Palliative actions

Relief of Displaced Persons/Refugees

The majority of food aid operations falling under this heading are for man-made disasters resulting in crises of mass exodus. This in turn almost invariably results in the collection of large numbers of people in camps or designated settlement areas where they have to be fed, as in most cases they have no resources with which to engage in productively and usually are not allowed to integrate into the economic life of the local population. The purpose of the food aid in these cases is to maintain the camp population on a small but nutritionally adequate ration. Within this population there may well be subgroups requiring special foods, such as severely malnourished infants, pregnant women, the elderly, and the infirm. On occasion, additional food aid may be required to provide incentives for work on essential infrastructure, wells, shelter, etc. This generally requires a commodity that is not available in the regular ration and has value in the community or with the local population, where it may be bartered for fresh produce. It has been found that this purpose of providing an incentive is not achieved when more of the same food as in the rations is provided.

In most cases, influxes of this kind cause considerable material and social problems for the country accepting the refugees. Where possible the country will endeavour, naturally enough, to maintain that refugees are an international and not a national problem, so that it becomes the responsibility of the international community to take full charge of their welfare. In this way the purpose of the food aid is changed, strictly speaking, from a limited relief operation to that of a kind of international social service. Since solutions to refugee and displaced persons problems do not come easily or quickly, these operations constitute a long-term drain on food aid resources.

A further problem is that emergencies of this kind are largely unpredictable, while bilateral and multilateral food aid for development purposes has generally to be planned some time in advance of need and has to work within limited budgetary frameworks; these are never sufficient to meet total demands. Many of these food aid programmes are an integral part of overseas aid, so that an additional food allocation would be likely to result in a cut in some other aid component or a reduction in development food aid projects. This is true, for instance, for the British food aid programme. This problem, together with the increasing number of requests for emergency assistance, was one of the main reasons for the creation of the IEFR as indicated in Chapter 4. This provided flexibility but not much additionality. The latter came to be provided largely by voluntary agencies who were able to mobilize considerable support from the public. The purposes and objectives of these various organizations were not necessarily limited to providing food aid, but their contribution to food aid was frequently significant.

A useful degree of international co-operation generally comes into play in such crises of mass exodus. There have been sound precedents for this. In 1938 an Intergovernmental Committee for Refugees (IGCR) was established to assist the League of Nations High Commission for Refugees in settling large numbers of refugees from Germany and Austria. On 9 December 1944 the UN Relief and Rehabilitation Administration (UNRRA) was established. Its functions, together with those of the IGCR were taken over by the International Refugee Organization in July 1947. These functions were in turn taken over by the UN High Commission for Refugees (UNHCR). This organization was set up by virtue of a UN General Assembly Resolution in 1949 and became operational in 1951. All these activities, involving several million persons displaced following World War II, required the provision and management of food aid which was an integral part of their overall operations. By the time the UNHCR had become operational, the main work of resettling the post-war refugees had been accomplished, so that the organization became largely concerned with the implementation and supervision of the Convention on Refugees of 1951 which widened the definition of a refugee to correspond to the

UNHCR mandate to 'promote, organize, co-ordinate and supervise international action on behalf of refugees protected by former international agencies and on behalf of any person who is outside the country of his nationality (or in the case of stateless persons, his former residence) because he has been persecuted by reason of his race, nationality, religion, or political opinion and cannot, or does not, wish to return on account of such fears'.

Renewed movements of refugees in various parts of the world around this time led to the UN providing for a three-year programme for the UNHCR, running from 1955 to 1958, on the basis of voluntary contributions from government or private sources. This funding base was supplemented in 1957 by the creation of an emergency fund whose resources were derived from the repayment of loans that had been made to refugees under earlier programmes.

The UNHCR still has to raise the bulk of its funding for refugee relief operations by means of international appeals. In recent years these have been largely centred around the problems of Africa, although the continued exodus of large numbers of people from the earlier crisis centres in Vietnam and Cambodia continued to absorb a considerable proportion of total resources. In respect of Africa, funds were raised by a series of international conferences under the auspices of the UNHCR entitled International Conference(s) for Assistance to Refugees in Africa (ICARA). Monies raised by this means were used in part for the provision and transportation of food aid, for which the UN/FAO World Food Programme has now become the principal channel of procurement and distribution. The UNHCR field representation is also frequently made responsible for the co-ordination of the activities of voluntary organizations, some of which will have their own food aid programme, applied to the same general purpose of providing for the sustenance of refugees.

Famine and other Natural Disaster Relief

The provision of food aid for the purposes of relief from famine and other natural disasters was considered at length in the various discussions following upon the Hot Springs Conference and leading to the establishment of the FAO. Many of the large nations already had internal criteria for special food distribution for such purposes.

A concrete problem that arose was to define 'famine' and the criteria upon which relief could be given. A UN General Assembly Resolution of 26 January 1952 on Food and Famine referred to such emergencies as those caused by crop failures due to plague, drought, flood, blight, volcanic eruptions, earthquakes, and similar accidents of a natural character, but this did not settle the question of degree, that is at what level of emergency should food aid be supplied. Since it was agreed that famine was most prevalent in those countries where there was already a high incidence of malnutrition, some distinction had to be made between these two factors. For this they took the example of the Indian Famine Code which *inter alia* predicated:

(a) a probable degree of shortage of food supplies in relation to the usual consumption of the affected population;
(b) the extent to which the government concerned is dealing and can deal with the situation through its own resources and
(c) the effects of famine in fields other than food.[1]

These criteria remain valid under present circumstances in respect of emergency food aid. Finally, for the purpose of assessing the need for international action in the event of disasters, the following definition was arrived at: 'It is a food situation in which there are clear indications, based on careful and impartial study, that serious catastrophe and extensive suffering will occur if international assistance is not rendered.'[2]

The discussions at the fourteenth session of the UN Economic and Social Council at which this definition was elaborated also added a rider to the effect that famine emergencies arising from the aftermath of war and civil disturbances were excluded. This issue was then blurred in later discussions where it was considered that emergencies arising from natural causes might be aggravated by war or civil disorders and that emergency assistance including food aid could then be granted! In any event this hair-splitting resulted in the creation of two separate UN organizations—the one dealing with man-made catastrophes (UNHCR) and the other with natural disasters, the UN Disaster Relief Organization (UNDRO)—both with head offices in Geneva.

International action seems to have been somewhat weakened by these dichotomies and to have complicated the role of the World Food Programme in respect of emergencies. It can also have some curious side effects in the recipient countries—for example the 1.5

million or so refugees that came into Somalia in the early 1980s were all classified as 'refugees', even though they were ethnic Somalis and at least half of them were known to have been victims of drought. The reason was that the Somali government in its confrontation with Ethiopia wanted to highlight exodus for political and not meteorological reasons; this left UNHCR as the principal source of finance. In Djibouti the authorities were more pragmatic—refugees there from the same Ethiopian source were quickly segregated into 'refugiés' and 'sinistrés' when its government learned that there would be a UN sponsored drought mission coming, capable of unlocking additional funds!

Unicef, a large number of voluntary organizations, several regional organizations, and national organizations with international fields of activity, also operate in this domain. Some of these, such as the Swiss Disaster Relief Organization (Schweizerisches Katastrophenhilfskorps), the International Committee of the Red Cross (ICRC), and the Swedish Emergency Relief teams, have special competence and experience in natural disaster relief. There are many other organizations that address themselves both to natural and to man-made emergencies, and are sometimes able to provide food aid when requested, as part of their overall operations. Voluntary organizations (NGOs), through their greater flexibility are often called upon to provide short-term assistance immediately after disaster has struck, thus providing a vitally needed bridge between the event and the delivery of the larger but slower moving bilateral or international agency assistance.

The food aid requirements and the management of food aid for natural disasters are similar to those of the refugees and displaced persons, except that preventive actions can sometimes be undertaken before a mass exodus occurs. Return to normal conditions can also be expected sooner than is the case with refugee situations. It should be emphasized, however, that not every natural disaster requires food aid as part of the relief operation, whereas in the case of refugees it is always sooner or later required.

Recent events have shown that 'emergencies' are a very popular field with the media as well as with donors, and that considerable amounts of additional food resources can be made available to cope with them. There is a danger, however, that the quick response and large funding frequently unlocked by these events can lead governments to see this as an easier source of funds than requests for development projects. There is a detectable trend, for this reason, to dress up as emergencies, food deficits that are due to quite different causes, with the result that those causes are not properly analysed or tackled. In 1982–3 a drought emergency was declared in the north and central areas of Mozambique and a number of deaths were reported, yet there was still water in the rivers in the affected region. The emergency arose much more from government regulations prohibiting the free movement of produce from one district to another, forced delivery quotas for farmers, and the closing of retail outlets, than from lack of water.

On the positive side it should be remembered that since the end of World War II, and to some extent before that, famines and various emergency needs have led to a drive to establish strategic or emergency food reserves. This was partially achieved by the creation of the IEFR and the signing of the Food Aid Convention (see Chapter 4) and is now being pursued further with attempts to establish Food Security as an international action programme, placing much more emphasis on the creation of national reserves than on reliance on external inputs. The role of food aid in relation to these reserves, coming under the general heading of food security, is discussed in the section on Development, below.

From Relief to Development

The need to build upon some of the generous responses to calamities, either by tackling some of the problems that caused the disaster in the first place, or else by trying to introduce some resource-building activity into pure palliative actions such as refugee settlement, has recently led to increasing attention being paid to this previously little-explored area. Added motivation is derived from the fact that financial grants for purely developmental actions were becoming harder to obtain. From the recipient's point of view also, loan funds, even if available, would only add to the already acute debt problems in many countries.

This is easier said than done, however. Difficulties arise both on the donor as well as on the recipient side. The voluntary agencies, which have recently been assuming an increasingly important role in relief operations, have had to concentrate their attention on the effectiveness of the immediate operations. They need to have proof, preferably visual, of the positive results of their operations, in order to stimulate more donations to keep the momentum going. In the case of refugee emergencies, neither the recipients nor the host government want to see an end to the external inputs; the former for fear of a forced return to their country of origin or of starvation, and the latter for fear that the whole operation might be turned into a national rather than an international responsibility. It could also be argued that even multilateral agencies such as the UNHCR derive their funding base from appeals in connection with disasters rather than from finding solutions.

Development agencies handling capital and technical assistance as well as food aid tend to look upon these emergencies as a painful necessity. In the case of refugee operations, they are seen as being generally devoid of any beneficial longer-term returns for the host country. A further complication arises from the fact that most of the organizations and institutions in this area on the one hand and in the development field on the other, have their own fixed mandates, which in the case of the larger bureaucracies, are generally quite precisely delineated in order to avoid 'poaching' on one another's territory. This militates against the international organizations speaking with a single effective voice in this important area.

The UNHCR for instance, was not established as an implementing agency; that means it has to find a vehicle for its various programmes and actions, through which its funds are channelled. This vehicle may be a government agency, an international organization, a voluntary agency, or an independent institution. If there is to be a development activity, say, in a refugee settlement, such as education or training, it has to be contracted out to an international institution with the appropriate mandate (FAO, Unesco, the International Labour Organization (ILO), etc.) or to a voluntary body, through which the UNHCR funds will be channelled. Apart from this line of activity, UNHCR's mandate covers the legal aspects of refugee status, supervision of voluntary repatriation, and the care of refugees, duly recorded as such by them, but it does not have a development mandate. It had on occasion considered raising funds for this purpose, but the idea was hotly contested by the development agencies.

With the growing spread of repressive regimes and the improvement—if that is the right word—in their repressive techniques, the likelihood of voluntary repatriation of refugees becomes more remote. An innovative step to build a bridge between relief and development as a possible way out of settlement was taken in the preliminary recommendations of a UN mission to the Sudan in 1986. This proposed that, rather than the provision of additional funds specifically for refugees, a country accepting refugees should be entitled to additional development assistance to accelerate their absorption within the national economy. This could be achieved by adding acceptance of refugees as a factor in establishing greater eligibility for IDA credits and other forms of technical and capital assistance, including food aid. Food aid put to this purpose could then contribute to the host government's ability to begin to integrate the refugees, who with a training component and food aid during such training, could become productive members of the economy rather than a drain on national and international resources. In Africa, particularly in the Sahel region, such actions would be facilitated by the fact that ethnic groups often straddle national borders.

Even some quite modest food aid actions within refugee settlements can lead the way to some development, or if not development, then at least the prevention of further deterioration of the environment. In Somalia, for instance, the large refugee camps that were located in the rural areas had made a desert of their location over some 10 kilometres in radius due to the search for firewood, general movement of population, over-utilization of water resources, etc. In some of these cases food aid was used to undertake reforestation in the degraded area; in other cases sub-surface dams were built to improve water retention in the streams and to retain flash floods; in yet others agricultural production was undertaken on a modest scale to provide some fresh produce, but principally to prevent further soil erosion. The government would also give permission for refugees to work on sand-dune fixation outside the settlements with a daily food ration being provided on site: since the authorities did not have the cash to pay national workers there was no displacement of local labour.

The opportunities for development actions in connection with famine relief are much greater as there is far more interest in establishing the causes of a famine beyond the simple meteorological phenomena if only to warn of, or lessen the effects of, a repetition. Reserve stocks, storage capacity, price maintenance, etc. enter into the picture, and food aid is currently given for those related purposes. A recent famine in the Turkana district of Kenya, affecting mainly the large pastoralist population, led to food aid being used not only to provide these groups with cereals with which to purchase livestock to replenish their herds, but further to develop a series of administrative measures and structures designed to give much earlier warning of any new emergency to allow time to take preventive measures.

More recently in the case of the Sudan which had suffered from a serious and prolonged drought in many parts of the country, as well as a massive influx of refugees from Ethiopia, Chad and Uganda, a considerable amount of post-relief aid is being allocated to rehabilitation programmes, that is rehabilitation not simply of the drought victims but also of the environment. This is an encouraging sign that disaster prevention is beginning to be seen as a logical follow up to disasters themselves.

Voluntary agencies can also play an important role in this field. They generally have a much wider coverage of the rural areas of a country than the official organizations, which have to keep in close touch with central or regional government authorities in the main cities. This often enables the voluntary agencies to identify genuine needs or to become aware of crop failures, price rises or other signs of impending calamity, well before official organizations in the metropolitan area. Although a central government may receive pleas or data from outlying districts, it may have to deal with more immediate priorities and problems first. Again, even if major donor institutions have indications of shortages, crop or rain failure, etc., there is nothing they can do about the problem officially until a government request for assistance is received. Voluntary agencies generally are able to communicate directly with their head offices, who can then often alert the central authorities. It is, needless to say, far easier and less costly to take remedial action before a real crisis develops. Massive amounts of food aid are required once the stage of mass migration has been reached, but relatively small amounts, when correctly applied and at the right time, are capable of preventing such a disastrous sequence of events. It is in that context that the international early warning systems of the FAO and many national institutions have been developed. Regrettably, it is still difficult to attract sufficient international attention to these schemes to raise the funding they require for further improvement and refinement. The Latin adage *praemotus, premonitus*—to be forewarned is to be forearmed—is still valid in this field of disaster prevention.

The Band-Aid/Live-Aid organizers, for instance, have shown a welcome awareness of the problems of turning relief into development, despite the heavy emphasis on famine relief in their fund raising appeals; their allocation of the funds raised gives 20 per cent to the emergency itself, 20 per cent for the transport of food and supporting materials, with the remaining 60 per cent allocated to measures designed to prevent a recurrence of the emergency.

Development

The concept of assisting less-privileged countries to accelerate their progress might be singled out as one of the main themes of the second half of the twentieth century. It evolved both in conceptual and operational terms over the years and underwent a number of variations. It could be said to have originated in practical terms with the establishment of UNRRA and in the atmosphere of international economic and social co-operation immediately after the end of the Second World War. The main goal at that time though, was relief rather than development. The Marshall Plan introduced a developmental dimension but remained essentially a programme of assistance. Whether the large amounts of assistance now being provided from the developed to the under-developed, particularly in Africa, for relief, in which food aid plays such a key role, will follow the same evolution into true development is an open question. There is, however, no doubt as to the need to persuade events to take that course.

In development actions, there is not only the question of the purposes for which the food aid is provided to be considered, but also the mode of its provision. The first major differentiation in mode is that between what might be termed impersonal and personalized means of delivery of food aid. The former is the type of food aid that is supplied in bulk to government stocks, reserves, silos, etc., and is used by the government just as it would use national production of the same commodity. This means that the food aid is generally sold to the recipients or distributed through national relief schemes. This is impersonal food aid, in the sense that the recipient cannot tell the difference between it and national commercial purchase or production. In food aid literature this type of aid is known as programme aid. The most usual mode of delivery of programme aid is through concessional sales to governments, and in volume terms accounts for some 80 per cent of all food aid world-wide. The latter, personalized aid, is known in food aid literature as project aid and is directed or 'targeted' to certain designated groups of beneficiaries, or the institutions housing such beneficiaries. In these cases the recipients are aware that the commodities they are receiving are derived from food aid sources.

Food aid may also be used on occasion in the form of animal or poultry feed in connection with agricultural development projects. There is frequently a need for seeds, especially following a drought when farmers may have been forced to use their stock for consumption. Food aid does not generally address itself to this question. In the case of the international organizations the provision of seeds is undertaken on request and within financial constraints, by the Office of Special Relief Operations of the FAO and is not the prerogative of the World Food Programme.

Food aid delivered in any of the foregoing modes may be put to a wide range of purposes. It is convenient to group these under the headings of Programme Aid and Project Aid.

Programme Food Aid

The programme type of food aid is generally provided for the purpose of some form of budget support, and in this sense is an indirect form of financial assistance, using commodities that the country would normally have had to purchase commercially, or in the event of inability to purchase, to forgo. This budget support then becomes the equivalent of import substitution or balance-of-payment assistance. Such actions theoretically allow foreign exchange to be freed and used for development purposes. In practice, though, the bulk of this type of food aid comes in the form of concessional sales, that is an arrangement between donor and recipient to sell the commodities on the local market through government outlets; the revenue derived from such sales ('counterpart funds') being used for certain developmental purposes which will have been spelled out in the donor–recipient agreement. If the food aid in this mode has been supplied as a loan, it is expected that the developmental objectives will result in increased production, enabling the recipient to repay the donor in cash. Food aid provided in this way operates within the framework of the surplus disposal and UMR arrangements described in Chapter 4. Due consideration also has to be given to the possible disincentive effects on agricultural production (see Chapter 11).

Under the general heading of budgetary support, there are a number of more specific purposes:

(a) *Foreign exchange savings.* Food aid results in a net saving of foreign exchange when it is provided in grant form and is a commodity that the government would have to purchase were it not for the food aid. In the case of a loan or credit it amounts to a delayed payment. Transport cost savings also result when the donor supplies the food aid c.i.f. (cost, insurance, freight) to the port of delivery, since under commercial purchase arrangements these would be payable by the recipient. Internal transport costs remain the same as for commercial transactions. This type of food aid is particularly relevant to food deficit countries with low export earnings, or countries labouring under balance of payments difficulties as a result of heavy indebtedness or for other reasons.

(b) *Local currency generation.* These funds are generated through the sale of food aid commodities on the local market, normally through government, or government controlled outlets. There is generally an element of conditionality in the donor–recipient agreement, the most common stipulation being that the proceeds shall be used for actions designed to increase agricultural production or rural incomes. The funds are known in the food aid literature as counterpart funds, and as indicated in Chapter 2 are often deposited into special joint (donor–recipient) accounts. These funds may be used for the purchase of local foods for other development projects, for incentive measures for local farmers, financing public works such as access roads, storage, and distribution or marketing facilities, purchase of fertilizers, pesticides, tools, and equipment for agricultural production. The relative importance of this type of food aid depends, of course, on its volume in relation to government expenditure. In some cases it can form a significant proportion of total government revenue. It is estimated that net receipts from the sale of food aid in Bangladesh in recent years has averaged 8 per cent of government revenue.

(c) *Food reserves.* Food aid, particularly in cereals, can be used to create national reserve stocks, which not only cushion price fluctuations but also limit sudden demands on the budget to purchase at high prices in times of shortage on the local market. In emergencies they provide a buffer for speedy relief pending the arrival of emergency food aid.

This form of food aid originated in the surplus disposal era but the direction of its purpose has gradually been changed to assist the lower income and food deficit countries. Although there has been a general trend on the part of the donors to ensure that the benefits, either direct or indirect, from the food aid are used for development purposes, generally, in the agricultural sector, governments are still in a position to use the funds for less productive purposes such as arms if they are so determined.

Recent experience with development projects using food aid has shown that there is frequently a need to provide some complementary inputs such as transport facilities, tools, current expenses, and so on. This has resulted in there being a number of cases where programme and project types of food aid have been combined, the programme mode being used, through sales, to provide the cash for the required complementary inputs. Strictly speaking, the sale of food aid in the grant type of project food aid is prohibited under the terms of the donor–recipient agreements, as this would have a depressing effect on local producer prices. Nevertheless, it could be argued that providing food as a wage in return for work is in fact a sale. It is also certain that quite a lot of food aid finds its way into local markets. This is frequently done because the recipients wish to exchange some of their food aid staples for fresh produce. After all, once the intended beneficiary receives his food aid, it becomes his property to do what he pleases with, though of course there will be pressures for him to use it to nutritional advantage.

In some project agreements allowance is made for the disposal or sale of a certain percentage of the food aid to defray local administrative or transport expenses; when this happens, it is known as 'monetization'. It has been increasingly used in recent years to overcome some of the red tape and bureaucratization associated with the distribution of food aid.

Project Food Aid

There is a wide spectrum of uses of which project food aid may be put, and in order to bring some order into the categorization of these various purposes, a breakdown used by WFP is useful:

(a)   projects for the development of human resources;
(b)   projects for the development of socio-economic infrastructure;
(c)   projects of a directly productive nature;
(d)   price stabilization and national food reserve projects.

Other organizations may look at the question of use, differently;

 (i)   food aid for vulnerable groups;
 (ii)   food aid for humanitarian purposes;
(iii)   food aid for income generation;
(iv)   food-for-work;
 (v)   institutional feeding;
(vi)   natural resource conservation.

Yet others will be found to take a modal approach divided into direct distribution (relief, emergencies, refugees, etc.); institutional feedings (clinics, hospitals, schools, etc.); food-for-work (use of food as a wage good); human settlement (virgin land development).

Whatever the method used, project food aid is now almost exclusively intended for the food deficit and low income countries, and with priority within those countries to the least privileged groups. This means that the beneficiaries have to be identified in order to establish the purpose of the food aid in the project. In terms of the share of total resources for project food aid, assistance to vulnerable groups and for poverty relief predominates.

The WFP categorization and its subdivisions cover most of these fields. The categories and subdivisions are as follows:

(1)   Human resource development.

(a)   *Food aid for mothers and pre-school children.* Pre-school children and mothers are considered as a vulnerable group since they are more exposed to the risk of malnutrition, and since the effects of malnutrition in this case are particularly pernicious. This category of food aid is generally distributed through Mother and Child Health Centres (MCH), clinics or hospitals. In some cases kindergartens serve as distribution centres for children of tender age at risk. At clinics and MCH centres distribution of food aid often acts as an incentive for mothers to bring their children for immunization and other simple checks that could detect actual or incipient malnutrition. The attendance of mothers at such centres also provides an opportunity for nutrition education in connection with the food, as well as family planning information.

(b) *School feeding in elementary and secondary schools.* Food aid in these instances may range from a morning snack of milk and biscuits for primary school children—particularly in rural areas where they have had to walk long distances without a breakfast beforehand—to full board in a residential secondary school. Food aid for these purposes is also sometimes provided through a network of school canteens prepared by a centrally located kitchen and distributed by isothermic cans to schools, as was done in the case of the national programme in Algeria.

Although the purpose of this type of food aid is generally stated as a contribution to academic improvement, nutrition education, and better retention rates, it should not be forgotten that it also represents a considerable cost saving on the institutions' budgets. In some cases the additional purpose of using such savings for improving the school infrastructure is included. In other cases the project agreement may stipulate the encouragement of school gardens, partly with a view to providing some fresh produce for a school canteen and partly to give the curriculum a practical dimension oriented towards agricultural practice and the value of nutrition. In practice, however, school gardens are rarely successful unless there is community participation and motivation; otherwise they are abandoned during the school holidays.

(c) *Vocational training institutions, youth camps, pre-vocational centres.* Institutions in this category are generally selected for aid purposes on the basis of their training being relevant to agricultural production, such as agro-mechanical or agricultural schools. Youth camps may serve for skills training among adolescents who may also have been school drop-outs. Conditions of distribution are usually similar to the foregoing category of secondary schools. In other cases food aid may be a partial replacement of apprenticeship schemes which are not widely available in many developing countries on account of lack of sources of revenue from business and industry. In the case of day schools or day students, food aid is generally provided through a canteen service, in which the institution contributes some items of a perishable nature that are not part of food aid. Food aid may further be linked to courses in domestic science and nutrition education, using some of the commodities for demonstration purposes over and above the feeding of the students.

(d)   *Literacy and adult education courses.* Attendance at these categories of human resource development activities is, all too frequently, predominantly male and difficult to maintain over an extended period without some form of incentive. The provision of food aid either in canteen form or as a weekly take-away ration for attendance is an effective incentive factor.

(e)   *Hospital patients, convalescents, the aged.* The purpose of this category of food aid is to provide the basic components of a diet that will accelerate recovery. Many serious illnesses, such as gastroenteritis and anaemia, in developing tropical countries are brought on by insufficient resistance in the body due to undernourishment or other food deficiencies. There are also many TB out-patients in this category, whose cure depends on regular medical dosages; food aid, as in the case of the MCH centres acts as an incentive for attendance.

(2)   Projects for the development of economic and social infrastructure.

(a)   *Public health programmes.* Food aid can be used for the purpose of assisting nurse training institutions along the lines of school feeding as most of these institutions are boarding. It can also be used in a food-for-work mode for well-digging, sewage disposal, etc. It has also been used as an incentive payment to public health workers undertaking field visits.

(b)   *Housing, building, public amenities.* A number of low-cost housing projects and self-help construction programmes have been stimulated through the provision of food aid. This is generally supplied in the food-for-work mode where the food is part of the wage. In public housing schemes this makes possible a considerable reduction in the wage bill for labour, so that available local funds can be used for further material or equipment purchases. On other occasions it has been found that the provision of food aid, often in a canteen mode, has been an essential element in attracting labour to construction sites, especially in rural areas or in cases where food cannot be readily purchased with the local currency. In self-help schemes it is an important motivational factor. Public amenities often consist of the planting of gardens in urban settings, the creation of green belts to prevent erosion, urban terracing to prevent subsidence, canal construction for flood control, and so on.

(c) *Transportation, communication.* Food aid here is generally supplied for road construction work in the food-for-work mode. This has often been an important factor in the development of access roads for rural markets, which would not have had sufficient priority within local budgets.

Access roads to rural schools have also been constructed on this basis; not only facilitating the supply of food for institutional feeding but also improving educational efficiency by allowing better supervision of teaching, supply of textbooks, etc.

(d) *Community development.* Food aid for this purpose is frequently channelled through voluntary organizations, for many of which community development forms an important part of their activity. Since many such projects are of short duration and frequently need to change location and mode, the backstopping provided by the personnel of a voluntary agency on site ensures effective use of the food aid.

(3) Projects of a directly productive nature.

(a) *Land development and improvement.* These activities are usually undertaken through the food-for-work mode. The purpose can range from simple soil conservation schemes (wind break tree planting, bunding, sub-surface dams, etc.) to large irrigation schemes, even involving earth dam construction. Improvement can also take the form of sand-dune stabilization or as a compensation for leaving land fallow to recuperate.

(b) *Land settlement and agrarian reform.* Settlement and agrarian reform schemes frequently involve the displacement of families to new sites or the opening up of virgin land. The purpose of food aid in such cases is to provide the settlers with an adequate family ration until they are able to bring the land into production. This generally takes the form of a weekly distribution of family rations, on a full ration scale for the first year and a half for a second and final year.

(c) *Assistance to refugees.* Although the bulk of assistance for refugees comes under a special category there are elements that can be considered as being in the project category for which purposes food aid may be allocated. This may take the form of encouragement of special skills for which training is required, for use in nutrition education and demonstration, and as a wage good for infrastructure work within a camp. To be effective food aid used for such purposes needs to contain commodities different from those offered in the basic ration, as there is otherwise little incentive to work. Certain development activities may also be undertaken with food-for-work in and around refugee camps, such as reforestation etc.

(d) *Crop production and diversification.* Food aid can be used as an incentive to crop production. This will be particularly applicable in cases where planting is undertaken after a drought, as a result of which the farmer would probably have had to use so much of his resource base (money, livestock, stored crops, and seed) that he has insufficient means left to purchase the food required for the labour intensive effort involved in preparing the land and planting. Food aid can also stimulate diversification of crops, the development of new varieties, or the introduction of new technologies, by reducing the farmer's dependence on the revenue from his existing crops for his survival, and thus enabling him to cushion the drop in production and revenue that the introduction of new routines usually brings about. Food aid is also provided in some farmer training centres as an incentive for attendance, or as a recompense for following agricultural extension advice.

(e) *Animal production and dairy development.* Food aid is also sometimes used for the purpose of providing animal feed, particularly where there is a need to rebuild herds after a drought or other food crop failure. A more common approach is the use of food aid milk powder to build up a market and distribution system using a mixture of reconstituted milk from the powder and local milk. With an increasing market derived from the food aid milk, local producers are provided with a remunerative outlet for their local milk. As their production builds up, the expectation is that the food aid will be able to phase out. This was the principle behind the 'Operation Flood' in India that developed large milk producing co-operatives. It was also used for dairy development in Kenya. In other cases, such as Algeria, it was used to ensure a regular supply of dairy products (milk, cheese, yoghurt) in the State Milk Marketing Board (ONALAIT).

(f) *Forestry projects.* Food aid is frequently used for the purpose of supporting reforestation schemes as well as seedling nurseries. This is usually implemented through the food-for-work mode. This type of action is particularly relevant in arid areas, and food-aid-assisted development projects of this type have been operated in Iraq, Morocco, Algeria, and the Sudan. Some of these projects have been instrumental in halting desert encroachment and even in bringing about local climatic changes when continued over a longer period.

(g) *Fishery development.* There is considerable potential in a number of developing countries for the encouragement of fish farming—either in the form of hatcheries for restocking lakes and rivers, or in large ponds for production of mature fish for consumption. This additional protein source can lead to an improvement in local diets. Such projects are generally implemented through the food-for-work mode.

(h) *Industrial projects.* Food aid commodities are frequently provided to processing plants in developing countries for the local production of weaning foods. A considerable amount of foreign exchange is allocated for the import of these relatively luxury items for urban centres. In these local processing operations only part of the ingredients are supplied under food aid, others, perhaps sugar or cereal-meal, being provided locally. These activities also help to build up local light industries and competence in food processing.

Food aid can also, of course be used in the food-for-work mode for the construction of industrial infrastructure (buildings, roads, etc.), or as part payment for industrial workers, as was done in the case of miners in Turkey.

(4) Price stabilization and national food reserve projects.

(a) Food aid can provide a useful cushion against price fluctuations in staples. In order to achieve this purpose, delivery needs to be timely and in sufficient quantity to make an impact on the given situation. In this respect, local purchases and triangular transactions, in which a donor will acquire food locally either for use as food aid in that country, or in a third country, are particularly relevant. Such actions help to maintain prices for producers, which might otherwise begin to fall in times of good crops or rise when shortages threaten, which leads to speculation on the market. A similar cushioning effect can be provided by food aid agencies purchasing or delivering commodities to create or replenish national food stocks. These latter measures come under the general heading of Food Security, a principle that is being actively promoted by the Committee on Food Security in the FAO and in the World Food Council.

(b) Food aid commodities have also been used to build up the initial capital stock of certain types of agricultural co-operatives, to provide them with a working capital for their members.

The foregoing list is by no means exhaustive, since food aid is a developing dynamic and there have been many new and significant expansions in its use over the last quarter-century—a process that is likely to continue.

A number of voluntary organizations are also involved in quite large-scale developmental food aid operations. Many are well known on the world scene, such as Oxfam, Catholic Relief Services (CRS), the Lutheran World Federation (LWF), CARE, and latterly Band-Aid. In some cases they act as channels for the operation of part of some bilateral food aid programmes. Quite a large proportion of the US PL 480 Title II project food aid is channelled through CRS and CARE. This latter organization was established at the end of World War II under the title 'Co-operative for American Remittance to Europe' and was later amended to meet the changing needs to 'Co-operative for America Relief Everywhere'. Apart from the fact that this agency handles in the region of $US 200 million per year in food commodities, transport, and supervisory services, it has developed interesting programming principles. Their programmes fall into roughly the same general categorizations as other donor organizations, namely, food for nutritional purposes, food-for-work, food as an incentive, emergency feeding, and food for exchange for local currency (monetization). Of particular interest, in a qualitative sense, is the list of standards that are part of these general principles.

(a) All food aid projects must provide a clear statement about the intended participants, the nature and scope of the problem(s) being addressed, the results sought and how they are to be achieved, a specific time frame, and the plans by which they are to be monitored and evaluated.

(b) All food aid project proposals must set down minimum expectations of inputs, results, and conditions deemed essential for success. If these conditions cannot be met, the project cannot be justified and should not be undertaken.

(c) All food aid projects must be assessed for their potential impact on domestic agricultural production and consumption. The food aid provided is to be a net addition to the local food supply and never a disincentive to domestic production.

(d) All food aid projects must comply with rigorous standards of accountability. Wastage and diversion must not be allowed to subvert project objectives or interfere with the equitable distributional effect of food aid as a resource transfer.

Where a project entails establishing physical infrastructure provision must also be included for its maintenance.

These principles bring home the fact that a mere physical distribution plan is not sufficient in itself. There is also the question of the quality of the programme, for instance, does it live up to standards in terms of the commodities themselves, their delivery, the concept of the programme, and its purpose?

References

1. UN ECOSOC, *Food and Famine: Procedures for International Action in the Event of Emergency Famines from Natural Causes*, Document E/2220 (New York, 14 May 1952).
2. FAO, *Report of Working Party on Emergency Famine Reserve*, Council Document 16/14 (Rome, 1952).

6 FOOD AID:
What kinds of food and why?

One of the first things that have to be taken into consideration in planning and carrying out food aid programmes and projects is the question of availability. In the earlier days of food aid programmes, as shown in the historical chapters, surplus disposal was the main factor in determining what might be available for use overseas. At that time the type of food was thus determined by surplus availability alone, and no questions were asked about national eating habits, or the nutritional value of the food delivered in relation to the requirement. The only important caveat was that food aid using surplus produce should not cause disruption in the normal commercial market. This caveat was designed to protect producer price levels and international sales prices and quantitites, rather than the market in the recipient country.

Experience gained in the operation of surplus disposal, at that time mainly in post-war Europe, showed that there were serious disadvantages in this type of food aid: it was not always available when needed, it might not get to where it was needed, more than one product might be needed to solve undernourishment, and so forth. All these considerations led to the gradual development of programmed approaches. There was a process of tackling the questions of: the timing of availability; then diversification of available products; then questions of suitability and adaptability to local conditions. This latter consideration became particularly important when non-European regions became involved. The type of food aid available in the earlier years was, after all, the food used as staples in North American countries since they were the principal providers of surplus commodites at the time. Diversification, say, from wheat and maize into dairy products, canned fish and meat, oils, etc., provided the possibility both of handling food aid in a nutritional context, and of targeting it to those most in need of such nutritional succour.

At present the single commodity type of food aid programme,

say, wheat, maize, or rice, is usually channelled into the general support type programme or US Title I type of assistance as described in Chapter 4. It is, however, the targeted programme of projects that involves questions of nutrition, suitability of commodities, evaluation of its effect, and so forth. This has also given rise to a number of specialist terms and considerations which may not be familiar to those not involved in food aid operations.

In the technical jargon of food aid, the selection of commodities and the scale of rations distributed in any given programme or project has come to be known as the 'food basket'. Ideally this 'basket' should provide a specific amount of energy, calculated in terms of given amounts of calories and protein derived from cereals, milk, meat, fish, oils, and so forth. The commodities chosen for this 'basket' should furthermore correspond as closely as possible to the normal eating habits of the persons receiving the food aid, that is, the beneficiaries. This is seen as a means of minimizing the problems that often arise in accepting unfamiliar foods.

In practice, though, a number of other factors come into play and usually lead to various compromises having to be made. For instance:

(a) the desired or requested commodity may not be available from the donor(s), or may not be so at the right time or in the right quantity;

(b) nutritional requirements may vary according to type of activity, to location and to season;

(c) there may be some local production, say of cereals, available for purchase, these should then be bought and not included in the food basket from external sources;

(d) due to delivery time-lag, decisions as to the required commodity and its quantity need generally to be taken some six months in advance of requirement;

(e) the limited shelf life of certain commodities under conditions of high humidity and/or temperature needs to be taken into consideration;

(f) the local transport capacity and storage facilities may be inadequate;

(g) there may be unprogrammed changes in requirements.

As indicated earlier these conditions do not apply to food aid commodities for concessional sale or for augmenting national stocks, even though these account for around 60 per cent of food aid flows. (In 1983–4 the USA shipped 4,986,000 tons of cereals under Title I programmes out of a total cereal food aid of 5,655,000 tonnes.)

Nutritional needs

Customarily, the first step in establishing the commodities required for a given food basket is to set out the broad nutritional needs, since these deal with categories of foods rather than specific types of food within a given category. In the majority of cases, the basket will be found to contain: cereals, milk or milk products, edible oil, fish, meat, or pulses (as a vegetable protein source), and occasionally dried fruit or sugar. This categorization allows an initial review of the local requirement, as well as of local and external availability, to be made. The nutritional requirements can then be reviewed in greater detail. When reviewing the particular foods within each category, there is an interplay between availability from donor(s), local purchase possibilities, acceptability by the recipients, and the possibility of creating new and unsustainable eating habits.

The various types of interplay commonly encountered may be outlined as follows.

Cereals

Cereals are the most readily available of the commodities from the traditional donor community. They account, in fact, for almost 90 per cent of all food aid in volume terms (8.8 million tonnes in 1983–4 as against only 0.9 million tonnes in non-cereal food aid) and about 75 per cent in value terms (owing to the higher cost of other commodities).

Within the cereals category, wheat and maize (corn in US parlance) are the most readily available commodities. Statistics relating to cereal production and to cereal food aid are generally broken down into three groups, namely, wheat, rice, and coarse grains. The coarse grains may comprise maize, barley, rye, sorghum, or oats, but maize is the largest component in this category.

Within these three major categories of cereals there is, however, no particular or necessary correlation between world cereal

Table 3. Comparison of food aid allocations of cereals with world production and traditional donors' production

Cereal type	Percentage share of		
	World production estimates	Traditional donors' production	Food aid allocations
Wheat	30	40	81
Maize	43	57	10
Rice	27	3	9

production in the traditional donor group of countries and actual food aid allocations. The averages in recent years expressed in percentages of total cereals are shown in Table 3. The major cereal exporting countries were shown to have stocks of 66 million tonnes of wheat and 109 million tonnes of coarse grains and rice in 1983–4. This means that there is generally a sufficient cushion of stocks available in these categories to be able to meet requests, even if these exceed the quantities specified in the Food Aid Convention and the International Emergency Food Reserve as indicated in Chapter 4.

(a) Wheat.

Wheat and wheat products (flour, pasta, etc.) are in such general use in countries with temperate climates that it is often forgotten that these products might not always be desirable elsewhere. There is also the question of the end-use of the product that has to be taken into consideration. If wheat has been shipped as bulk grain, some kind of processing will be needed before it can be consumed as bread, pasta, or flapjacks. In most of the recipient countries such processing can only be undertaken in a large urban centre. The milling capacity there may already be fully utilized or bags may be in short supply. By far the greatest proportion of wheat in food aid is, however, destined to central government grain stores to form part of the national stock which can be drawn down when required for processing. This accounts for the very high skewing of food aid deliveries in favour of wheat as shown in Table 3. In the case of targeted or project food aid, destined perhaps for rural communities some distance from the port of entry, processing becomes a problem. For this reason wheat is frequently sent as flour rather than as grain. Although this solves one processing problem, it gives rise to three others, namely: (i) there is a volume loss of around 15 per cent in milling, depending on the extraction rate; (ii) there is a loss of nutrients as shown in Table 9; (iii) flour, usually bagged in thin cotton sacks, has a limited shelf life in hot and humid conditions.

Since wheat is not a staple in most of the recipient countries of food aid, the import of this commodity will not have adverse effects on local production and the market, but it has other side effects. In many developing countries bread has become a 'status' product consumed by better-off urban populations. There is consequently no difficulty in acceptance, but it tends to build up eating habits that can only be sustained either by continued food aid, or by expenditure of foreign exchange on a product that could easily be replaced in nutritional terms, even if not in status terms, by the use of local cereals such as maize, sorghum, millet, or rice. If the market for bread is enlarged as a result of food aid, then that aid will have done a disservice to the country. These kinds of consideration have to be taken into account in the design of a food aid basket.

(b) Maize (corn).

As shown in the foregoing Table 3, there is considerable production of maize in the traditional donor group of countries. In the USA alone the 1984 maize harvest was estimated at 192 million tonnes. Maize is a staple in many parts of Africa, Latin America and the Caribbean. In the case of Africa most of the local maize is of the white variety, whereas the maize available in food aid programmes is almost exclusively the yellow type. In the African sub-Saharan region, yellow maize is looked upon as animal feed and therefore has no 'status' value, even though in nutritional terms the yellow variety is preferable. In case of emergencies where starvation threatens, the acceptability problems of yellow maize can be overcome, but in less extreme conditions it may be necessary to mix yellow with white maize in a milling process, gradually increasing the proportion of yellow over time until a critical acceptance point is reached. In the longer term the problem can be overcome by the introduction of higher yielding yellow maize varieties by planners.

(c) Rice.

Rice is a staple in most parts of Asia and is also consumed in many parts of the developing world where it is not a staple, but looked upon as a 'status' food used in the better-off families or for special occasions. The bulk of the world's rice production is in Asia, where in 1984 an estimated 420 million tonnes out of a world total of 456 million tonnes was produced. Relatively little is grown in the traditional food aid donor countries, the chief suppliers being the USA, Australia and Japan.

Food aid rice is generally shipped parboiled or polished to eliminate parasites and improve shelf life. It can, however, be eaten boiled without any other preparation or processing. In the choice of rice in a food aid basket, besides low availability, the following factors need to be considered:

   (i)   the cost is on average double that of wheat or maize;
   (ii) it does not provide any particular nutritional advantage over other cereals (see Table 9 for nutritional values);
   (iii) in many countries it is a status commodity (i.e., is it like providing cake rather than bread?).

(d) Other cereals.

Various cereals, not widely cultivated in the traditional donor countries, are often requested by developing countries for inclusion in the food aid basket, the most common being sorghum and millet.

Sorghum is grown in the USA and some is being made available for food aid. However, there is a problem of variety similar to that in the case of maize, in that the US sorghum is the red kind whereas that generally consumed in sub-Saharan Africa is the white, which is apparently easier to prepare for consumption. World market prices of sorghum are approximately the same as those of maize, so unlike rice it does not raise cost/benefit questions.

Pulses and Tubers

In tropical and sub-tropical countries a wide variety of beans, peas, tubers, and roots form part of the traditional diets and provide valuable nutrients at low cost.

The lower-cost varieties most commonly grown in temperate climates are lentils, chick-peas, and cow-peas and in recent years some of these have become available in food aid in response to requests from developing countries. Other items common in the tropics such as cassava (manioc) or yams (sweet potatoes) are not provided in food aid.

The availability of pulses in food aid allocations is quite limited. They are provided mainly by the EEC countries and the USA. From the recipient point of view, pulses take a long time to soak and cook, giving rise to higher fuel and water requirements.

Fruit and Vegetables

Perishables such as fruit and vegetables are not provided under food aid programmes, since this would require refrigeration, which would be both impractical and prohibitively costly. Moreover, many of the countries receiving food aid are exporters of tropical fruits and other agricultural products to the developed countries. In such cases the high market price and small quantities involved enable air freight to be used.

Dried fruits such as apples, apricots, figs, and pears are sometimes made available in small quantities in food aid programmes. Most of these commodities are provided by European donors.

Fresh fruit and vegetables frequently come into the recipients' households, not only through their own cultivation but also indirectly by means of an exchange of food aid commodities in the local markets for these fresh products. The addition of fresh produce is important from a nutritional point of view as a source of vitamins, particularly vitamin C.

Milk and Milk Products

Milk is usually considered an essential nutritional component in any food aid package, particularly where children and young mothers are involved.

In food aid programmes, the milk is supplied in powder form and may either be dried skimmed milk, generally known as DSM or NFDM (non-fat dried milk) or as whole or full cream milk known as DWM (dried whole milk). In recent years, as a result of the European Economic Community's Common Agricultural Policy (CAP) large amounts of DSM have become available in food aid programmes. The EEC now produces twice as much milk as the USA. In its 1984 food aid allocations the EEC made available 122,500 tonnes of DSM. At that time world prices were running at around five times the price for maize, that is in the region of $US700 per tonne. Dried whole milk, at nearly double the cost and less readily available, is reserved for use in food aid programmes for intensive care and nutritional rehabilitation of severely undernourished children or in cases where the mothers are unable to breast-feed.

Although it might be assumed that milk is universally acceptable, this is not always so. The milk powder provided in food aid is, of course, cow's milk. In a number of societies where milk is not a normal part of the diet, milk fed to infants can cause diarrhoea and other rejection symptoms. In other cases it may need to be mixed with sugar before being digestible. To the horror of food aid operators, reporters have sometimes seen recipient mothers selling donated milk powder in the market in exchange for sugar, not realizing that this was the only way of getting her child to digest the reconstituted milk. In other cases recipients may have been used to buffalo or camel's milk, but not cow's milk.

Another practical problem that frequently arises with milk powders is the operation of the reconstitution process. This requires both clean water and heat as well as clean and suitable utensils. If the milk is being used in an institution, general hygiene and storage are required. Contamination of the milk through polluted water, dust, etc. can cause serious medical problems, particularly if the recipients are already undernourished.

In the case of feeding programmes for larger institutions, or for distribution to a wide network of centres, many of these problems are overcome by providing the milk powder to a central dairy products plan that can not only reconstitute the milk, but also produce yoghurt and cheese from the powder. This approach was adopted in Algeria where food aid DSM for a large national school feeding programme was processed by ONALAIT, the national agency for the distribution of all milk products within the country.

Another frequently used milk product is butter-oil or ghee and this is also available in some food aid programmes, particularly those of the EEC. In nutritional terms this falls into the category of fats and oils. Butter-oil is generally packed in large round cans holding five to ten kilograms depending on the manufacturer. This makes the product more suited for institutions or large centres than for family distribution. Its cost is, however, about twice that of vegetable oils.

Processed cheese in cans is also sometimes available in food aid, but suppliers are very limited, Scandinavia being the principal source. Although cheese is nutritionally very beneficial, the cans tend to explode when stored under tropical conditions. This makes it a very popular product with the local rodents, but not with store-keepers. It is also not a normal item of consumption in recipient countries.

Edible Oils

Butter-oil, referred to above, is frequently classified as an edible oil, but this description usually applies to the vegetable oils made from maize, rape, soya bean, sunflower, ground-nuts, etc. These oils are highly prized commodities in most recipient countries, not only because of their unusually high value on the local markets, but also because frying is considered one of the safest means of cooking where ambient hygiene is difficult to ensure and water may be in short supply. It is also an essential ingredient in the many types of pancakes and flapjacks that are made and eaten in many areas.

There appear to be no problems of acceptability of the various vegetable oils supplied under food aid programmes, although packaging and transport can give rise to difficulties as shown in Chapter 8. The requirements for these products in food aid programmes usually run well in excess of availability.

Meats and Fish

These are seen as the most desirable source of animal protein but their supply in food aid is limited owing both to availability and to cost.

Fish is the more available of the two categories, and is supplied in food aid either in dried salted form or canned, the former being the more frequent, with supplies coming largely from Scandinavia and Germany. Dried fish needs, of course, to be kept dry during transportation and storage, and requires a good supply of clean water for soaking, which may not always be readily available. In some areas fish is appreciated as much for the salt it yields as for itself. There appear to be very few taboos connected with fish as a food, but this is not the case for meat.

Taboos have to be taken into careful consideration by food aid programmers. There is not only the question whether certain kinds of meat may not be acceptable according to region, such as pork or beef, but also whether it has been ritually slaughtered or not. Labels are of little help as they get torn off or are not understood by the recipients. They can even mislead; there was a case of a donation of baby food being rejected even though it carried a picture of a smiling healthy baby. On enquiring into the cause of the rejection, the donor was told by the recipients that they were really not in the habit of eating children. The simple task of opening tins of meat or fish, where the canner fails to provide built-in openers, can also be hazardous, and can give rise to considerable frustration, not to mention wastage.

Sugar

Sugar has only quite recently become available in food aid programmes. This has been partly in response to the problems of inacceptability of milk in some areas without sugar, and also partly to increased supplies and falling prices, particularly in the EEC. They are the principal suppliers for this food aid, but quantities are naturally very limited. Also, there is always a suspicion among donors that it might be used for father's tea rather than for the children's milk.

Blended/Processed Foods

A number of blended foods have been made available in food aid, mostly in the form of fortified cereal blends. The most familiar of these, which has been available for a number of years from the USA, is corn soya milk (CSM) which is a composite of maize-meal/ DSM, soya flour and a small quantity of sugar. It can be used to make a nutritive gruel or porridge. It can also be used as an additive to other dishes. Similar blends under various trade names are available from European food aid sources. These products are particularly useful in infant nutritional rehabilitation programmes. Availability is limited and costs are relatively high.

Changes in Availability

Changes in the availability of various commodities for food aid may occur as a result of crop fluctuations in the producer countries and changes in world market price, as well as changes in food aid

Table 4. Commodities allocated under the International Emergency Food Reserve programme in 1984 and 1985 (in metric tons)

Commodity	1984	1985
Cereals	620 638	758 867
Pulses	13 419	3 545
Edible oil/fat	19 194	21 508
Milk powder, whole/skimmed	3 996	7 051
Corn soya milk	8 193	20 060
Complete food biscuits	–	216
Sugar	434	500
Tea	–	20

requirements. All these variants had long been seen as obstacles to longer-term planning of food aid, particularly those in which it was essential to maintain nutritional norms, such as programmes in favour of children and other at-risk groups such as pregnant women, the sick, and the elderly.

Regulatory mechanisms were gradually built up to ensure a minimum flow of food aid, the most important of these being the Food Aid Convention and International Emergency Food Reserve, described in Chapter 4. The former currently applies to cereals only, although proposals are being made to include items such as milk products and fish under the Convention. The IEFR provides cereals as well as other commodities from pledges either in kind or in cash.

The quantities of the various commodities allocated under the IEFR programme give a good picture of the types of compromise that are made between availability and the needs of people in emergency situations, who are usually wholly dependent, for a while, on food aid. The figures under this programme for 1984 and 1985 are shown in Table 4.

Nutritional Requirements

There is, naturally, an interplay between availability and nutritional standards and requirements. The pressure on donors to provide commodities to meet these requirements is particularly strong in the case of programmes for children and vulnerable groups, and

Table 5. Energy intakes of New Guinea adults

Location	Body weight (kg)		Energy intake per day (kcal)
Coastal	Males	56	1940
	Females	47	1420
Highland	Males	57	2520
	Females	51	2100

Source: Agricultural Development and Nutrition, A. Pacey and P. Payne (eds), published by arrangement with FAO and Unicef (London, and Boulder, Colorado, 1985).

has a considerable influence on availability. The setting of nutritional standards also has the advantage, from the food aid programming point of view, that a quantification of the food and nutritional requirements, on the basis of the estimated number of beneficiaries by category, can be made some time in advance.

Recent nutritional research has led to the development of measuring malnutrition in terms of low energy intake rather than insufficient protein or vitamin intake alone. Energy is provided through carbohydrates, fats and oils, proteins, minerals, and of course water. A nutritionally adequate diet is one in which all the necessary nutrients are included in sufficient amounts to meet body needs. These body needs will vary according to the type of activity engaged in, and energy intake norms for these various categories have come to be worked out to provide indicators for planning purposes.

Although nutritionists are in agreement as to the amounts of energy, minerals, and vitamins, etc., yielded by various types of food, they are not in agreement as to precisely what human needs are, under a given set of conditions, for maintenance (of body functions, etc.), growth and activity. Requirements may vary according to location or social group, or even between individuals of the same weight, height, and age. Ethnic groups with lighter bodies or bone structure in warm climates have a lower requirement than heavier persons in cold climates. A study of adults in New Guinea showed considerable variations according to location and sex, as shown in Table 5.

All such variations complicate the task of setting a precise line below whch malnutrition (a major concern of many food aid programmes) can be said to start. A series of studies carried out in

Table 6. Variations in estimates of food energy requirements for a moderately active man (body weight 70 kg)*

Year	Energy requirements (kcal)
1943	3000
1958	3200
1968	2800
1974	2700

* Estimated by the US National Academy of Sciences.

India by local and expatriate nutritionists to establish a poverty threshold based on energy intakes showed a variation ranging from 2250 kcal to 2700 kcal per day. In other studies, however, pastoralists and nomads have been found to be able to adapt to intakes as low as 1600 kcal per day over protracted periods.

Another relevant point is that until fairly recently, most of the longer-term studies upon which nutritional norms have been based were carried out in temperate climates in developed economies. Yet, even there, estimates vary. For example, four successive estimates of food energy requirements for a moderately active man with a body weight of 70 kilograms made between 1943 and 1974 by the US National Academy of Sciences are given in Table 6. The 16 per cent fall in estimated requirements over this period is not the result of improvements in the process of estimation, nor of any change in levels of activity, but must be attributed more vaguely to climates of opinion and, perhaps, concern about obesity.

With these cautionary remarks in mind one can now look at the rather 'cut and dried' nutritional norms and corresponding tables.

In these statistical tables energy requirements are shown in kilojoules (kJ), megajoules (MJ), or more frequently in kilocalories (kcal). One kilojoule is equal to 0.239 kilocalories. Proteins, fats and oil are expressed in grams, while minerals and vitamins are shown in milligrams (mg). Unless otherwise indicated the figures represent daily requirements.

There is considerable variation in the energy requirements of adults according to types of activity. The results of sample surveys of (a) miners in Canton (China) and (b) rural women in Guatemala are given in Table 7.

Another survey of a group of housewives in the Philippines showed an average daily energy expenditure of 2,040 kcal while a

Table 7. Daily energy requirements of (a) miners in Canton and (b) rural women in Guatemala

Type of activity	kcal used per day	
	During working hours	During off-work hours
(a) Miners in Canton		
Ore porting	2 615	1 198
Ore dressing	2 032	1 270
Hammering	1 912	936
Prop setting	1 892	914
Drilling	974	1 283
(b) Rural women in Guatemala		
Yearly average	1 058	927
Planting season	999	877
Harvesting	1 024	926
Non-agricultural season	1 020	912
Physiological status		
Pregnant	1 071	973
Lactating	1 051	840

similar group of shoemakers showed an average of 2,712 kcal. Energy requirements are naturally higher in cold climates, but the present recipients of food aid live predominantly in tropical and sub-tropical areas of the world.

Surveys and studies of this type have led to the elaboration of average energy requirements of groups of beneficiaries of food aid by general type of activity. The FAO, in conjunction with the World Health Organization and nutrition experts, use the following calculations given in Table 8, which have been widely accepted by food aid programmers to assess the required energy intakes by age group and physiological status. The UN–FAO World Food programme has used these data to draw up the table of requirements by general category of food aid programme. The four categories covered are institutional feeding, hospital feeding, refugees/displaced persons in camps, and food for work programmes.

In order to provide the food needed to the recipients in these categories it is necessary to find out how much of a given commodity or selection of commodities is required to yield the energy and protein needed. Yields in terms of energy and nutrients from

Table 8. Calculations of required energy intakes by age group and physiological status (used by FAO/WHO)

Category of recipient		Approx. weight (kg)	Energy needed (kcal)	Protein needed (g)
Children	0–1 year	7.3	820	14
	1–3 years	13.4	1 360	16
	4–6 years	20.2	1 830	20
	7–9 years	28.1	2 190	25
Youths				
Male	10–12 years	36.9	2 190	25
	13–15 years	51.3	2 900	25
	16–19 years	62.9	3 070	25
Youths				
Female	10–12 years	38.0	2 350	29
	13–15 years	49.9	2 490	31
	16–19	54.4	2 310	30
Adults				
Male		65.0	3 000	37
Female				
Moderately active		55.0	2 200	29
Last half pregnancy			2 550	38
Lactating			2 750	46

Source: FAO Nutrition Paper No. 23, Rome 1982.

the main categories of food aid commodities mentioned earlier in this chapter are given in Table 9.

Armed with these data food aid programmers can proceed to the choice of the actual commodities to be used in a given programme. The choice will depend upon the interplay between availability, local custom and production, finance, timing, and of course, the nature of the situation that requires food aid. Although it is relatively simple to work out the energy requirements for a group of people who may need basic sustenance for a limited time, or for a food supplement to a household diet such as in most food-for-work types of project, there is generally a lot of 'fine tuning' needed in respect of the given situations requiring food aid.

The recipient group may, for instance, be found to be anaemic due to lack of iron in the local diet or to lack of food altogether; this means that a selection of commodities giving a higher iron content would be necessary. Alternatively, cases of deficiency of vision may

Table 9. Yields of energy and nutrients from various food aid commodities (per 100 g edible portion)

Commodity	Energy (kcal)	Protein (g)	Fat (g)	Calcium (mg)	Iron (mg)	Vitamins (mg)				Niacin
						B1	B2	C	A	
Wheat grain	332	12.7	1.8	60	7.6	0.35	0.12	0	0	3.6
Bread (white)	261	7.7	2.0	37	1.7	0.16	0.06	0	0	1.0
Maize (yellow)	364	10.0	4.8	13	4.9	0.32	0.12	4	50	1.7
Rice	364	7.0	0.6	6	2.4	0.17	0.03	0	0	5.4
Corn soy milk	380	20.0	6.0	1000	18.0	0.80	0.80	40	510	8.0
Lentils	340	23.0	1.0	68	7.0	0.5	0.3	0	0	1.3
Soy bean	405	33.7	17.9	183	6.1	0.71	0.25	0	27	2.0
Milk – DSM	360	36.0	0.7	1290	0.6	0.35	1.80	7	8	0.9
Milk – DWM	490	23.5	24.0	900	0.7	0.24	1.23	4	318	0.7
Vegetable oil	890	0	100.0	0	0	0	0	0	0	0
Butter oil	862	0	97.8	0	0	0	0	0	600	0
Meat (average)	220	21.0	15.0	0	1.9	0.15	0.19	0	0	3.2
Fish (salted)	270	47.0	7.5	1600	2.4	0.10	0.36	0	33	4.4
Sugar	400	0	0	0	0	0	0	0	0	0

have been detected in children, due to lack of vitamin A. Vitamin B1 from thiamine, B2 from riboflavin and B6 from niacin help the body to metabolize carbohydrate and other nutrients. Lack of B1 can cause beri-beri, lack of B6 causes pellagra, lack of C lowers resistance to infections, and so forth. In cases of rehabilitation after prolonged malnutrition, energy-rich food with the full range of minerals available is required. Table 9 gives the average contribution to these requirements by the main categories of food generally found in aid programmes.

The foregoing shows the importance of close collaboration with health and medical requirements in the planning and implementation of food aid programmes, particularly when children and various vulnerable or at-risk groups of people are concerned. Giving food to a child with intestinal virus or parasites means that the food is wasted by passing through the body without benefit; conversely a child who has been medically treated for these conditions will relapse if there is no proper food to go with the treatment. Cooperation of this kind naturally takes place where food aid is given to institutions such as Mother and Child Health (MCH) centres and clinics or used in feeding hospital patients.

The attention paid to nutritional requirements varies from donor to donor. In general it is the larger donors and their dependent non-governmental organizations, who have the funds to carry out surveys and a range of commodities at their disposal, that pay the greatest heed to recipient requirements and recipient conditions and devise specific programmes or projects to suit a given situation. Those donors with fewer commodities at their disposal may simply make arrangements for the commercial purchase of a required commodity, or else make a contribution in cash or kind to a regional or international organization such as the EEC or WFP, or to a large voluntary organization, which will then be responsible for integrating these contributions into the overall food aid package.

An important element in such contributions is the cash component. Not only is cash required for transportation and distribution in a number of cases, but it also enables the acquisition of local products and complementary inputs into food aid projects—that is to say, non-food items such as tools, utensils, technical assistance, etc. It will be noted that most of the considerations and data in this chapter so far have been donor based rather than recipient based. This arises on account of the annual budgeting processes of most of the donor countries. Estimates of requirements in kind and in cash have to be drawn up well ahead of the budget exercise so that forward global estimates of requirements have to be made. Much, but not all, is covered by the Food Aid Convention and the International Emergency Food Reserve. Adjustments in national and multinational programmes frequently have to be made in the light of unforeseen emergencies or of changing priorities. Programming flexibility is also enhanced through annual contributions or pledges to international organizations who can then use these pledges to mount multi-annual programmes and projects. Pledges in cash add an important element of flexibility to the programmes since they enable purchases to be made locally or regionally. This has the double advantage of providing the producer country with the equivalent of an export order (since payment is made in convertible currency) as well as making savings on transport, time, and cost. From a health and nutrition point of view, it enables one gap in food aid programmes to be filled, namely, that of providing fresh produce such as fruit and vegetables.

Other means exist of introducing flexibility into the longer-term overall commitments of donors; these may be summarized as follows.

(a) *Commodity exchange.* Situations may arise where a given commodity in an agreed food basket has not been delivered, perhaps owing to transport bottlenecks, spoilage, pilferage, etc. These can sometimes be overcome by borrowing the commodity from other projects or from governmental stores, to be repaid when the food aid commodity arrives;

(b) *Monetization.* A certain percentage of the food aid commodities may be allowed to be sold either by the Government or by the recipients, for exchange with products locally available and more suited to local tastes and requirements than the food aid imports;

(c) *Triangular transactions.* A country in a certain region may have an exportable surplus of a commodity required for food aid in a neighbouring country. Commercial export does not work because the recipient has no funds for such purchases. Food aid cash contributions can then be used to purchase the commodity from the producer and deliver it under food aid to the recipient. For instance, in the early 1980s, Zimbabwe had a large stock of maize which was used in this way for food aid programmes in neighbouring African countries. With no other buyers in prospect Zimbabwe would have had storage and disposal problems had it not been for this international purchase programme by the UN–FAO World Food Programme. A failure to use the stocks meaningfully could have had negative results on future maize production. The World Food Programme has led the way in establishing this type of transaction as a recognized food aid method that is of considerable benefit to producer countries in the developing world.

7 FOOD AID:
How to get it there?

Crucial to the effectiveness of all types of food aid are its delivery systems. Much continues to be written in the Press and in specialized literature about the value and quantity of food aid, but much less about the delivery systems—that is, until something goes wrong. In fact, much of the criticism of food aid in general stems from an insufficient flow of information about the operation of the delivery systems and the constraints of time, costs, commodity availability, and losses, that affect the three main links in the delivery chain, namely: transportation, storage, and distribution.

These three links in the chain provide a convenient framework for a review of the operations and their problems at each stage, so as to give a clearer picture of the whole chain of operations, generally known as 'logistics'.

Transportation

In the majority of cases delivery of commodities from donor country to recipient country involves the use of ocean freight. Overland transport with its different method of operation, will be considered separately in Chapter 8.

Ocean Freight

Shipping companies world-wide work on a commercial profitability basis, so that ocean freight for food aid has to be paid for by some means. Funds for these payments are derived in various ways according to the type of food aid programme acting as the donor agency. Furthermore, there are variations in the proportions of the total transportation operation that donors are prepared to include in the freight contract or food aid agreement. These can range from only providing transportation within the donor community to port of embarkation, to the other extreme of paying full transportation costs, including the delivery to distribution points within, say, a land-locked country. Some of the concessional sales of programmes of bilateral agencies such as the Title I programme of US Public Law 480 have provided food, usually grains, for sale in the recipient country against local currency, on the understanding that ocean freight from port of delivery in the USA is undertaken and paid for by the recipient country. Although $US loans have frequently been extended by the donor to the recipient to cover such costs the charge remains incumbent on the recipient. In addition, in such cases, there is generally a requirement to use only the vessels of the donor country. However, the most common practice for food aid programmes in which food is intended for specified categories of consumers (generally known as 'targeted' aid) is that of the cost of ocean freight up to port of entry in the recipient country being provided as part of the food aid donation. In the case of land-locked countries cost of transit rail or road freight from discharge port to nearest frontier railhead in the recipient country is included in such packages. The other extreme, in which costs for inland transport from port to distribution points are either partially or wholly covered, relates to the various special programmes for disadvantaged categories within the group of least-developed countries, or disaster areas within the affected countries.

Payment of freight costs can also affect the quantity of food aid actually delivered to a recipient by a donor. Multilateral food aid programmes such as the World Food Programme operate on the basis of volume (tonnage) actually delivered. Some bilateral programmes, on the other hand, allocate a given value amount to a food aid budget or a specific food aid programme. This value amount is then used to cover the cost of the purchase of the required commodity as well as loading, freight, unloading, and insurance. In other cases, part of a given quantity of a commodity may be sold to defray the costs of transport, freight, bagging, containerization, etc. In either case the amount of food actually received will be less than would appear from the figures given in the donor's pledge. That is to say, a donation of 100,000 monetary units (the equivalent of, say, 1,000 tons of cereals at commercial rates) would in fact only yield say 650 tons of cereals actually delivered, the difference being absorbed by the freight costs. Obviously, both commodity prices and freight rates fluctuate considerably, both seasonally and from year to year, so it is not possible to draw up a simple table showing the ratio between commodity and transport rates by type of commodity. As a rough guide, at 1985 prices the ocean freight for bulk grain from a United States or European port to, say, East Africa would amount to about 30 per cent of the cost of the grain. In the case of ports with no bulk handling it could rise to 50 per cent and in the case of some land-locked countries delivery costs can more than equal the cost of the commodity.

Choice of Carrier

A food aid programme's choice of carrier is largely determined by the prevailing factors of time, cost, volume, and cargo handling facilities. The time component is largely determined by the programme requirements. Thorough account has to be taken of seasonal freezing of river estuary, port, or inland seas in northern latitudes. For instance, in the case of a programme designed to provide food security in a recipient country through the regular or periodic restocking of national supplies with sizeable shipments of bulk grain, regularity is more important than transit time; consequently, the programmer is able to choose the less costly but still reliable means of ocean transport. In other cases time may be the crucial factor in order to relieve malnutrition or famine. In those cases the programmer will need to select the fastest means of delivery, and may at times even have to resort to diverting less urgent cargoes of the same commodity already on the high seas en route to another recipient.[1] The fastest means are usually modern vessels plying recognized trade routes. Those trade routes do not necessarily coincide with the required destinations of food aid shipments, and even where they do, their freight costs are usually higher. Furthermore, such fast carriers generally have a number of regular commercial customers, and space may be limited or even not available when required for food aid shipments. Since humanitarian considerations cannot be expected to guide the activities of commercial shipping operators, food aid programmes often need to have recourse to chartering arrangements. Such arrangements are particularly valuable whenever the shipment is large enough to warrant the use of the full capacity of the vessel, either in the form of a single shipment to a designated port of call, or as several smaller packages to the total capacity of the vessel, for off-loading at several ports in a region, for instance at Port Sudan, Hodeida, Asab, and Djibouti in the Red Sea region.

Maritime practice divides chartering arrangements into two categories: 'time-charter' and 'voyage-charter'. Under time-charter arrangements, the charterer hires the vessel for a given period of time and can take it to any port(s) he may require within the specified time. A voyage-charter specifies the type and quantity of cargo to be carried from one stipulated port to another at an agreed rate. Rates for time-charter tend to be the more economical; however, the charterer takes on all the ancillary costs of chandlering, loading, unloading, and various other related fees; furthermore, if a port should be congested and loading or unloading delayed, the operation may not be completed in the time expected by the charterer, so that extra expenses or cost overruns, known as 'demurrage', may be incurred. Since freight carried on voyage-charter terms is for collection at one port for delivery to another, any delays become the responsibility of the owner of the vessel, who will cover such eventualities by including the risk element in the charter price; this accounts for the higher rates charged for this operation. Rates charged by ship-owners offering vessels for charter will vary according to the market conditions: rates are naturally lower when shipping capacity exceeds demand. Chartering provides a useful regulator of freight rates, since the major freight lines may have to adjust their rates for normal cargo operations if competition from charter parties becomes too stiff. For this reason many of the major companies operate a charter department as well as a regular freight department so as to provide a dual tariff system. The major companies, in respect of normal freight and passenger operations, form regional or country groupings of all flags plying certain routes or regions; these are known as 'conference lines'. These 'conferences' cover various regions, such as the North Atlantic conference, the Baltic and White Sea conference, etc., and set common tariffs for various categories of cargoes within the areas they cover.

Although there may be considerable variations in the price advantages of chartering over regular cargo service, an across-the-board average of cargoes of various types from the Americas, Asia, Australasia and Europe to a range of recipient countries, showed that charter rates at 1984 prices, for food aid averaged $US45 per tonne as against $US125 for regular cargo services.

Categories of cargoes and load factors have to be taken into consideration in the choice of a vessel for food aid. Although economies can generally be made by the use of large shipments, this is not always possible, not only on account of programme requirements, but also because of the facilities at the port of unloading. An 8,000 to 10,000 ton vessel may draw between 20 and 30 feet, depending on her hull construction and the temperature and density of the water; there are a number of ports that have less depth of water than that, so that a smaller vessel might have to be used, or the cargo off-loaded into lighters, causing extra costs and losses. Regular cargo services are aware of such problems but it is not unknown for charter parties to overlook them.

Food aid involves various types of commodities, as was seen in Chapter 6. For shipment on regular cargo services differing rates will apply for each type of cargo. The most economical rates are for cargoes such as bulk grain where the available capacity is fully utilized. Commodities in round cans or drums such as butter-oil or vegetable oil will occupy much more space than their actual volume. The differing rate calculations take into consideration the overall space occupied by the consignment, that is the total volume taken up in a ship's hold. Shipping practice equates one long ton weight to 40 cubic feet or one metric ton to one cubic metre and will charge whichever rate is the most beneficial to the owner of the vessel. A ton of bulk grain would be charged at the weight rate but a net ton of bagged grain would be over the weight/volume ratio and be charged at around 48 cubic feet. These problems are avoided in the case of a time-charter where it is up to the charterer to make best use of the space available in the chartered vessel; alternatively, the unused space between, say, drums could be filled with some other commodity, but this is rarely practical.

Stowage and Stowage Plans

Every merchant vessel is required to draw up a stowage plan showing where each consignment is placed and to have this plan accessible at ports of discharge. Certain commodities may require special handling which raises the question of stowage planning. The vessel's stowage plan has to take into consideration these handling requirements, as well as the need to unload as rapidly as possible in order to avoid incurring any fines or penalties that might have been specified in the freight contract. Speed of unloading will depend furthermore on the availability of stevedoring gangs or mechanical unloading facilities at the port. When these are insufficient or lacking, unloading has to be undertaken using the vessel's own tackle, which is often slower. In this process cargoes that can be moved relatively easily from the quayside (such as crated goods that can be fork-lifted) are unloaded first and large consignments of such items as bagged maize that would pile up on the quayside and either require the vessel to move to another berth or cause delay in unloading are left until the last. However, if a vessel were carrying, say, 1,000 tons of bagged maize the master would not put the rest of his cargo consisting say of 100 tons of engine oil in 5-litre cans on top of the maize since any leak would contaminate the maize and he would be liable for damages. Other commodities such as dried fish have to be stowed where there is no risk of humidity, others may have to be stowed away from heat sources (engine-room, boilers, etc.), or may require special ventilation and temperature control to prevent spontaneous combustion (certain grains, etc.). All these factors affect not only freight costs of food commodities but also loading and unloading time at various ports (known as the 'turn-around time') which can in turn affect the delivery time of the commodities. Incorrect stowage can, in addition, cause loss or damage through subjecting some commodities or their containers to too much pressure, so that they burst and perhaps contaminate or render inedible other commodities. Incorrect stowage in a hold may also result in commodities being off-loaded in the wrong port; although such errors are the responsibility of the vessel owners who have to pay for the re-routeing, they will give such non-profitable operations the lowest priority and the ensuing delays can easily upset the operation of a whole food aid project.

Port authorities also play a role in the discharge of cargoes and the time taken for the operation, particularly in congested ports where each vessel is given a set time for discharge and/or loading. If the operation is not completed in the given time, or if the port can only handle one hold at a time of a large vessel, the vessel may have to move out to roads and wait another turn to discharge the remainder of the cargo. If this happens for liner-term vessels, the master or owners have to make a calculation of the cost of the extra running days involved in a wait, against that of redirecting the remaining cargo from another port and paying the transport costs back from there. In either case the food aid shipment would be delayed; in the case of reshipment this could amount to several months.

Ancillary Costs

The cost of the commodity and freight charges are the principal but not the only costs in the delivery system at this stage. Costs are incurred for marine insurance and for superintendence. Insurance costs, though moderate under normal operating conditions, can rise steeply or even be refused by the insurers if the cargo is passing through a declared danger zone that could arise from blockades or from hostilities or threatened hostilities and it is precisely to such areas that food aid for emergencies often has to go. Similarly, freight rates themselves can rise in such cases. In addition freight rates may be subject to a 10 to 20 per cent surcharge in cases where a vessel is carrying cargo for a port known to be generally congested, in which a delay in berthing may be expected either continually or seasonally. In some cases such delays have amounted to several weeks, particularly in African ports such as Port Sudan, Dar-es-Salaam, Berbera, Douala, Lagos, etc.

Services known in maritime practice as 'superintendence' are generally carried out by major marine insurance companies such as Lloyds and consist of a certified statement of cargoes discharged and their condition; such superintendence reports form the basis of claims against the owners for damage to cargo or against the port of loading in the event of 'short-loading': that is to say, loading less than the amount stipulated in the bill of lading. In the case of a vessel having to leave a port before completion of unloading or of any discrepancy, such deficiencies are recorded as 'short-landings' and will form the basis of claims against the vessel for redirection of the remaining cargo.

Charges are made by port authorities under various headings: anchoring; berthing; piloting; tug dues; light, radar, or radio beacon charges; health charges; or, in the case of discharge outside the main port, of lighterage, that is, transhipment from vessel to shore by means of lighters or barges. Although these charges are absorbed into the overall freight charges under liner-terms or voyage charters, the charges can vary considerably from port to

Table 10. Ancillary charges at two ports in Bangladesh, both using the system of discharge into lighters (1983–1984)

Charge	Cost per metric ton*	
	Chittagong	Chalna
River dues	5.50	6.50
Landing charge	7.00	7.00
Landing tally	1.92	0.77
Terminal charge	nil	nil
Loading charge	nil	nil
Siding	6.70	6.70
Stevedoring	10.52	19.94
Weighbridge	1.05	
Miscellaneous	3.37	
Lighterage	72.80	36.40
Gunny bags†	204.00	204.00
Storage	22.00	22.00
Unloading		
Reloading	88.44	88.44
Resale of gunny bags†	−120.00	−120.00
	303.30	271.75

Exchange rate = 24.50 takas per $US
Total cost per ton   =$US 12.37   =$US 11.09

* Charges in local currency (takas).

† Gunny bags purchased for bagging bulk grain were resold after delivery of the grain.

port and the service is not always commensurate with the charges levied. This has the effect of regular cargo vessels tending to avoid such high cost/poor service ports so that food aid shipments may have to make charter arrangements to reach those ports directly. Table 10 gives an example of such ancillary charges at two ports in Bangladesh, both using the system of discharge into lighters; it shows the cumulative costs per metric ton of food aid cargoes in local currency (takas).

In 1983–4 ocean freight for bulk grain from US port to Bangladesh by the more expensive standard freight rate was $US27.50 per ton so that these various port and handling charges added 45 per cent to the ocean freight costs.

A further example from Port Sudan not involving discharge into

Table 11. Ancillary charges in Port Sudan, not using the system of discharge into lighters (1986)

Charge	Cost per metric ton* (£S)
Stevedoring	10
Landing charge	1.25
Porterage	1.60
Clearance charges	1.00
Transport from jetty to warehouse	5.50
	19.35
+ 2% commission to state shipping company	.38
	19.73
Approximate exchange rate = £S 2.40 per $US Total cost per ton = $US 8.22 per ton	

* In Sudanese pounds.

lighters is given in Table 11. With freight rates at approximately $US29.50 per ton from US port to Red Sea port these charges represented an addition of just under 30 per cent to the ocean freight costs.

These figures are based on the exemption from taxes and customs duties applicable to aid shipments and on the higher liner rates. At charter rates the freight would be considerably less, thus increasing the proportion of the port and handling charges to around 50 per cent over the ocean freight costs.

In industrialized countries, ancillary charges can vary considerably. The pilotage charges for a 10,000 ton vessel to London's Tilbury docks in 1985 amounted to approximately £4,000, whereas a vessel of the same tonnage could be piloted into Le Havre for the equivalent of £1,500.

Distribution

Overland Freight

Overland freight in the context of commodities from food aid donor country to food recipient country is virtually limited to com-

modities purchased in a developing country through food aid programmes funded by the traditional donor community on the basis
of 'triangular' transactions as described in Chapters 4 and 5. This
type of transaction is fairly common in the commercial world, particularly within the Eastern bloc's Comecon partners, where a
recipient country may effect payment for, say, Soviet natural gas to
a third country in a different commodity, leaving that third country
to complete the transaction by delivering yet another commodity to
the Soviet Union in final settlement. In respect to food aid, however,
the multilateral organizations, WFP and FAO's Office of Special
Relief Operations (OSRO) have taken the lead in adapting this system to the benefit of developing countries. The best documented of
such operations was the purchase of white maize from Zimbabwe
covering the period between July 1981 and late 1983. A status
report prepared by WFP in December 1983 showed a total of
406,372 tonnes purchased in this manner from Zimbabwe. The
funding was derived from WFP's international resources, from
international pledges to the International Emergency Food Reserve
(IEFR), and from other bilateral donations. The maize was bagged
in Zimbabwe and the greater part railed from there to Maputo in
Mozambique where WFP and OSRO provided logistic and supervisory assistance to the authorities to handle receipt, distribution, and
transhipment of the commodity. Approximately one-third of the
total tonnage was distributed within Mozambique; the remainder
was earmarked for other recipients in Africa. The total tonnage
delivered per recipient country is shown in Table 12. A further 973
tonnes were delivered to Mozambique in 1984 bringing the total
delivered to 407,345 tonnes.

The more common use of overland transport occurs in respect of
transhipments of food aid consignments to land-locked countries
from a port of entry in a neighbouring country. For instance, Arica
in Chile serves as the port of entry for Bolivia; the port of Dar-
es-Salaam, already heavily engaged in trade for Tanzania itself, also
serves as the port of entry for goods to Burundi and Rwanda, as
well as for Zambia and Zaire over the Chinese-built Tanzam rail-
road; more recently since the closure of the rail link between
Malawi and Nacala in Mozambique, traffic for Malawi is also
being handled through Dar-es-Salaam. Thus, in the case of commodities for Southern Zaire, two transit countries would be involved,
namely Zambia and Tanzania. Some countries, though not strictly

Table 12. Overland deliveries of white maize from Zimbabwe to various recipient countries via WFP and OSRO (from July 1981 to late 1983)

Country	Delivery (tonnes)
Angola	31 340
Bebin	2 500
Botswana	14 350
Cape Verde	2 135
Chad	2 140
Ghana	3 120
Kenya	6 000
Lesotho	5 861
Mali	6 580
Mozambique	143 668
Niger	13 000
Senegal	400
Somalia	7 000
Swaziland	6 888
Tanzania	135 920
Upper Volta	6 545
Zambia	18 655
Total	406,372

speaking land-locked, have supply difficulties due to their geographical position—Paraguay, for instance, can receive small tonnage vessels up the Parana river to the capital Asunción, but in most cases it proves more economical to tranship at an Argentine port. Zaire is another such case; the northern parts including the capital are served by the Zairean port of Matadi, but due to absence of overland rail connections between there and the southern parts of the country the latter are land-locked and have to be served via Dar-es-Salaam, or via East London in the Republic of South Africa via Zimbabwe and Zambia.

In these various transhipment operations many of the complications of entry and exit and customs clearance are avoided owing to the existence of an international commercial practice known as a 'through bill-of-lading'. This is designed to enable commodities to be discharged at port of entry into a bonded warehouse—that is, a warehouse for goods not cleared through local customs. These commodities can then be loaded directly on to railway wagons to the country of destination under customs seal until the frontier of that country is reached. Despite the facilities provided under these arrangements the paperwork involved can still cause quite considerable delays, especially if the country of destination and the country of entry happen not to be on good terms at the time. There were frequent disputes between Zambia and Tanzania about the 'disappearance' of railway wagons which were found to be used as temporary storage by one or other stationmaster or forwarding agent.

One of the more frequent constraints encountered in these transit operations is the availability of railway wagons or of trucks in the right amount and at the right times. In addition, the rail transport systems of some countries operate networks with different gauges. Bangladesh and Tanzania have systems with both standard gauge (that used in Europe) and metre gauge; others have standard gauge and narrow gauge. Wagons are not readily interchangeable from one gauge to another. Wagon availability is dependent not only on the obvious factor of locomotive availability and maintenance of plant and track, but more frequently on the question of turn-around time. At times of heavy goods movement, wagons may not be able to unload because of lack of space in customs or transit warehouses, and have to wait on a siding until space is available. In other cases difficulties may arise in tracing the consignee or in getting payment from him, with the result that wagons will be tied up pending settlement and so forth. All such incidents, some of which may be cumulative, can cause serious delays in food shipments involving transhipments. Even though perishable goods are not used in food aid, there are nevertheless commodities that can suffer from excessive heat in closed metal railway wagons in hot sun, or from humidity due to leaks in rail wagon roofs or in tarpaulin coverings during rainy seasons. Questions of pilferage and so on are discussed in Chapter 9 following sections dealing with losses in general.

Air Freight

The use of air transport for large-scale food transport operations was convincingly vindicated through its use in the relief of some two million people in the western sectors of Berlin during the 319 days of the Russian blockade of the city in 1948–9. However, the cost of such operations in men, equipment and management is well beyond that available to food aid operations, unless the necessary expertise and equipment are made available by the air force of one or more donor countries.

In recent years air transport for food emergencies has been made available in the case of the Sahel drought in the early 1970s, in a flood emergency in Somalia in 1981, and most recently in various parts of Ethiopia for famine relief.

The most economical use of aircraft for food emergencies is the air drop technique, which allows larger capacity aircraft to be used. The food aid, in specially designed packages to withstand the shock, is dropped out of the tail-gate of a cargo aircraft flying at low altitudes. For this, a relatively slow moving propeller or turbo-prop aircraft such as the *Hercules* is best suited. This technique avoids the need for landing strips, which are often not available in the areas required, or when they are available they can only accept smaller aircraft of limited carrying capacity.

Because of the limited tonnage that can be carried in air-lift operations for food aid, it is necessary to select commodities that will provide the maximum nutritive or recuperative value in proportion to their weight and volume. Blended foods such as soya-fortified flour and full cream milk powder are frequently used in such cases. It also has to be borne in mind that food alone is not sufficient in many types of emergency. There is the obvious need for shelter, blankets etc., but also the less obvious one of fuel in the case of villages in a flooded area, cut off from their normal supplies of wood or charcoal for boiling water, preparing food and so on.

The cost of civil air transport operations for food aid is increased by the fact that the load is generally only taken one way, that is, there is no return payload as is the case with most commercial air freight operations. This is obviously not a problem when the air transport is provided free of charge by a donor. Although the procedures for road and rail transport of food aid within a given country are well established, authorizations for the use of aircraft owned and operated by foreigners tends to be much more complicated and is often met with suspicion. This can result in permission being given to land only in the capital and not at provincial airports which are often nearer to the areas of the emergency.

The time taken in obtaining such authorizations can often defeat the purpose of using the aircraft—namely, speed of delivery. The Swiss Disaster Relief Unit have developed a number of innovative steps that get around this type of difficulty. Agreements have been drawn up between them and countries that are known to be struck regularly by natural disasters. Although not all such disasters require food aid for immediate delivery, the procedure established is relevant to food aid emergencies. At present the Swiss have agreements with the following countries:

Ivory Coast	Peru
Greece	Rwanda
Kenya	Tunisia
Malawi	Turkey
Pakistan	Yugoslavia

Furthermore, the Unit's ability to provide quick response to disasters is enhanced by a supply of some 15,000 different items of equipment liable to be needed in such cases, kept in their own warehouses. A roster of volunteers available for urgent missions of two to four months' duration is kept, so that supplies provided can be efficiently used in their various fields.

The greater part of food aid is delivered to the recipient government at port of entry or frontier railhead, at which point the donor responsibility ends and recipient responsibility begins. Humanitarian assistance for emergencies or voluntary agency aid for specified groups, however, is frequently carried at donor expense to destination.

The operation of the logistics chain from port of entry onwards is discussed in Chapter 8.

Reference

1. This occurred in the case of the 1980/81 emergency in Somalia when a cargo of cereals destined for the Far East was diverted to Mogadiscio while in the Indian ocean.

8   FOOD AID:
How to distribute it?

There is nothing particularly new about the art of distributing food to groups of people at varying distances from ports or other points of discharge. The Romans, after all, were able to supply their campaign armies in Europe and the Near East from their granaries in North Africa without the help of engines or radio. However, the operation of a modern logistics chain from various points of supply to a number of different inland destinations still needs to be run rather like a military operation, especially when emergencies or large-scale programmes are involved. All these operations require efficiency, proper timing, and accountability. Unlike the military, however, food aid donors have to pay great attention to cost factors without sacrificing efficiency, and discipline has to be replaced by a spirit of voluntarism or some other incentive.

The last link in the food aid delivery chain, that is, the final distribution to the recipient, is the most 'visible' and quite naturally attracts the most attention. It is generally determinant of the 'image' or perception of the whole operation, with little attention being paid to the earlier stages. It is also at this point that any accumulated errors or delays will naturally begin to show up most clearly—or disastrously, as the case may be.

Perhaps more importantly, this last stage in the chain is the one over which the donors have the least control, since the action and movement takes place within the territory of the recipient country and, barring special arrangements, has to follow all the norms and administrative procedures of that country. Consequently, it is that stage of the operation that is of greatest concern to most donors. This concern frequently expresses itself in requests to undertake evaluations, participate in monitoring activities, cost/benefit studies, and so forth. It often becomes the most frustrating stage of the operation for the recipients just because of this donor concern.

As indicated in previous chapters, in the early days of food aid operations in developing countries most donors were in reality quite happy to see their responsibility end at the port of delivery or railhead, knowing full well the relative weakness of the transport and surveillance systems, weakness of adminstrative support available and payment difficulties—especially in times of crisis when national services would certainly be over-stretched.

It was gradually with the shift of emphasis in donor policies from surplus disposal to programmes and projects designed to benefit certain underprivileged or 'target' groups that questions about the effectiveness of distribution were raised and means sought to ensure delivery to destination. At the same time many recipient states also came to believe that some external assistance to the logistics of food aid operations in-country would not only save them some headaches but, perhaps more importantly, induce the donors to continue their supply of food aid on the basis of improved efficiency and assured targeting.

An additional problem is that the more precisely the target groups are defined and supplied, and the smaller they are, the more complex the delivery of food aid becomes. Complexities raise costs; one result of this has been a reluctance on the part of donors to accept small-scale projects with widely diversified target groups, unless the operation can be handled through some form of contractual arrangement with a voluntary agency or related to other ongoing externally funded projects. Continual compromises had been, and are still having to be made between costs and efficiency. While donor countries and the various interest groups advocating food aid there are keen to have as much assurance as possible that the food is getting to where it is intended, they are not often willing to make the additional contributions that such requirements entail.

These considerations were also partly responsible for the categorization of deliveries to Less Developed Countries (LDCs), Most Severely Affected Areas (MSAs), landlocked countries etc. Within these special groups donors would often be prepared to defray part of the transportation costs within the country on the grounds that a low-income recipient country could not be expected to meet these costs fully itself without sacrificing other priorities. The simple answer, of course, is for the recipient country to defray transportation costs by selling part of the food aid to meet the costs. This was initially looked upon with dismay by many of the protagonists of targeted food aid who maintained that every grain of donated cereals must be seen to have been eaten by the intended recipients.

More recently, however, many donors finding it easier to provide food than cash for transportation have been taking a more relaxed view and are now espousing the cause of monetization, that is the exchange of food for local currency, even when the food aid was a grant and not a concessional sale.

An even simpler solution to transportation and distribution problems is for the food aid donors and operators not to be involved in those problems and their related costs at all! This can be achieved when distribution is carried out on the basis of entitlements of one kind or another. Much of the food aid provided domestically to underprivileged or target groups in the USA is handled by means of food stamps which entitle the bearer to buy food at designated commercial outlets up to the amount indicated on the entitlement. These are generally issued on a weekly basis and can be sent to the recipient by post and it is up to the commercial outlet—usually a normal supermarket—to ensure that the stamps are not used for the purchase of luxuries, drinks, etc. This system can work well in cases where the normal commercial food outlets are constantly well stocked and the recipients have no particular difficulty in reaching the point of distribution. In other variations of this theme, distribution can be made on the basis of ration cards or supplementary ration cards for certain vulnerable groups requiring extra nutrients. This system, with a number of levels of entitlement for the ordinary population, is in use in mainly socialist countries. As in the case of food stamps, the system works well for as long as the ration cards are honoured. In a number of African countries employing this system, there has often not been sufficient food in the outlets to provide the stipulated ration. Apart from removing the transportation problems away from the food aid providers on to general retailers, the system has the great advantage of not requiring any special logistics or other exceptional handling arrangements, and is consequently less costly to operate. It cannot, however, be expected to work in conditions where there is not a well developed normal commercial or state controlled distribution system, capable of providing the required commodities on a regular basis as required. The system is also open to falsification of the stamps or cards or the sale of these entitlements to others.

However, until some such radical or technological solutions are found, food aid operations still have to face the more classic problems of storage, inland transport, and final distribution, which are discussed below.

Storage

The level (in terms of volume) at which food aid to developing countries from all sources is now flowing over and above normal commercial imports, coupled with the need to effect economies of scale in shipping operations, has resulted in the need for an expanding network of storage facilities in nearly every food aid recipient country. It has to be borne in mind that in the case of commercial transactions, food importers are unlikely to order commodities in excess of the storage and distribution capacity available to them, as this could result in substantial financial losses. In the case of food aid, the recipient government is normally expected to provide the necessary storage; when the amount of food aid exceeds the government's available storage capacity—which can often occur, especially in the case of emergency food aid—serious bottlenecks and losses can arise. Since, furthermore, food aid is considered by many recipient governments to contain elements of unpredictability in terms of quantities, types of commodity, and delivery times, it is not an easy task for the national authorities concerned to get funds from the national budget for food aid alone. Recently, some positive means have been developing that help to overcome these problems; these relate to the increasing priority being given by a number of developing countries to the establishment of food security schemes which require the positioning in-country of reserve stocks, usually cereals. Such food security schemes have been receiving encouragement and some financial support from multilaterals and bilateral sources. Such long-term storage schemes require large as well as high-quality storage in order to protect the grain from humidity, rodents, birds, insects, and other contamination but have the advantage of providing a time-buffer between the need for food aid and replenishment of stocks from donor sources. In this manner many of the surges in sudden food aid requirements can be evened out and more effective delivery planning initiated.

Under existing conditions the development of high-quality and large capacity storage such as silos with mechanized loading and discharge facilities to and from ships carrying, say, bulk grain, have generally only been developed in those countries that have had either a major grain export or import requirement, both conditions presupposing a reasonably advanced state of development. However, the majority of developing countries that are in most need of food aid at present have been neither major exporters nor importers of grain in recent times and have consequently not felt the need to build up transport, storage, and distribution networks to handle such flows.

Regional variations in eating habits further affect the type of storage commonly available. In Latin America maize and wheat are staples; in sub-Saharan Africa staples comprise maize, sorghum, millet, and cassava; in East and South-east Asia rice is a staple. In some instances storage may have been constructed for other agricultural exports from developing countries, such as cotton or other vegetable fibres, which are of considerable bulk, but the storage requirements for these products are different and far less stringent than those for food products.

The first link in the storage chain for incoming food aid consignments is storage available at the port of entry. It is accepted practice for all goods to be off-loaded from ships to customs warehouse pending customs clearance and other formalities, and food aid is not exempt from such procedures. Since space is generally at a premium inside the port area, the practice is to allow a short period of 48 or 72 hours of free storage for commercial consignments in the port, after which time rental, known as 'demurrage' is charged by the port authority. Some port authorities may extend this period in the case of large humanitarian donations of foodstuffs. This simple and logical procedure can, nevertheless, cause problems for food aid donations. Except in the case of some emergencies and the special programmes for the least developed countries (LDCs), recipient countries' governments are usually given title to the food aid once it has been discharged into the port of entry. Bills of lading are made out in the first place either to a ministry or government institution or to a representative of the donor, who would then endorse it, in almost all cases, to a government agency. That agency or ministry is then assumed to effect customs clearance, paying or claiming exemption from local taxes and arranging for transportation to a non-bonded store available to it. In those cases where the recipient agency has funds of its own to defray such expenses, problems are unlikely to arise. However, in those cases where application has to be made to a treasury or a ministry of finance for the release of the necessary funds, several days may elapse before payment can be made, which means that demurrage is incurred, and the sum orginally requested and authorized may not be sufficient, so that a supplementary authorization has to be sought and so forth. Solutions to such questions are often found, especially in emergency situations, by the donor's agent settling the charges and then reclaiming from the recipient country's treasury in due course. Rather similar problems can arise in respect of unloading cargoes into the customs shed, which will involve the use of stevedore gangs. Regrettably, many commercial operators with goods to discharge from their vessels are prepared to pay a 'bonus' over and above the government or port authority rates, so that the incentive of the work gangs to handle government cargoes is considerably reduced. Discharge of food aid may thus be delayed and additional charges for berthage and demurrage incurred. These minor details are mentioned merely as illustrations of the types of problem that food aid personnel encounter and have to solve, in the normal course of operations.

The handling of food aid commodities on unloading and transfer to port storage is an area of concern to all parties. In the case of a port having bulk grain handling facilities, enabling shipment of grain in bulk carriers from donor port, there is a considerable saving in time, cost, and handling. Savings arise, not only in respect of reduced handling charges and quicker turn-around time for the vessel, but also through the elimination of the costly process of bagging grain in 50 kg or 100 lb sacks. The major grain-producing donors are able to make bulk grain available pretty well on request, but the bagging of a consignment prior to shipment can delay delivery to port by several weeks and adds considerably to costs. In cases where a recipient country is likely to require fairly regular deliveries of food grain over an extended period, whether on food aid or commercial purchase account, the cost of constructing a bulk handling silo at the principal port of entry would soon be amortized and would result in considerable cost savings on commercial purchases, besides allowing larger quantities of food aid to be received within the donor financing ceiling.

The handling of commodities other than grain generally presents fewer problems, owing to the lesser volume involved. However, it is worth noting that many donated commodities are bagged or packed for the type of mechanized handling found in developed countries (conveyors, stackers, fork-lifts, pallets, etc). In most cases, discharge in developing country ports is more labour intensive— and rightly so. However, bags of, say, wheat-flour, carried one by one on the backs of stevedores and then dropped from some four or five feet on to the accumulating pile or on to a concrete floor can easily rupture. Spilled flour is a messy business at the best of times, but under conditions of prevailing humidity or during tropical rainy seasons it is so much worse. More importantly, mould and contamination can spread to other sound bags. In some instances, though, thought has been given by donors to this type of problem. To cite a specific example, rice donated by Japan was sent in bags of woven polypropylene fibre, which even when accidentally dropped from ship's tackle from three or four metres, have still landed intact.

Another common product in food aid consignments is dried skimmed milk powder (DSM); US producers usually call it non-fat dried milk (NFDM). This product is generally shipped in 25 kg or 50 lb bags consisting of a polythene inner envelope and two layers of kraft paper coverings. Under normal conditions this packaging is perfectly adequate, but a puncture in the inner plastic under tropical humid conditions will cause the powder to 'cake', making it unsuitable for distribution to clinics, health centres, etc., since the caking is frequently accompanied by mould and other contamination. Spoiled DSM can still be salvaged for animal feed as a last resort. Higher-priced commodities such as edible oils, canned meat or fish, sugar, and tea present few storage problems due to their lesser bulk and stronger packaging. Such products are frequently containerized, however, to reduce pilferage.

Once cleared from port storage, commodities have to be on-forwarded in accordance with the food aid programme agreements or requirements. Commodities in transit to other countries sometimes have to make use of rail wagons as temporary storage, while in the case of in-country operations the goods are sent directly to central or regional warehouses. In this latter case proper storage conditions take on a greater significance since the goods are likely to remain there for a longer time. Proper storage conditions require adequate ventilation, achieved through orderly stacking on hard standing and on pallets. Stacking height needs to be limited to prevent the rupture of containers or bags in the lower layers; the pallets provide ventilation under the stack and prevent humidity rising through the stack from the ground. Warehouses also need to be protected from rodents and birds and may require periodic fumigation, particularly where pulses and maize are concerned. Proper stacking also facilitates counting and inventory as well as general warehouse management. Considerable losses may occur through neglect of these procedures. A number of studies[1-3] have been undertaken to estimate post-harvest losses in various parts of the world, showing a mean percentage loss ranging from just under 1 in the best cases to around 8 at the other extreme: these studies cover food production; in the case of food aid, losses can still occur in transportation, but in storage, losses or lack of them are related directly to warehouse management and adherence to prescribed norms. Management in this context also covers maintenance of premises and equipment, and the training and supervision of the staff involved.

There is a rather too facile assumption in some donor circles that all such minutiae are a 'government responsibility', often without ascertaining how the government concerned is expected to discharge its responsibility, especially when the commodities involved may be unfamiliar, with the result that there is no established routine for their handling, and when funds for staff orientation or training are unlikely to be available. In certain instances national authorities implementing food aid programmes have seized the opportunity provided thereby and initiated extensive training programmes for the staff involved in the various stages of the operation, thus making a positive contribution to the development of the national logistics and transport infrastructure. Relevant examples of this can be found in the case of school feeding programmes in Algeria and Brazil (Cantines Scolaires and Companha Nacional de Alimentacão Escolar (CNAE) respectively), that were initiated through multilateral assistance as pilot projects in one part of the country and then developed by the authorities into national programmes with considerable recurrent cost and development inputs by government, providing for staff, training, established posts, and equipment.

In the context of emergency projects with food aid storage is more complex, in that the areas of emergency are very often outside the areas covered by the existing national transport and storage infrastructure. As a result, special storage points may have to be set up, which may be of little or even no relevance to the national economy once the given emergency is over. The development of semi-permanent storage facilities based on inflatable plastic structures, requiring only a concrete or other hard standing and an air-pump, provide adequate responses to such problems.

A further important component of storage is that of record-keeping. Weekly or monthly reports showing entries, stocks and their distribution enable food aid administrators to maintain a balance between supply and consumption so that any discrepancies due to losses or deterioration can be quickly established.

Cost Implications

From the general tone of reports in the media on food aid operations, it is easy to assume that the whole process is a free gift to the recipient country concerned. In fact, other than in the case of special emergency relief, food aid is still costly to recipients. Storage is one important element of this cost configuration. Silos, warehouses, go-downs, etc., often have to be rented for the food aid, especially in times of exceptional requirements. Even when such facilities are government owned and available they still have to be maintained and staffed. In either case records have to be kept and security of facilities maintained. It can then be argued that a government would, in any event, have to incur similar expenditures if the food were purchased by them on a commercial basis; this argument, however, overlooks the fact that a government would not necessarily order the same type of commodity, in the same amounts, or from the same sources. Most donors require detailed reporting of deliveries, stocks, and distribution that place an additional administrative burden on the recipients. Even in the case of voluntary agencies' programmes—as opposed to government-to-government food aid, there is still an insistence on reporting and supervision, the latter often being carried out by the voluntary agencies' personnel on the ground. The rationale behind such requirements is that, the more realistic the reports, photographs, film interviews, etc. that can be obtained from the field, the more likely is the agency to be able to ensure continued support from its national funding base.

Inland Transport and Distribution

As indicated earlier, the last link in the delivery chain, the distribution of food aid to the intended beneficiaries, is the component that
attracts the most attention and the one over which the donors have
least control. From the point of view of reporting and of media
coverage, the shipment of a few thousand tons of grain run into a
silo and sold on concessional terms to a parastatal grain marketing
board, gets little attention since it is hardly distinguishable from
other normal commercial transactions. The actual handing out of
food to the beneficiaries, on the other hand, is highly newsworthy,
as demonstrated by the recent media coverage of famine and
drought victims in the Horn of Africa. It is at this level that judgements on the efficacy of food aid tend to be made, highlighting the
successes or failures, depending on the objective sought by the
viewer. Effective distribution is, however, dependent on the whole
of the back-up organization in the other segments of the delivery
chain. These are generally much less 'visible' and newsworthy and
consequently attract less comment. Inland transport, in the same
way as storage, is costly to the recipient country, except in the case
of certain special externally funded cases mentioned earlier.
Furthermore, the priority that governments need to give to food aid
in accordance with the terms of donor agreements can mean that
transport and personnel have to be diverted from their normal task,
which can have adverse development side effects.

In some countries with long coastlines or navigable river systems
coastal shipping or motorized barges may be used, but the bulk of
food aid transportation is overland by rail or by road haulage. Any
movement of goods—including food—entails a risk of damage,
loss, or contamination. These risks are increased in cases where
haulage is over bad roads or involves transhipment from rail to
road transport *en route.*

Cost Implications

The problem of availability of road transport applies in the same
way as the availability of railway wagons mentioned earlier; availability in turn affects the cost configuration. In the case of rail transport, there is a limit to the availability of wagons so that there is no
flexibility in the system, which is generally a state monopoly, unless

wagons are diverted and someone else's goods delayed instead. Tariffs are set for each category of merchandise, so that the cost structure is also predetermined. In the case of road haulage, however, there is generally a measure of flexibility, since private operators supplement the state or parastatal transport fleets. These private operators will, however, charge higher rates than the state system but derive their livelihood from the fact that the capacity of the state system is often well below the normal transportation requirements of the economy. If the food aid is given to the government to distribute internally, it is bound to use state transport, and delays may well arise before such transport can be made available. Even when private transporters are able to offer rates which are competitive with the state system, there is frequently a reluctance on their part to accept government consignments, due to the delays in receiving payment for their services. Under these circumstances, voluntary organizations with sufficient funds to defray either the differential between the private and state rates or the total transport costs are able to ensure quick delivery, though at a higher cost. Multilateral organizations such the World Food Programme have standing arrangements to make payment of 50 per cent of internal transport costs for the group of Least Developed Countries (LDCs), which has the advantage of being payable in convertible currency, enabling the transporters to acquire the often much-needed supply of spare parts, tyres, etc; these arrangements also enable the use of any available transport, whether state or private.

Costings for road transport are based on what is commonly known as a 'tonne/kilometre' or 'ton/mile' rate, in developing countries these base rates normally being set by governments, for use with the national transport system. Even on the basis of the official rates, the cost to the recipient, particularly in the case of land-locked countries where fuel costs—barring local production as in Bolivia—tend to be higher. These official transport rates, apart from distance, also take into consideration the state of the roads on a given itinerary and the season when the journey is to be undertaken. Data from a recently newsworthy land-locked country—Chad—show a variation in the tonne/kilometre rate from CFA francs 118 for journeys from the capital, N'Djamena (formerly Fort Lamy) to the northern desertic regions, down to CFA francs 51 over the better roads to the south and centre. Since the distance from N'Djamena to Faya Largeau in the north, for instance, is

1,015 km, the cost per tonne of food to that destination amounts to CFA francs 119,770 or approximately $US280. If grain were being transported in this way, the cost would be approximately twice that of the commodity landed at port of entry in Nigeria or Cameroun at that time. Furthermore, a footnote to these official rate tables indicates that there is a 35 per cent surcharge for transport in the rainy season, and this—despite many years without rain in the northern parts—is deemed to last for five months! A calculation made by the government and the donor community showed that the cost of the distribution of the 80,000 tonnes of food aid required in 1985 in connection with drought-displaced persons in various parts of the country amounted to around $US8.5 million.

The practice of charging extra for bad roads and/or for rainy seasons is in fact widespread. The wear and tear on the vehicles over poor roads is that much greater, and such deterioration of equipment takes on greatly increased significance in developing countries where foreign exchange restrictions often make it difficult to obtain spares, tyres, and so on, and limit the possibilities of effective vehicle maintenance. Good quality feeder roads can do much to off-set such losses, since these can be made with local materials and labour, whereas vehicles require foreign exchange and consume more fuel over bad roads. It has been jokingly said that only very rich countries can afford to have bad roads.

In certain large-scale operations of food aid, particularly in the case of longer-term emergencies, the transport capacity of the state concerned is completely overwhelmed, so that considerable external support is required to build up and sustain the corresponding transport fleet and logistics chain. This is particularly the case in the relief of large refugee populations, since with some justification the host country can claim that the refugees are an international rather than a national problem and should be supported by international rather than national efforts and funds.

A large-scale operation of the above type was established in Somalia in the early 1980s to organize the supply of food and other essential materials such as medical supplies and construction materials to over 1,000,000 refugees who had been settled in camps scattered all over the interior of the country. This integrated logistics system received donations of trucks, mobile workshops, water-tankers, and so on from a number of donor countries. The UNHCR purchased fuel and hired the US organization CARE to operate a large logistics and monitoring team and to run mechanical workshops for vehicle maintenance and repair. Technically the CARE team operated as a distinct unit within the Somali National Refugee Commission, but were in fact responsible for the receipt of all refugee relief cargoes coming in to the two main ports of Mogadiscio and Berbera; for their proper storage and inventory, their subsequent transportation to the refugee camps, and their final distribution there. The food aid was provided through the UN–FAO world programme who also assisted in the co-ordination of donations outside the WFP programmes themselves.

In certain exceptional circumstances, air transport has been used to get food aid to its destination in time. In more normal operations air transport becomes too expensive, especially in the case of high bulk cargoes such as cereals. Impassability of roads or other high-cost factors in overland transport, or security problems, may force a decision to use air transport. Chad, with the high internal transport costs referred to earlier, was a case in point.

A survey team of the International Committee of the Red Cross and the League of Red Cross Societies visited the northern and central regions of Chad in mid-1982 and found disastrous food shortages in the nine northern and central prefectures, requiring the supply of at least 3,000 tonnes of food over a two-month period for some 400,000 persons. The rainy season had made most roads impassable. In August of that year an appeal for international assistance was made jointly by these two organizations, together with the UN Development Programme and the UN Disaster Relief Organization.

The operation ran from 1 September to 5 October 1982. At the end of that period sufficient road transport could be organized to take over delivery of the food aid to the various outlying districts affected by the famine. The complexity of such an operation can be judged on the basis of the range of responses to the international appeal.

France provided a Hercules aircraft with 20 ton capacity together with operational costs for fifteen round trips; technicians to repair a DC3 and a DC4 aircraft that had belonged to Air Chad; and the equivalent of $US75,000 to the voluntary organization, Aviation Sans Frontières, for the repair of another DC4 aircraft in Chad.

The League of Red Cross Societies provided Swiss francs 300,000 towards the cost of the air bridge;

The Netherlands government provided a Hercules aircraft and funding for 20 round trips;

The US government provided a Hercules C130 aircraft for 10 days at an estimated cost of $US500,000;

The UK government leased a Hercules C130 aircraft from Air Botswana at an estimated cost of £140,000;

The EEC provided the equivalent of $US500,000 towards the operational costs of the air bridge. This was channelled through the UN Disaster Relief Organization;

The International Committee of the Red Cross leased a second aircraft from Air Botswana for 13 days' operation;

Unicef provided 17 tons of medical supplies for the stricken population.

In this period of approximately five weeks, a total of 88 flights were made with 111 landings at destination to deliver a total of 1,448 tons of food—at a cost, however of over $US2 million. This works out to about $US1,400 per ton of food delivered and is obviously not something that can be undertaken every time there is a food shortage.

References

1. Lipton, M., 'Post-harvest technology and the reduction of hunger', *IDS Bulletin*, vol. 13, No. 3 (Brighton, 1982).
2. Adams, J. M., and Shulter, G. G. M., 'Losses caused by insects and micro-organisms' in Harris, K. L., and Lindblad, C. J. (eds.), *Post-harvest Grain Loss Assessment Methods*, American Assocation of Cereal Chemists (1978).
3. *Prevention of Post-harvest Food Losses—A Training Manual*, FAO (Rome, 1985).

9 FOOD AID:

How to make sure it got to where it should?

As indicated in the previous chapter, donor concern over the efficacy of the distribution systems in recipient countries, and the controls set up to ensure that the food actually reaches the intended
beneficiaries, frequently led to donor requests to recipient countries
to permit the mounting of various kinds of evaluation or review
missions and studies, or even to post their own monitors to the
recipient country. In this way, end-use became a nagging concern
not just for the donors but also, by reflection as much a worry for
the recipient countries wishing to ensure a continued flow of donor
food aid.

There are many who argue quite strongly that any concern over
control on the part of the donors is ill founded, since it is none of
their business once the food aid has reached the recipient country.
As the historical evolution of food aid programmes has shown, this
was the view held by most of the donors originally—admittedly,
not out of any particular concern for the feelings of sovereignty of
the recipient country, but rather because, at a time when food aid
was essentially a question of shovelling out surpluses, no one very
much cared what happened to the food provided it arrived safely at
the port of destination. Furthermore, at that time almost all the
food aid came in the form of cereals, and the greater part of those
consignments was shipped in bulk, with the result that any one
donor's cereals were pretty well indistinguishable from another's,
or for that matter from locally produced grain, once they all ended
up in the same silos. However, with the growth in the volume of
food aid, and the increasing amounts of taxpayers' money in the
producer countries going into price support or production subsidies, questions began to be asked. Also, various rumours and
reports were circulating to the effect that food aid was probably
going to support armies rather than deserving civilians, or that food

aid donated to one country was being sold to a third country. A spectacular case of the latter occurred in 1963 when the vessel *Star of Alexandria* put into Anaba harbour in eastern Algeria carrying a cargo of US Title II maize donated to Egypt, along with a load of Russian rockets and hand-grenades all destined for the guerrillas in Angola, some of whom were being trained in Algeria. The vessel blew up spectacularly in the harbour and what remained of the maize was sold in the local market in Anaba. A rather more legitimate reason for concern about food aid shipments was the possible disincentive effect of large shipments on local prices and thus the depressive effect on local production. These various concerns also brought about a shift in emphasis in food aid programming away from concessional sales and loans and/or credits, and into more grant aid. By the early 1960s grant aid became almost synonymous with project aid in which various conditions relating to recipient categories, modalities of operation, etc. were laid down in an agreement between donor and recipient. Once this happened both donor and recipient had an interest in seeing that the terms of agreement were respected, and that in turn meant controls, supervision, and so forth. Many of these projects stipulated the provision of a range of commodities designed to maintain or improve a certain nutritional standard. Consequently, it was no longer a question of delivering undistinguishable cereals, but bagged or canned commodities all bearing donor marks of origin and almost all of them carrying an indication prohibiting their sale.

Despite all this, those who argue in favour of scrapping controls maintain that the initiative for them came solely from the donors and not the recipients, and still maintain that it would be preferable just to give the food away or write a cheque instead. The problems of writing a cheque were fully explored in Chapter 3. Just giving the food away runs into another set of problems: it smacks of a hand-out and many recipients do not care for charity hand-outs, they are looked upon as denigrating and as an act of paternalism on the part of the donor. Furthermore, in many countries this practice revives memories of the 'company shop' syndrome or other practices of a food-for-work nature dating from colonial times. Those who argue in favour of scrapping all controls out of respect for sovereignty also tend to forget that since the end of World War II the world has been moving towards systems of interdependence and that obdurate independence is in a sense reactionary. If no man is an island, then neither is any country—even the small island economies! Many developing countries, too, operate from their own resources various types of domestic food aid programmes that are not supported by external donations, such as school or supplementary feeding programmes, all of which are subject to accountability and are appropriately monitored. In many such instances funds come from both public and private sources; the latter are just as anxious to see proper management and utilization of the funds as any external donor.

A curious paradox arises from the fact that almost all grant type food aid stipulates free distribution, while as indicated above there are many to whom hand-outs are anathema, not only for socio-historical reasons but also because they tend to upset carefully structured price control and subsidy policies. A case of this kind arose in Zambia in the late 1970s when the UN, on the basis of information available to them, declared a regional drought emergency in a district of southern Zambia and insisted on free distribution. The government would not agree to free distribution unless everyone in the country got the same, but there was not enough food aid for that. After a lot of discussion the government felt that it would be acceptable for the party and the army to make a free distribution, but to that the donor objected. In the meantime the rains had come.

Any resistance to free distribution is, however, put aside in the case of real emergencies, particularly in the case of refugees and other crises of mass exodus. In such instances donors are generally encouraged to mount their own monitoring and control operations, as this is seen by the host country as a means of disengaging from the responsibility of providing for the upkeep of these groups, and putting that responsibility on to international shoulders.

In practice, targeted programmes or any food projects that stipulate a selective distribution require some kind of control to ensure that the conditions are met. Food aid provided, say, to a vulnerable group, malnourished children, drought victims, and so forth confers a certain status or 'privilege' on that group which has to be maintained through some kind of control. Since such food is furthermore distributed free of charge, it is not unnatural that persons outside that designated group, who have to pay for their food or may not even find any available, should covet the free food. Consequently, without controls, the food would get to all and sundry and the whole purpose of the targeting on the most deserving groups would be vitiated.

In practical terms, the definition and operation of the required controls to ensure this proper distribution of the food aid is one of the most complicated and controversial in the recipient countries and perhaps one of the least popular facets of food aid practice, even when it is carried out entirely by local administrators. Controls are either dictated by shortages or the establishment of privileges in the above sense. Food aid given as budget support through large inputs of cereals is designed, after all, to permit the recipient government to get into a position where basic supplies are adequate, market prices stabilized and control systems rendered superfluous. When given in the form of project aid to a specified target group, it is intended to bring that group up to a level of nutrition or food availability compatible with that of the general population. At that point the need for controls and for targeted food aid should fall away. However, until such a time as these rather Utopian conditions come about, food aid operators will have to have recourse to some form of regulatory and supervisory mechanism.

In this context it is mainly the targeted or project type of food aid that calls for comment. Concessional sales of bulk grain, or even of grants in that form, under programme food aid do not differ in essentials from normal commercial transactions of the same commodities, and are subject to the various checks and controls on discharge etc. as described in Chapter 7. Possible losses are confined to a narrow field of operations, say, from ship to silo or port to central warehouse. Donor responsibility (and therefore concern) ceases upon acknowledgement of the receipt of the agreed quantities by the recipient government and upon settlement of any insurance payment claims.

A number of control techniques are practised both by donors and recipients in respect of project food aid; these may be classified under the general headings of monitoring and evaluation, each with a number of variants suited to local conditions.

Monitoring

This category of control is essentially designed to answer the first preoccupation of most donors, 'What happened to my food aid?'

Its main objective therefore lies in the field of accountability. Monitoring may be defined as a continuous overview of a given activity with the aim of establishing how far the various inputs into the project or activity are able to satisfy its stated objective(s) and to provide corrective action as and when there arises any deviation from, or non-fulfilment of, that objective. Monitoring, consequently, enables a satisfactory quantitative control to be operated and can indicate whether the food aid is getting to where it is supposed to go.

Evaluation

Evaluation, generally complementary to monitoring, is basically designed to answer a wider concern frequently voiced by donors, namely, 'Is my food aid being used to best effect?' Put in another way, monitoring can indicate whether the food aid is getting to its designated target, but it cannot answer the question as to whether this is actually the best place for it to go. That latter question involves qualitative considerations and a measure of value judgement which could lead to changing or modifying the objectives themselves. Monitoring can only operate within the framework of prescribed objectives.

Various practical applications of these main functions are used in connection with food aid programmes and projects.

Monitoring Techniques

There is naturally a considerable variation in the monitoring requirements according to: the size of the food aid operation; the isolation of the beneficiaries from, or integration with, the general population; their concentration in one location or their scattering among many different points; the absence or availability of good communications, and so on.

In recent times the largest type of operation has been food aid programmes for refugees or for otherwise displaced persons concentrated into settlements or camps. Many operations of this type are supported entirely by external assistance. Apart from ensuring that these persons do not create any security problems for the host government or impinge adversely on the national economy, the national authorities generally prefer to leave all questions of the welfare of these people to the external agencies. This means that the monitoring will frequently be carried out solely by foreign experts. This was done in the case of the large exodus of ethnic Somalis from Ethiopia in recent years. There monitoring was carried out by a large team that covered the ports of entry, the main stores and distribution points, and each of the refugee camps in the country—34 locations in all. This team was provided by CARE, the same non-governmental organization providing the logistics support mentioned in Chapter 8, operating under a sub-contract with UNHCR for the purpose. This system was able to provide all the necessary quantitative data on commodities discharged from port, checked on to central stores, transported to regional stores and finally distributed to the camps. This was a sophisticated and costly operation, supplied with its own radio communications network that ensured the flow of food aid to a refugee population that rose at one period to 1.5. million.

Similar large operations in other parts of the world have given rise to other forms of distribution control. In the case of the Kampucheans driven out of their country by the Vietnamese invaders the United Nations established a special organization under their aegis—the United Nations Border Region Operation (UNBRO). In the case of the earlier—and smaller—crises in Ethiopia in the late 1970s the International Labour Office supplied experts to mount an operation known as the Emergency Transport Unit (ETU). This controlled the inland distribution from port of entry (Asab) to central government stores, but in that case the government did not wish to have any expatriate presence involved in the allocation of the food aid to the beneficiaries; as later developments showed, this was used as much for political as for humanitarian purposes. Although this was regarded as scandalous by some, others saw it merely as an exercise of the recipient's sovereign rights. Be that as it may, the fact remains that all monitoring exercises face various kinds of constraints and their success is generally proportional to the amount of recipient country's co-operation or disengagement, as the case may be. There is also the simple truth that human nature is inventive—monitoring controls are largely set up to thwart attempts by the non-entitled to get the food aid. For each new control measure introduced the non-entitled are quick to think up some new means of evading it! Some of the more realistic food aid operators maintain that there is no generally valid formula; it is merely a question of keeping one step ahead of the game.

To cite a case in point, in a settlement of Angolan refugees in Zambia in the late 1970s, distribution control was carried out by the issue of a ration book for each head of family, with copies of the details on file in the project office to check for alterations, etc. The number of children and dependants in each head of household book was indicated by crosses put by the project office down the side of the card. It was found that new crosses were being added each week by the recipients when the distribution was made. The project office countered this tactic by punching out all the space below the last legitimate cross. Attempts were made by the beneficiaries to fill in the holes and write in new crosses but this was too easily detectable. The next event the monitors noticed was the large number of 'lost' cards requiring replacement—the 'lost' ones were, of course, being used to get a double ration by dint of sending different family members to different distribution points on ration distribution days—and so on.

Other types of limitation can be placed on the effectiveness of monitoring. In the Somali case, despite all the efforts put into ensuring accountability and low losses, the monitoring team did not decide on the numbers of refugees entitled to the ten-day ration. That was a complicated question decided on between donors, the UNHCR, and the National Refugee Commission, and depending on the availability of food aid. This became known as the 'numbers game'. Although the monitors knew that the rations given out were well in excess of their reasonably accurate estimates of the real numbers, there was nothing they could do about it other than supply information. For doing this they were often threatened by the army personnel in charge of the camps, since it was 'customary' for the commander to get 50 individual rations for himself and 25 for his assistants. This meant that the camp commandants could take home a quarter of a ton of cereals every ten days.

In the smaller targeted operations working within the recipient country's administrative system, there is much greater national participation in the monitoring process. In institutional feeding, schools, clinics, and hospitals entitlement is based on attendance. This places a burden of record keeping on the national staff. A boarding school with all students entitled becomes a simple food management operation, with storekeeper's accounts of entries and exits. In other cases only some of the pupils may be entitled, which complicates the control issue. In clinics entitlement will be based on the judgment of the medical staff, for reasons of undernourishment, at-risk status, etc. The data thus collected are then fed into the quarterly, or sometimes monthly, reports that most donor agencies require. Very often replenishment of the food stocks is made contingent upon receipt of the required reports; this can take a lot of time for the nurses and assistants in a clinic or MCH centre in filling out often quite complicated forms—time that could well have been better spent on looking after their clients; hence the need to keep control forms as simple and straightforward as possible. It has often been found that items of information requested and obtained with patient form-filling has subsequently not been used by those requesting it.

In food-for-work projects control can be carried out in the same way as a pay register, with workers taking their ration entitlement home on given days from designated collection points. In some cases the food aid is provided through a canteen, with estimated quantities for the average number of workers present plus a percentage for wastage in cooking and for the kitchen staff.

Evaluation Techniques

Monitoring, then, can provide a range of quantitative answers in respect of food aid operations, particularly questions of end-use. It can also indicate whether an operation is efficient in terms of its stated objectives and can even provide the justification for the termination of a food aid operation. It cannot, however, say whether the food aid could be better used somewhere else or be applied in a different manner. Questions that go into validity of the project itself are largely qualitative and are handled by means of an evaluation process.

An evaluation will rely heavily on data provided by monitoring operations but will go beyond these into basic questions about the suitability of a project of a particular type in a given set of circumtances. Evaluations are often encouraged in order to make recommendations to donors and recipients for improvement of the operation, changes in objectives or purposes, the selection of beneficiaries, methods of distribution, and control of the food aid, etc. It has become fairly general practice for donor organizations not to extend the agreed 'life' of a project or programme without first undertaking a detailed assessment of its overall performance and the impact it has made.

One of the most frequently discussed issues in food aid literature on this subject is the question of impact. This has obvious qualitative implications and assessments of impact have become very popular with donors who still insist on quantification of impact. This sounds rather like squaring the circle. Its importance lies not so much in the assessment of performance, but rather in its use as a tool for modifying project design in food aid operations, making them more responsive to needs, even to the extent of changing the objectives or modes of operation of on-going operations.

A useful methodology for achieving this was developed by Unicef. This involves assessing (a) the percentage of a target population for whom the food aid is (i) available, (ii) accessible, (b) who makes use of it and (c) who are given the quality of service that brings about a positive change. For instance, if a given food commodity is available to 80 per cent of the target population, but only 40 per cent of them are actually making use of it, then there must either be a problem of acceptability of that commodity or there is perhaps an abundant local supply of it. In another case a commodity may be available to 90 per cent of the target population, but only 60 per cent have access to it; then there is doubtless a problem of distribution. Change in any of these components will affect the impact rating as shown in Figure 1.

The first question to be settled in any impact assessment exercise is to determine for whom it is intended, and then what it is intended to demonstrate. The usual reaction to such a question is that the assessors are naturally making an unbiased overall study, but in almost all cases the piper calls the tune. One also has to take into account the end users—do they have right to comment? After all, consensus rather than objectivity tends to be the predominant consideration in multilateral organizations; especially if the *post factum* evaluation is likely to contain some unpalatable conclusions.

These views were put succinctly by Amartya Sen in his paper on Food Entitlement and Food Aid Programmes at The Hague seminar

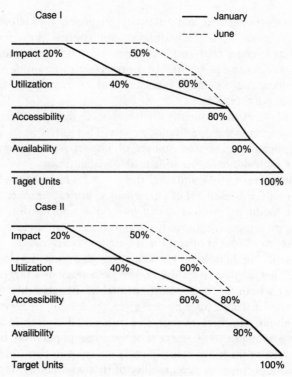

Figure 1. Illustration of weight of various factors in impact assessment.

in December 1982; 'the assessment of the role of aid must depend on the perspective', and it is useful to be clear about two central issues:

(a)   The assessor issue: from whose point of view are we assessing the aid question?
(b)   The control issue: what control does the assessing agent have over the use of food aid?'

One can see that from a donor point of view, the assesssment may range from satisfying itself on simple tonnage delivery data to creation of new markets or up to end-use assessment. From an executing agency point of view—whether national or international—it would be seen in terms of internal project efficiency, other elements being brushed off as being outside the terms of reference or simply someone else's responsibility. From the recipient's point of view, it may be seen as job creation, budget support, acceleration of sectoral objectives, relief from the burden of balance of payments, even negatively, as an extra charge to recurrent costs.

If it is possible to design projects in such a way that ease of evaluation becomes an important factor, then conversely it should be equally possible for impact assessment to be concerned with project design, since it is by being concerned with design and choice of project that some parameters other than *post factum* assessment can be established. Rather than trying to find out only what happened in the case of a given project, it would be more logical to find out what its potential was, and then make a comparative assessment on that basis. In order to achieve that end, it would be necessary to devise a methodology that could be used in both directions, that is, what did it look like and what might it have looked like?

Many thorny questions could be circumvented by a more effective assessment of a programme or project potential. On many occasions donors, executing agencies or governments have to write up the project justification in glowing terms to get access to supplies in competition when some other project or region is doing just the same thing. The result is too often over-optimism which results in recrimination and search for culprits, when it doesn't perform to expectations. It is at the stage of project design, of course, that the most effective inputs can be made, as amendments can be included painlessly before crystallization takes place. A review of many of the effective evaluation missions carried out by WFP will show that a number of the recommendations consist of measures to rectify lack of foresight at the project formulation stage. Difficulties arise in the implementation of recommendations of this type, as project and programme formulation divisions tend to regard such activity as an interference in their internal affairs. One also has to contend with the popular view that evaluation should really only serve to highlight success and justify further aid.

One of the main problems in getting action from assessment that can be meaningful in terms of development or other criteria is that the documentation tends to be exhaustive and perforce massive, even when brought down to an effective résumé. There are still far too many parameters to deal with for a decision maker to act expeditiously.

Evaluations, furthermore, tend to be costly, not only in terms of transportation and remuneration for the external officials involved, whether expatriate or national, but also in terms of the time that national administrators—probably already heavily overloaded—have to spend in connection with evaluation studies and missions. Donor administrators may have spent a considerable amount of time in discussion and negotiations with their own authorities and with the recipient government or institution just to get the programme going in the first place. They do not like to be told that, in reality, they got it all wrong and should have started off on quite a different basis. Also, changing procedures that might involve a new set of departments or officials is not always easy for the recipient authorities. There is also the fear that negative comments or recommendations might induce the donor to transfer his assistance elsewhere, or else that the national administrators concerned might be seen as having given their ministry or country a bad image, with foreseeable consequences for the individuals. Constraints of this kind can often act against the objectivity of evaluations.

Even so, evaluation remains the most readily available means of ensuring (in the interests of the recipient as much as of the donor) that the food aid is getting to where it should and that that destination is in fact the place or the mode in which it can make the greatest positive impact.

Reference

1. Sen, A. K., *Food Entitlement and Food Aid Programmes*, in WFP/ Government of the Netherlands Seminar on Food Aid, The Hague, 1983.

10 FOOD AID
Who gains from it?

It is pretty obvious that those who should gain most from food aid are its intended recipients. Frequently, however, this question is asked in a pejorative sense, with the questioner looking for instances of profiteering on the part of the producers and purveyors of food aid, and of the various bureaucracies involved, rather than seeking illustrations of its beneficial impact on the recipients. In order to clear up some of these misconceptions, this pejorative view will be discussed first. Further background information on food production and the financing and channelling arrangements practised in food aid operations will be needed before judgements can be made about where profiteering or other forms of abuse are most likely to occur.

As indicated in previous chapters, food aid may be given in the form of a loan, a credit, a sale below normal market price, or a free gift. It may be offered by governments, by international bodies, by regional institutions, by voluntary groups and agencies, or by individuals. Whatever the channel used for effecting the transfer of food aid from donor to recipient, a value transaction of some kind is involved, either in the form of a monetary settlement—whether a deferred one or not—or in the case of a voluntary contribution an opportunity cost—that is to say, the recipient person or organization concerned would have been able to use their time or their resources on something else by forgoing the donation. Whatever the source of funds or the channelling, such considerations are irrelevant to the producer since, unless his contribution is a free gift, he will be paid anyway. Free donations have sometimes been made by producers; this was the case with wheat growers in the UK for African famine relief recently. The Mennonite community in Canada has also frequently made donations of maize and wheat for food aid.

All such transactions offer alternative potential for gain or for loss. From a donor government's point of view, an assessment has to be made as to whether the indirect benefits to be derived from a grant or the concessional sale of food as aid would be of greater value or interest overall than, say, spending the equivalent sum on road maintenance or improved social services at home. Even in cases where an agricultural surplus is available, it still might be more in the national interest to allocate it for longer-term food reserves, for domestic food aid programmes, for conversion into alcohol, or for use as animal feed, rather than disposing of it as food aid.

Since the largest component in total food aid flows is cereals, it can be expected that the growers and purveyors of the different categories of cereal would have some say in food aid policies. There is no doubt that the farmers' lobby and the American Farm Bureau Federation in the USA played an important role in getting the PL 480 legislation passed by the US Congress. At that time, as indicated in previous chapters, falling grain prices on the domestic market, due to mounting production and limited commercial outlets, led to pressure for surplus disposal through food aid. In that sense the producers and transporters of cereals certainly gained from the institutionalization of food aid. Whatever the possibilities of gain were through the PL 480 programme, it must be seen in relation to the overall commercial sales of the agricultural products covered by this aid programme. During the first thirty years of the PL 480 programme's operation, the food aid component represented only 11 per cent of total overseas commercial sales by the USA of those same agricultural products in the same period.

Current figures for food aid in cereals from all donors were just under 10 million tonnes (1984–5) out of a total world production of 1,625 million tonnes. In the case of the USA again, food aid in cereals in 1984–5 amounted to just over 7 million tons out of a total national production of 340 million tons in that period. It can thus be seen that there is much more room for profiteering in areas other than food aid, which represents only a marginal proportion of the cereals market. The fact that food is bought under government contract does not represent any exceptional status either, since most donor governments make purchases of food for their own institutions (schools, prisons, etc.) and for their armed forces.

The institutionalization of food aid in the major producer/donor countries was certainly a factor in price maintenance, from which the producers stood to gain, but this must also be seen as a benefit to the whole economy rather than simply to one particular sector of it. Furthermore, price maintenance measures, together with production incentives, had been in operation in a number of countries well before the internationalization of food aid.

The Producers

Producers of cereals and other agricultural products suitable for food aid have, nevertheless, to judge their production requirements on the basis of their assessment of the total quantities they can expect to sell through government intervention agencies or the normal commercial market, as well as estimating the minimum amount needed to cover their outgoings. Government purchase of food for food aid is not effected through client farms or enterprises, but orders are generally geographically distributed and rotated so as not to create imbalances. In most of the large producer countries, cereal production has now come to be regulated by a number of conventions and agreements designed to ensure a consistent availability of cereals as a cushion against climatic variations and thus against price fluctuations. The amounts taken up by food aid play only a minor part in these wider schemes. The best known of these regulatory bodies is the International Wheat Council, details of which were given in Chapter 4. There are also less known regulatory mechanisms at the national level. In the case of the USA, the Department of Agriculture, within the framework of its various subsidy and stabilization programmes, will indicate the area of land and the types of crops to be grown on it in order to be eligible for government support. Controls of this type do not leave much room for manoeuvre, though some producers have resorted to trying to increase their yields per hectare on the agreed land area so as to increase their profits, but even here measures are being taken by the US Government to link yield to area.

The existence of large cereal surpluses is generally taken to indicate that there must be a considerable element of profitability in the production process. This is doubtless correct since increased production is the result of investment and hard work. However, the development of such surpluses has not been on account of food aid, but rather that food aid began to be seen as a safety valve for the surpluses, which then needed some regulatory and disposal measures.

The USA has had longer experience in such regulatory mechanisms than most of the other traditional donors. American and Canadian growers in the immediate post-war period were encouraged to grow more cereals in view of the presumptive needs of and markets in war-torn Europe and the Far East. Initially it was assumed that disposal of the crops would be through normal commercial sales, or at least within a wider funding arrangement such as the wartime US Lend-Lease agreements with the United Kingdom, or even within the framework of an international Food Bank as proposed during the initial negotiations on the establishment of the UN Food and Agriculture Organization in Quebec in 1945. It was largely the recipient countries' inability to make payments in convertible currency that accelerated the development of institutionalized and government supported food aid, rather than the sudden realization of the need.

In the case of the European Community, cereal surpluses have been built up over the years for reasons relating to the Common Agricultural Policy (CAP) established under the Treaty of Rome and not for reasons related to food aid, which only arose later once the surpluses became available. Whatever objections may be raised to the overproduction of cereals, no major food aid programme would have been possible without them. Regulatory measures are being introduced to contain the surpluses within reasonable limits. These have become unpopular with large sections of the European farming community, for whom the CAP was very beneficial, but again this state of affairs is not to be blamed on food aid. Historically the introduction of agricultural subsidies and the increased production that resulted from them in the USA was one of the instruments that President Roosevelt used in his National Recovery Act in the mid-1930s to pull the country out of the great depression. The development has been cited as an argument in favour of the view that an increase in consumption and availability of food leads to further increases in agricultural production. Food aid derived from donor country agricultural surpluses can, with careful management, act in a similar way to stimulate production in recipient countries.

It can be seen from the foregoing that food aid for the producer of agricultural products offers no more benefits or opportunities for abuse than do the normal commercial transactions. In the general area of food production and supply it is, in fact, in the areas of handling and processing that larger profit margins exist.

Handling and Processing

Taking the case of a simple breakfast cereal, only 20 per cent of the cost to the consumer is attributable to the raw materials in it; the rest goes into processing, packaging, publicity, and of course, profit. Most of these additional elements are cut out or reduced in the case of food aid. Packaging is reduced since by far the largest proportion of cereals food aid is shipped in bulk in grain-carrying vessels; publicity is limited to stencilling standard indications of product, quantity, grade, and origin on bags which are used for a small proportion of food aid, either for ports that have no bulk handling facilities or for food aid projects that need monitored distribution. The most common processing operation in food aid programmes is the conversion of grain into meal—either maize into maize meal or wheat into flour. In these operations there is a larger profit margin.

In view of the larger profit margins in processed foods, a number of companies in the business try to persuade national and international food aid sources to purchase from them such items as freeze-dried meats and vegetables or other packaged and processed foods. Since the cost in relation to the nutritive value is very high and insufficient to compensate for the savings in volume to be transported these approaches are generally resisted by donors. In addition the average recipient has no experience in handling such products and incorrect preparation, far from bringing benefit, could result in food poisoning.

For instance, the cost of milling and bagging wheat flour, based on an average cost over 27 years of operation of the US PL 480 programme since its inception, amounted to $US16 for every ton of wheat milled. In the milling process there is generally a loss of 20 to 25 per cent of the original volume of grain milled. This means that altogether, at least 40 per cent over the cost of the grain equivalent must be allowed. In the case of the corn soya milk (CSM) described in Chapter 6 and used for nutritional rehabilitation, the costs of the

Table 13. Relationship of tonnage to value for various food aid commodities

Commodity	Tonnage (% of all PL 480 cereals)	Value (% of all PL 480 cereals)
Wheat	63.5	53.0
Corn (maize)	8.0	6.2
Sorghum grain	5.1	3.2
Rice	6.2	15.3
Wheat-flour	8.9	10.9
Corn-meal (maize-meal)	0.85	1.25
CSM	0.75	2.32

Source: Foreign Agriculture Service of the US Department of Agriculture, *Food for Peace*, Annual Report, Washington, DC, 1982.

processing are considerably higher. The raw materials consist of mixed soya and maize-meal, milk powder and a small quantity of sugar. Mould sets in rapidly if the product is exposed to moisture. It is therefore packed in two strong kraft paper outer bags plus a polythene sealed liner. The average cost of CSM per ton over the 27-year period of PL 480 operations was $US259, much of the extra cost being due to the special bagging requirement and the blending process.

Some idea of the cost factors involved in processing and bagging in relation to the value of the staples can be seen from Table 13, derived from the 27-year average of the PL 480 operations.

Rice generally averages around twice the price of wheat in its unprocessed state, but for food aid operations it is generally shipped, refined, parboiled, and bagged, which boosts the costs.

In the case of non-cereal food items, a higher degree of processing is involved. Taken at current average prices, soya bean oil in bulk (i.e., not in cans or drums as would be required for food aid) costs around $US450 per ton, while the cost of 1 ton of soya beans is just over $US200. In addition there is a marketable residue after the extraction of the oil, which further increases the margin between the raw material and the processed product price. Finally the current pro-forma cost of a tonne of soya bean oil for programming purposes packaged and canned in 1-gallon or 5-litre containers is just over $US1000 per tonne. The foregoing data show that food processing and packaging operations can often cost more than the commodity itself and that there must be considerable scope for profit at various stages of these operations.

Simply taking data from food aid allocations and deliveries, it is easy to assume that all these operations benefit only the donor country and its agro-industries. This is not necessarily the case since in many instances, processing is undertaken after arrival of the food aid in the recipient country. The most common of these processes is the conversion of wheat into flour and maize into maize-meal. In the non-cereal category, the most frequent activity is the reconstitution of milk powder into milk and in some cases also into yoghurt and cheese. In this way food aid transfers some of the benefits and opportunities of the processing operations to the developing countries. These can be regarded as secondary benefits or 'spin-off' from the initial food operation. Against this view, however, two arguments are frequently put forward: firstly, that the controls in many of the processing plants in the recipient countries are not as rigid as in the industrialized ones, thus giving greater scope for profiteering; and secondly, that the profits accrue to the wrong group of persons. In practice the two are interrelated. Most mills operate on a given extraction rate (i.e., how much grain husk is removed in the milling process and the degree of refinement). Any variation in this rate—which is easy to manipulate mechanically—will result in gain or loss on the whole operation. Consequently the less the controls the greater the scope for manoeuvre. By profits accruing to the wrong groups, it is meant that those millers most likely to be involved in large processing operations of food aid wheat or maize are likely to be in the upper-income bracket already and living in large urban centres. They are consequently not in line with the present emphasis on food aid programmes assisting the lower income and vulnerable groups.

Be that as it may, one of the great advantages of in-country milling is that it can be undertaken as and when the need for the product arises. When wheat-flour or maize-meal is delivered already processed in a food aid allocation, it has to be distributed and consumed, or processed into bread, etc. rapidly in view of its very limited shelf life in hot and humid climates. In most developing countries the extraction rate in wheat milling is around 85 per cent as opposed to standard 72 per cent in the US. This higher rate results in a coarser and therefore more nutritious flour, which is an indirect benefit to the recipient.

A further compensatory factor in milling in-country—even allowing for local profits accruing—is that the total costs to the recipient country will be less than when the product is received already processed. If the processing is undertaken in the donor country the costs become part of the total food aid budget. So, if these processing costs in the donor country are eliminated, then more cereals can be delivered for the same food aid budget. Even allowing for quite considerable wastage or extravagant profits at the recipient country processing stage, the net amount of food aid received as flour would be greater, due to the lower processing costs and higher extraction rates. These considerations become particularly important if the food aid in question is in the form of a loan rather than a grant.

Transportation, Storage, and Distribution

The other large group of people who benefit from food aid operations are those involved in its transportation, storage, and distribution. As indicated in Chapter 7, most food aid operators and programmers keep a tight rein over ocean freight rates, leaving little room for manoeuvre. However, conflicts of interest can arise between farmers and shippers. A proposal was made in the USA to change the standing arrangements under which half of all government generated cargoes had to be shipped in US flag carriers. The maritime lobby was interested in raising this to 75 per cent in respect of food aid—the reason being that the US merchant fleet is relatively uncompetitive and relies quite heavily on this obligatory diversion of government freight to its benefit. The agricultural lobby, keen to maintain US competitiveness in agricultural products, wanted to exclude all food aid from this provision. The agricultural lobby was finally able to have all Title I shipments excluded from this amendment.

The amount of food aid cargo shipped from the donor countries is marginal in relation to the total amount of goods handled there. But in some of the recipient countries it may represent a considerable percentage of the total incoming freight, leading to an overburdening of all the existing port, handling, storage, and internal transport facilities. When the increase is manageable and within the absorptive capacity of the facilities such increases are beneficial in

Table 14. Comparison of imports of commercial food aid cereals by low and middle income developing countries in 1974 and 1984

Developing countries (groups)*	Commercial cereal imports (×1000 tonnes)		Food aid cereal imports (×1000 tonnes)	
	1974	1984	1974/5	1983/84
Low income	22 774	26 430	5 611	4 870
Middle income	41 418	86 980	2 390	4 718
Totals	64 192	113 410	8 001	9 588

* All the low income countries are recipients of food aid but not all those in the middle income group.

terms of increased activity and revenue; when they are in excess of that capacity they can be damaging. Grain consumption in recent years in the developing countries has been progressively outstripping local production in many areas, largely, it seems, due to the need to meet the high volumes required in urban centres. A study of the grain handling and transportation facilities in developing countries carried out by the International Wheat Council in June 1985 showed that this growth became particularly noticeable after the passing of the US PL 480 legislation, and was seen as one of the most remarkable features of the world grain economy. In the early 1950s these imports totalled around 15 million tonnes, two-thirds of which was wheat. Within a decade this volume had doubled and by the early 1970s had reached 45 million tonnes and within the following decade had doubled again. The figures are corroborated by the World Bank annual statistics giving data up to the end of 1982.

Table 14 gives the breakdown according to the World Bank classification of low and middle income developing countries as well as the food aid element in the total trend.

Bangladesh accounted for 38 per cent of the food aid in the low income group in 1984 and 27 per cent in 1983 while in the middle income group Egypt accounted for 26 per cent in 1979 and 44 per cent in 1983. The drop in the amount of food aid to the low income group between 1974–5 and 1983–4 is due to India's share dropping from 1.5 million tonnes to 0.37 million tonnes in that period.

In many of the present food aid recipient countries the transport infrastructure evolved to serve the needs of an economy where there was no heavy reliance on external imports of basic foodstuffs and whose ports may have been designed to handle less bulky cargoes, or perhaps mineral exports and industrial imports, such facilities not being easily adaptable to food requirements. Overburdening of existing facilities results in increases in handling costs, inflation of some elements of internal transport due to the need to have recourse to private sector facilities, increased storage costs due to overburdening of government facilities, and so forth. All such distortions can lead to inflation of prices in various sectors, which would not be beneficial to the recipient country, even though some sections of the community who happen to be directly involved in the operations would benefit disproportionately.

The dilemma is that much of this overburdening could be diminished by capital investment in more adequate infrastructure specifically designed to handle such increases in food imports, but this could not be justified if there were prospects of food aid flows diminishing or if food aid were to serve its avowed purpose of working itself out of a job by increasing local agricultural production and nutritional levels. Recipient governments are becoming increasingly reluctant to countenance expenditure on infrastructure that may not be adequately utilized and which increases recurrent operating or debt-servicing costs. On the other hand, if a recipient country can make use of the opportunity presented by the influx of food aid imports as well as commercial imports to build up facilities that had long been planned, but not fundable, then such large imports would generate lasting benefits. The International Wheat Council's study referred to above aimed precisely to provide evidence of the needs of developing countries for assistance to upgrade their facilities. In many instances an abnormal influx of food aid under emergency programmes has enabled recipient countries to obtain external grants and technical assistance to build up or modernize transportation, storage, and distribution systems that have been of lasting benefit to the economy and which under normal conditions would not have been of sufficient interest to national or external investors. As mentioned in Chapter 7, relatively modest investments in grain silo installation and bulk handling facilities in recipient ports could make considerable savings on ocean freight both for commercial and food aid cargoes.

It is often assumed that food aid benefits food storage owners and operators (grain silos, edible-oil tanks, warehouses, etc.). In reality they stand to lose from food aid on the grounds that food aid is one means of relieving the pressure on storage in times of agricultural surplus in producer/donor countries. In the recipient countries the position is different. Government storage facilities may have been built for quite modest imports and a smaller population. When such facilities reach capacity, perhaps as a result of emergency food aid or unusual import needs due to crop failures and so on, private storage operators are called in to take the strain, and are then in a position to operate on a seller's market with resulting high profits. This again is an instance of benefits accruing to the wrong groups in terms of food aid priorities. The remedy lies not only in increasing temporary storage facilities but also in scheduling food aid deliveries and ensuring speedy distribution and utilization of the food aid.

Concern is often expressed about the apparently large number of administrators connected with food aid operations in developing countries, many of them expatriate, and of the benefits accruing to them. The largest and most 'visible' groups of expatriates are usually the volunteers, often extremely dedicated people rewarded financially only marginally above a local costs basis. Again it is the emergency programmes that call for large expatriate groups; the normal food aid types of programme and projects operate with a much higher percentage of national staff, with an expatriate presence only at the higher planning or policy levels, or in the logistics operation. Food aid does provide employment for quite a large number of national administrative staff in the recipient countries. This can be beneficial in the sense that such appointments, being derived from externally funded operations, are not subject to the often very stringent appointment conditions of Civil Service Commissions. In addition, they provide practical training in administration, accountancy, and logistics or storekeeping operations, for which it is often difficult to find adequate practical training in many of the recipient countries. Food aid projects also frequently provide new employment opportunities for women: in a food aid supported school feeding programme in Brazil, for example, all the operational staff as well as a high percentage of the senior executive and administration staff were women.

An analysis of the staffing patterns of food aid projects will show that the manpower requirements for those containing a range of nutritionally essential commodities targeted to specific groups of beneficiaries are much greater than, say, a budget support type of programme where in most cases a single commodity is passed directly to a central government or parastatal organization. Many of these target groups are in outlying areas and may also be widely scattered over a country in relatively small units. The transportation, storage, and distribution of food aid to them, together with the necessary accountancy, result in considerable administrative costs. Nor are these costs necessarily proportional to the quantities of food delivered: the distribution of even small quantities of multicommodity food aid is much the same as that for larger volumes (large refugee camps etc. are another matter). The bulk of these administrative costs fall on the government of the recipient country; some can be off-set when part of the food aid is allowed to be sold as 'monetized'. In the case of a budget support type of programme, costs to the government may be no more than the modest charges for discharging some thousands of tons of grain into a silo from the vessel. Furthermore the government is free to pay for any charges out of the sale of the grain through its distribution network.

Relative Benefits

These questions raise one of the more interesting aspects of the relative benefits derived from aid as between the different categories of people and organizations involved in its operation. Distribution of food aid to, say, a network of small Mother and Child Health (MCH) centres in rural areas will certainly alleviate the previously identified malnutrition among the clientele of the centres while also providing employment for some local clerks or storekeepers and extra business for truckers. On the other hand it will give a lot of extra work to the nursing staff and auxiliaries of the centres who will be required to fill out more forms attesting to the receipt of the food by the beneficiaries, along with evidence of improved growth rates of the children, etc. The staff will also have to break up the bags of milk powder or drums of oil into individual lots. In such projects the food aid will certainly benefit many of the undernourished mothers and children, but the staff of the centres could most probably have detected more cases or provided better follow-up had they been relieved of some of the administrative and distributive tasks. The administration of the whole project is likely already to have cost the government a number of additional salaried administrative posts as well as the related transport and handling costs. Consequently, the chances of their taking on extra staff at the MCH centres would be minimal. The food aid donor would not even consider picking up this kind of recurrent cost which would be seen as a government responsibility, probably enshrined in the food aid agreement. An assessment of a project like that would probably confirm to the donor that a satisfactory number of mothers and children had been benefited, but would probably not reveal how many more might have benefited if the staff had had more time, nor what the total costs to the government were per beneficiary.

This kind of dilemma has frequently been the raison d'être for the presence of voluntary organizations in the recipient countries. In a number of instances, organizations such as Save The Children Fund, Médecins sans Frontières, etc. have been able to take over much of the administration of supplementary feeding cum immunization programmes to the considerable benefit of all parties concerned. However, in many cases once this happens there will be detractors claiming that there is too much expatriate presence. Donors, though, continue to press for assurances that the food aid actually reaches the designated beneficiaries and has not been diverted into some non-humanitarian channels. Food aid in such cases can thus be said to provide confirmed benefits to the targeted beneficiaries, but at an added cost to the recipient government who probably requested the food aid in the first place because they did not have the budgetary resources to provide for the required services itself. The question that arises is whether the available food aid should be given to the government for sale, enabling it to provide the needed services—that is to say, sacrifice a large assured benefit to a small sector for a lesser/more uncertain benefit to a large sector.

This does not detract from the basic premise that food aid is given to satisfy hunger and that priority should go to the hungriest, but it emphasizes the fact that there is more than one way of attacking the problem of hunger and malnutrition. If food aid is to fulfil its basic tenet of being able to work itself out of a job, it is not enough to rely on palliative feeding operations, however essential they may be; it must also lend itself to a range of other actions relating to increased agricultural production, income generation, infrastructure improvement, access to markets, and so forth. A range of approaches to such questions was shown in the various types of food aid channelling in Chapter 5. There is, however, an important difference between a single project approach—which might be likened to applying ointment to a spot without asking what caused the spot—and a composite or complementary approach in which a number of food aid tools are applied collectively to the overall problems of poverty, malnutrition, lack of access to food, etc.

This is not as Utopian as it may sound. Throughout the 1950s and 1960s, India received massive amounts of food aid. It was taking such a large proportion of the total amount of food aid available at that time that donor circles began to wonder if it was not a bottomless pit, with no likelihood of national production improving or even of just keeping pace with the population growth. Yet India is not ony self-sufficient in cereals, but even has some exportable surpluses. The food aid generated counterpart funds— at one stage even more than the economy could usefully absorb— which were used to finance a range of agricultural development schemes, fertilizer development, improved storage and distribution systems, etc. Just as importantly, this food aid was locked into national development planning so that complementary resources of technical assistance, crop and phytogenetic research, or investment capital could be associated with the food aid as required. Many other instances on a smaller scale show that food aid with the necessary complementary inputs has a far greater impact and is therefore of greater benefit to the recipient than food aid on its own.

Benefit can also be obtained from food aid in its role as a stabilizing element through food security linked to national plans, or other schemes aimed at cushioning supply variations or price fluctuations. Few things have been found to be more unsettling to government, whatever its political colour, than an urban populace that has become hungry through the onset of food shortages, increased prices (as in Tunisia recently), or any other factor resulting in decreased access to food. The benefits of catastrophes avoided are not easy to quantify.

Some of the more positive benefits of food aid go unnoticed as they perhaps belong to this unquantifiable category and are neither spectacular nor particularly newsworthy, yet are frequently linked to this broader framework approach. Food aid programmes have often been instrumental in improving mother and child and health facilities, improving infant mortality and malnutrition statistics, operating nutrition surveillance, and various other related actions that lead to improved knowledge of food utilization and thus to improved living standards.

Although nutrition plays an important part in the satisfaction of hunger these foregoing considerations have led to the need to examine the role of nutrition in the broader framework of economic as well as food policies—giving stronger emphasis to the need to attack malnutrition at its root and to improve the general knowledge of how best to utilize available foods. These twin considerations are, of course, particularily applicable to young children. The particular benefit derived from food aid in support of children is that it is one of the few areas in which humanitarian and developmental goals are combined. The humanitarian appeal of children's programmes ensures a readier flow of support than is generally forthcoming for developmental projects, yet this humanitarian support to children has important development aspects. Lack of proper nourishment at an early age can cause lasting mental and/or physical handicap and thus hinder the proper development of the human resources available to a nation. A number of developing countries have well-developed Mother and Child Health Centres (MCH) and other health facilities for young children. Those that are in receipt of food aid for the customers of the centres are generally better attended than those without, so that the coverage of the population is increased through the food aid. Detractors argue that the mothers and children only come for the food, but even so, they are registered, their children's growth measured and they benefit from the associated immunization programmes. Such centres also provide information on optimum food utilization, and methods of preparation, enable mothers to detect the early symptoms of malnutrition, and provide them with some knowledge as to how to cope with it. A broader attack on malnutrition and hunger has, of course, to be linked to the various other facets of the problem such as increased agricultural production, with the possible use of food aid as an incentive, and so forth, as outlined in Chapter 5.

The range of options open in the use of food aid for optimum benefit to the recipients, indicates that flexibility is an important element in this process. Food aid may be used in the form of commodities for consumption or for sale. In the latter case they can be used to provide services and financial resources. A further need for flexibility derives from the fact that the overall problems of hunger and malnutrition and other forms of deprivation are not static. They may affect different groups of people at different times. Some problems are seasonal, some regional, others structural, and for each of these a different response is needed if the optimum benefits are to be derived from the food aid. Since the volume of food aid always remains modest in relation to overall food needs, careful planning of the resource (both the national and external inputs) is needed to obtain the wished-for catalysing or innovative effect. It is here that flexibility and ingenuity in adapting resources to specific requirements come into play.

Food aid is generally seen in terms of its benefit or value to recipients, which leads one to think in terms of individuals, but in many cases it is the economy that must be considered as the recipient. A recent study by the International Food Policy Research Institute (IFPRI) put forward the view that the world food problem is not really about food at all, but rather an aspect of the more general problems of poverty and unequal distribution of purchasing power among people and nations; it went on to say that a more balanced view would acknowledge that there are specific problems related to the supply of food which will not necessarily be solved by the overall process of economic growth, and that policies aimed at generating productive employment opportunities for the poor must be central to any long-term solution.

From another point of view, it can be argued that either the drive for flexibility in food aid programming is merely a cover up for the fact that no satisfactory formula has yet been found for the optimum use of food aid or else that changing delivery modalities are merely reflections of the pressures of various lobbies or donor interests. Food aid programming to be both of benefit to recipients and of sufficient benefit or interest to the producers and donors to motivate them to supply it, is a dynamic concept and cannot be satisfied by any single fixed formula. Research and operational experience can provide a number of valuable guidelines, but not an operational procedure that will be generally applicable. It was, in fact, the single fixed purpose approach in the early days of surplus disposal that gave rise to a range of side effects that led to the adoption of the more target-specific and flexible policies of later years.

11 FOOD AID:
When is it of no help?

In spite of the best use of planning and foresight in food aid programming, things can still go wrong, especially in cases of response
to crises, when the time available for a proper assessment of the
situation is short. After all, 'Murphy's law' states that anything that
could conceivably go wrong is bound to go wrong at the worst
possible moment. It is strange to see that, even though needs always
exceed the food aid available, there are cases where food aid has
been sent when it was not needed. A more frequent unwelcome
occurrence is the supply of food aid of the wrong kind, to the
wrong groups, or at the wrong time. A third and larger category
concerns unwelcome side effects of food aid in the socio-economic
and socio-psychological fields. The serious criticism of food aid is
directed at this last category.

Food Aid Sent when Not Needed

In respect of the first category, not every kind of crisis calls for food
aid in response, nevertheless in some cases it has been delivered.
Perhaps the best documented case is that in connection with an
earthquake in Guatemala in 1976, described in some detail in
Against the Grain by Tony Jackson.[1] The earthquake apparently
took place at a time when there was an excellent harvest in all parts
of the country, none of which was damaged by the 'quake. A few
items such as salt, soap, and sugar were in short supply for a short
time due to the collapse of many retail outlets, but even grain stored
in individual collapsed houses was retrieved by the owners. Nevertheless, a total of some 25,000 tonnes of cereals were brought into
the country and another 5,000 tonnes released from aid agency
stores, resulting in a glut and depressed prices for producers. In
such cases however, the initial despatch of food aid is not
unwarranted as there may not have been time to assess the extent of

the damage and therefore of the real needs. Furthermore, a number of aid and relief agencies concerned with rapid deployment in case of emergencies, such as the Swiss Disaster Relief, maintain a kind of ready-to-roll relief package, consisting of emergency rations, medicines, vaccines, tents, blankets, and generators, that can be put onto a cargo plane and rapidly flown out, together with a small group of support personnel experienced in disaster relief. This approach has proved its worth many times over. It is only when food aid continues to be sent, despite advice to the contrary from agency representatives and the government, that the criticisms become justified, as was evidently the case in Guatemala. However, a more generally applicable reason for a continued supply in such cases would be a lack of feedback from the country or a delay in acting upon it at the donor end. It is often lack of information about the real needs of the situation that causes errors of this type.

The Wrong Kind, the Wrong Groups, the Wrong Time

The second category of errors is more frequent: the supply of the wrong food, food at the wrong time, or food to the wrong groups. The difficulties of achieving what might be termed 'instant food aid' have already been described in Chapter 7. It is, however, interesting to note how impressions are built up from media coverage of some of these events. At the beginning of an operation, especially in emergency conditions, the criticism is generally that the assistance being provided is disgracefully little in relation to the needs—all with pictures in support—and that much more food aid needs to be sent forthwith. When more does arrive (it is assumed simply in response to the first criticism) it is then claimed that there is too much, that it was not needed, that it is being wasted, or that unscrupulous operators are enriching themselves, and so forth. Each of these allegations may well have some foundation in fact; they are all hazards familiar to food aid operators. The essential thing, however, is to maintain the perspective of the total operation. The question of 'unsuitability' often only arises in the later stages of the relief operation; the same product may not have aroused any criticism at the beginning of the operation. The implication is simply that 'choosiness' increases with satiety.

There are two further factors that have to be taken into consideration in these cases. The first is that basically donors provide what they have available, or in the case of emergencies what is immediately available, to avoid any criticism relating to delayed delivery. The second is the problem of what to do about numerous uncoordinated voluntary contributions that are liable to arrive, often donated by a large number of private individuals by no means in the upper income brackets. In practice it is very hard to discourage the generosity of donors of this kind. The most effective ways are: firstly, through media information and feedback from the scene of operations, giving potential contributors an idea of what is really needed (but even then there is bound to be some time-lag, and by the time the contributions arrive the situation may have changed again); secondly, by channelling such individual generosity through voluntary or international organizations like Oxfam or Unicef.

To give a small example of this type of problem: a flood occurred in 1981 in Somalia, beginning in the central region around Belet-Weyn where the Shebelli river comes down from the Ethiopian highlands and works its way south to where the Shebelli and Juba rivers meet in a delta region. The flood was caused by a heavy runoff from the rains in Ethiopia. The provincial capital of Belet-Weyn and several nearby villages were cut off, with people and animals concentrated in a few areas of slightly higher ground. The government appealed for assistance, especially air-lift capacity. The real requirement in the situation was for cargo aircraft with short landing and take-off capability or aircraft with air-drop facilities, to ferry food supplies from the capital to the affected areas—around 300 km. There were adequate stocks in the government warehouses in Mogadiscio to handle the situation. There was a secondary requirement for fuel since the powerhouse had been flooded and boiled water was needed for the clinic, and available supplies of charcoal were waterlogged. The response to the appeal was a motley selection of items all air-ferried at considerable cost, from Europe, North America, The Gulf States, and the Sudan. Food items ranged from Danish full cream in small cans, Turkish delight, corned beef (without openers), canned mutton (of which there was a surfeit in the area, as sheep were slaughtered before they drowned), down to more useful items like wheat-flour, sugar, and cooking oil. The British were among the first to respond with a useful plane-load of tents, medical supplies, rubber boots, and some inflated rubber dinghies with outboards and solid fuel. The two most useful responses in the longer term were from the French who provided a Breguet cargo plane from their air force base in Djibouti and from the USA with a load of pierced steel planking. The French crew shuttled their plane back and forth several times a day for over a week, adroitly landing and taking off from the unflooded half of an already short runway, which was just what was required in the first place. The American steel planking, of the type used to construct emergency landing strips, was most useful in the later phase, as the waters receded, to enable trucks to move across mud-flats to supply stranded populations. Most of the odd food items were from Somali families and their friends working in Saudi Arabia and the Gulf States who had collected them together and chartered an aeroplane, and it would not have been possible to say 'thank you for nothing'. Who is to say that they were not appreciated by the recipients—even if nutritionally inappropriate—since under normal circumstances an import licence would not have been granted for luxury items.

Problems of this nature can be resolved by means of co-operation and co-ordination among donors and between donors and recipients. In most cases this takes place with successful results, the only problem being that it takes time to organize. For this reason it will be found that criticism of this kind arises much more frequently in the case of emergency operations than with developmental ones, for which there is more time to study needs. If what appear to be wrong foods are sent despite consultation and co-ordination, it is most likely because of questions of acceptability as described in Chapter 7.

Distribution of food to the wrong groups does not generally come about by mistake, but much more frequently because of limitations in the practicability of ensuring 100 per cent accuracy in 'targeting' the feeding programmes. It has often been said that school feeding programmes, for instance, simply supply a food supplement to those well-to-do children who are able to have access to schools. Some well-to-do children may indeed be getting a snack or a meal from food aid in school lunches.

But what about the poorer children who are also getting the food aid; who are often sent out by their parents to a school with a food aid feeding programme just to ensure that they get at least one nutritive meal a day? In such cases the problem that faces planners of school feeding programmes is to decide whether to provide the food aid to the whole school, irrespective of the pupils' social or economic standing, or whether to carry out a kind of means test and give it only to the poorest children. Purists in the donor community often favour the second approach, the recipient governments and institutions the first. It is not only that the first option is easier to administer, but even more importantly, what child would gladly identify itself with the 'impoverished' group and be subjected to the scorn of its classmates? It is better to provide a nutritive meal to the, say, 80 per cent of children who are in need of it and risk over-indulging some of the well-off. In any event most of the really 'well-off' go to private schools in developing countries, while school feeding programmes concentrate on the state schools.

Inappropriate timing of food aid deliveries is often commented upon, and is frequently a justified criticism, but this raises the question of finding practical ways of solving it. The almost inevitable time-lag in initial deliveries, especially for large-scale emergencies, has been dealt with in detail in Chapters 7 and 8, but there are other areas that need further clarification. It is frequently said that food aid for drought relief in a certain area was all wasted because it arrived just in time for the rains. This kind of bald statement ignores some of the realities at the receiving end, whatever the merits of the delay argument. The onset of rains after a drought does not dispense with the need for food aid. In the first place, crops do not instantly sprout and ripen; in the second place, for some time one cannot be sure whether the rains are sufficient and prolonged enough to ensure a crop; in the third place, rains may disrupt normal activities by making roads impassable, etc., thus depriving many people of a livelihood and so increasing the temporary need for food aid; and in the fourth place, some kinds of cereal food aid can be used for planting when no other seed stock is available. In many types of resettlement or land development projects, food aid is given to settlers for the first year, to tide them over until the yield from their first crops becomes available. The same situation applies to food aid at the end of a period of drought. To cut off the aid, just because rain has fallen, means depriving the affected population of the means of recovering from the effects of the drought, which would certainly have left them without any reserves and probably without any seed stock—quite apart from inevitable decline in income and/or livestock that they will have suffered. In the case of pastoralists, too, cereal food aid has been useful in providing them with a means of restocking their herds after a drought, through barter transactions.

Other causes of bad timing have their origins in shipping delays, in losses of various kinds, or in a government's or an institution's inability to meet the costs involved in internal transport. In other cases there are regulations which bind food aid movement to the use of state-owned transport only; and this is often overstretched and under-equipped. All these various impediments have been detailed in other chapters.

It will be noted that the various negative elements that have been discussed so far in this chapter relate to the project or 'targeted' types of food aid and not to concessional sales, balance-of-payment or budget support programmes. Although, in volume terms, the latter group accounts for by far the greater part of food aid delivered to recipient countries, its delivery and administration is simple, not only because a much narrower range of commodities is involved (generally only bulk cereals and milk powder), but also because it is unusually channelled into existing central silos or stores and is designed to maintain an existing level of supply and distribution. Targeted food aid, on the other hand, can overburden distribution systems as well as overburdening the existing administrative structures through additional accounting and monitoring requirements. Emergency food aid is, of course, even more disruptive in that context.

Irregularity of supply in any category of food aid is disruptive. Under-supply of bulk or programme aid can cause national shortages of a cereal where there is a heavy reliance on cereal food aid, while over-delivery within a given time-frame can cause port or storage congestion. In essence these problems are quantitative rather than qualitative.

Unwelcome Side Effects

It is in the third category, the unwelcome side effects of food aid in the socio-economic and socio-psychological area, that the qualitative elements are most apparent. It is in this field that much of the debate about the pros and cons of various types of food aid still continues. There is always room for improvement in programming methods and policies.

The disadvantages that are most generally commented upon fall into the following broad categories.

Dependency — on the continuing supply of food aid;

Disincentive — to agricultural production and the undertaking of necessary reforms and adjustments;

Distortion — of existing habits and traditions.

Dependency

The dependency proposition maintains that aid, including food aid, is addictive, acts as a brake on development, and merely serves as a tool to perpetuate the dominance of the donors. In reality the issues are not nearly as clear-cut as that bald statement would imply. The setting in which the food aid is given seems more determinant than the food aid per se. The following two examples from projects of an identical type may serve to illustrate the point.

The first project provided food aid to around 10,000 Angolan refugees in a settlement provided by the Zambian Government in the north-east of the country. Each family was allocated a one-hectare plot of virgin, well-timbered land and a voluntary organization provided some tools and equipment for the community. Family rations of around 2,500 kcal per person were to be given for the first year, to provide subsistence until a crop could be harvested. In the second year the rations were halved and then phased out.

The second project, in southern Somalia provided similar food aid to a slightly larger number of displaced nomads from the north whom the government tried to settle on good land with water available for irrigation. Food aid was to be provided for the recipient group until such time as it 'graduated' into the status of a self-sustaining unit.

In the first case the food aid did continue longer than foreseen, largely due to new arrivals that caused some inequalities, but the greater part of the original settlers had completed their clearing and planting and had become self-sufficient within two years. Not that they merely grew sufficient to feed themselves from their own crops but rather, being good farmers and entrepreneurs, they found that there was a good livelihood to be made in producing and selling vegetables in a town some 20 kilometres distant. This enabled the food aid to be phased out.

In the second Somali case the settlement was run on the lines of a kolkhoz or collective farm and the population were those left from an attempt to collectivize over 200,000 nomads, the majority of whom managed to get back to their pastoral habitat, leaving behind the ones in this project. After more than eight years of supplying food aid to these remaining settlers no progress could be seen to result from the food aid, despite extensive complementary inputs in the form of farm machinery, feeds, fertilizer, irrigation and extension services. Under threat of having the food aid stopped by the donor after that period, the government finally—on an experimental basis so as not to deviate from ideological principles—allowed the settlers to receive one hectare plots as their own property. Within a few months a marketable surplus of rice appeared, and later, other crops, enabling the food aid to be phased out progressively.

In both cases there remained a small percentage of the settlers who were unable to become productive.

Addiction or dependency did not occur in the first case; it did occur in the second. However, as the final result showed, it was not on account of the food aid but of the socio-economic constraints under which the settlers had to operate. There remains the problem of the residue of settlers who did appear to become dependent on the food aid and were not able to emulate their fellows despite being offered the same conditions. Such persons are more likely to be in the category of those who in any society would need to fall back on social security at some time, in one form or another. It is thus more logical to see them in that light rather than as mere addicts to food aid. The existence of food aid admittedly allowed them to fall back on it, but so would the existence of any other form of social security.

The second proposition of the dependency theory quoted—that food aid perpetuates the domination of the donors—is based on a criticism of the justification given for the creation of surplus disposal food aid, particularly in the case of the USA, where it is stated that these activities are designed not only to stimulate development in the recipient country, but also to stimulate growth of commercial exports of cereals and agricultural products to the recipient countries. The dependency view is, then, that food aid is an indirect means of institutionalizing these commercial donor interests, on the basis that the growers get paid anyway by the donor government, which is probably less risky than competing for export orders. This argument had validity for as long as the bulk of food aid was based on surplus disposal and for as long as there was only one principal supplier of cereals, namely the USA. Surplus disposal has been progressively replaced by the programme and project concept, with clearly defined terms between donor and recipient. Furthermore, the USA is no longer in a dominant position; the European Economic Community, Canada, Australia and the Nordic group all have their food aid programmes with cereal components. Recipients are thus able to avoid dependency by judicious acceptances from a range of potential donors. An increasing proportion of food aid is also being given by donor governments through international channels (WFP) rising from 12.9 per cent in 1972 to 23.6 per cent in 1983.

There are cases of a different form of dominance not explicit in the dependency proposition quoted, namely that of donors facilitating government dominance in a recipient country. Adequate food supplies are a requirement for political survival for even the most autocratic governments, and many ask for assistance to import food to stabilize an otherwise untenable situation.[2] In some political systems food can be used as a political reward or punishment system through rationing, control of retail outlets and restricted access canteens. Ration cards or other forms of entitlement are then only made available to the political élite or the politically acceptable, dissent may be punished by the refusal of a ration card or other access to food. The most recent example of this syndrome is the use of humanitarian food aid to Ethiopia which is denied to those families and children who happen to live in rebel-oriented Tigre and Eritrea, and which serves to assist what *The Times* of 11 October 1985 describes as the inhumanity amounting to almost genocide of the forced resettlement programme being put through by the Dergue.

Another aspect of dependency, and generally less commented on, arises from the success of a food aid operation rather than from its failure. This seems to apply particularly to settlement projects. In many examples of refugee and displaced persons' settlements, for instance, the food aid combined with various other externally provided complementary inputs of health and education services, can make the settlement better off than the surrounding villages or towns, especially when the settlement is in a location far away from major population centres. This type of success acts like a magnet on the nearby outside population who begin to find ways and means of participating in these facilities. In this way additional pressures from new interest groups build on the government and the donors to maintain such a desirable situation, thus making the phasing out or termination of food aid more difficult. An unending commitment to support settlements of this type has to be considered as dependency on food aid. The causes of the dependency, however, lie not so much in the food aid *per se*, as in the failure to resolve the international political problems or the civil strife that caused the influx of refugees or displaced persons in the first instance, and in the failure to improve living standards outside the settlements. It has been suggested as a way of ending such dependency that aid to the countries that create refugees should be cut off until something is done for the refugees.[3]

At the national level it is quite possible for states to become dependent on the budget-support type of food aid, especially in times of economic adversity such as crop failures, fall in export prices, etc, that would make commercial purchases of food difficult or even out of the question. These cases of dependency have, however, to be seen in relation to other possible means of maintaining food supplies within the available budgetary resources. In fact, to become dependent on food aid in this context is no worse than incurring additional foreign debt through loans. Credit facilities for food aid are generally more easily negotiable than financial credit and even though the going service charges for food aid credits (such as the US Title I) are slightly higher than, say, credits from the World Bank's soft loan facility, the IDA, these charges as well as the principal can frequently be repaid in local currency rather than in foreign exchange. In addition, over two-thirds of food aid is provided in the form of grants (in 1983, 70.6 per cent as against 62.9 per cent in 1973).

An unwelcome side effect of dependency is what is tantamount to withdrawal symptoms. These can occur when there is a need to move from a mass or group feeding situation to a developmental process, such as might arise in efforts to integrate a displaced persons' camp into productive activities in society. The camp population will have become used to receiving food for no activity and will find it hard to accept a normal relationship between food and productivity. Such transition is also complicated by the fact that the necessary food they are able to acquire through productive work may not be as great as the basic welfare ration, so that any progressive phasing out would come to look like a penalty for having worked. In many instances the termination of a food aid project, when looked upon as an end to dependency, can have very negative effects, especially if it is linked to the welfare of children, say, in a school feeding project. It is in this context that the programming function takes on great importance as the means of ensuring that such projects are not embarked upon by the donor without firm assurance that the institution and the government will be able to assume responsibility for the continuation of the project once the food aid phase has come to an end. This was a point made quite forcefully in a note on Special Feeding projects submitted by the Executive Director of the UN/FAO World Food Programme to the Intergovernmental Committee in April 1968 which stated that 'special feeding projects are by definition of a continuing nature ... whose continuation will require constantly increasing resources year by year ... while WFP cannot indefinitely support such programmes ... more harm may be caused by the untimely interruption of a well-managed food programme than perhaps by having abstained from the project in the first place.'

Disincentives

Human beings and thus human society, unless challenged or sufficiently motivated, will always tend to take the path of least effort. An important criticism of food aid is that it removes that challenge and motivation and is consequently no help to the objective of development.

One of the most serious implications of this disincentive effect is its possible influence on government policies. A government may know that certain structural reforms would be necessary to remedy certain types of food shortages, or inequitable access to food, but is hesitant to take the necessary measures knowing also that they would be unpalatable to one or other section of the community and would lead to increased social tensions. Food aid then becomes a means of avoiding such difficult choices while at the same time ensuring that there is no particular discontent due to food shortages—especially in the politically sensitive urban areas. This has come to be known as the 'soft option'. In short, food aid under such conditions can help to maintain a status quo and take away the challenge to do something about the structural problems that were giving rise to the need for food aid in the first place. The intention of food aid is basically to promote development and so improve the quality of life, especially of the poorer sections of the community. If it in fact goes to maintain the status quo, then it is most likely that priority will go to the administration, the civil service, the armed forces and the local urban population rather than to the poor, especially the rural poor, who would be a more appropriate target for food aid. In this way the objective of the food aid is altered and goes to those in less need of it. This development apparently took place in Bangladesh in 1980.[4]

The theme of the potential disincentive effects of food aid on agricultural production has already filled many volumes. The central argument is that food aid will discourage farmers' own production efforts since not only may a local or a national availability of food through food aid reduce the market for local products, but it can also undercut them in price. This latter is especially the case where growers have been able to sell on a parallel or 'black' market at considerably more than the official (and generally subsidized) price through government outlets. Other arguments suggest that, on the contrary, food aid enables farmers to retain more of their production and improve their nutritional status since the food aid will reduce the pressure on them to sell at low controlled prices or make obligatory deliveries to feed the urban population. Yet others, while admitting the depressive effect of food aid on producer prices and thus possibly on agricultural production in general, maintain that crop diversification and other adjustment factors will soon re-establish the balance. The most important among these latter viewpoints is the argument that increased demand for food from increased employment and development is made possible by the increased resources and national revenue generated through food aid and counterpart funds. This school of thought also points to the fact that a number of previously large recipients of food aid such as India and Colombia have now 'graduated' out of the recipient class to become exporters of food products themselves.

The great advantage of the polemic about the possible disincentive effects of food aid is that it brings increasing and necessary awareness to donors and recipients alike of the measures required to avoid such effects.

Although most of the literature on disincentives revolves around cereal food aid, its effects can be felt in other areas. In the earlier days of food aid programming cases have been documented of imports of milk powder, which virtually eliminated nascent local dairy industries in the recipient country. Many such defects have been overcome as a result of improved food aid programming as well as a wider understanding of the mechanisms underlying the phenomenon. This is well illustrated by the massive imports of milk powder into India under a multilateral food aid project entitled 'Operation Flood' which, far from inhibiting local production, became the basis for its growth. These imports and their reconstitution into fresh milk built up a nationwide distribution network with adequate hygiene and stable prices. Local producers were encouraged to contribute their production which, because of stable prices, also increased until a point was reached where the scheme could operate without external imports. Much of this local production came from the poorer rural families. Although India still imports milk powder, this is used either for buffer stocks in the event of seasonal or local shortages, or for conversion into less essential products such as yoghurt, cheese, or ice cream.

Distorting of normal food habits

Food aid can bring about changes in traditional consumption habits. There is not necessarily any disadvantage in this so long as the changes result in improved nutritive value at no increase in cost and no food habits are introduced that cannot be subsequently maintained through local production.

Probably the commonest change that has been brought about in recent decades is the introduction of bread into many areas of the world, partly as a result of acquired European food habits, but also following upon quite large imports of food aid wheat. Bread in the earlier days was largely consumed by the better-off urban populations. The habit has been spreading to other areas and bread is quite frequently included in school meals and baked from food aid wheat-flour. This only becomes a problem, or at least a growing concern, in those areas where wheat is not a normal crop and does not grow well, such as in tropical Africa. Nevertheless, the disruption caused by food aid is minor compared with that caused in other areas such as baby foods and infants' milk preparations that are imported commercially at considerable cost in foreign exchange and are tending to replace breast-feeding in many developing countries.

Disruption of Other Traditions

Food aid is also known to cause disruption through migration towards free food distribution centres. These effects are particularly noticeable in pastoral or nomadic societies with their high mobility. The knowledge that food aid was available in Nouakchott, the capital of Mauritania, certainly attracted a large number of nomads from the desert areas, many of whom have become squatters around the town. It is perhaps not only the food aid that contributes to this phenomenon but also the constant insistence of many aid agencies and experts that nomads must be settled and that pastoralism is a state equated to abject poverty. Food aid thus tends to be given for this purpose and leads to the destruction of a traditional way of life, which in reality is the optimum means of obtaining a livelihood from the hostile environment of the semi-desert regions of Africa and other parts of the globe. Food aid would be better directed at maintaining the pastoralists in their habitat and complemented with improved animal husbandry techniques, etc., and with the provision of cereals for barter, with which to restock their herds when losses have occurred through drought. Most pastoralists have a fine appreciation of how much human and animal population the environment will carry. Food aid can upset this by allowing an increase in the populations to take place over and above what the environment can actually bear, thus leading to undernourishment or the flight of some members to the towns.

There was a rather similar case in Somalia, where to the developers' astonishment some nomadic dignitaries came to protest over the installation of new wells at which camels could get water. These dignitaries maintained that the action was destructive to their society as it would lead people to increase their herds beyond the carrying capacity of the area in terms of forage, etc. In other words, development was cancelling out the in-built regulatory systems of the society. In the case of Mauritania, food aid provided to some nomadic groups who had temporarily fled to the towns to avoid involvement in Polisario incursions, played the same role there as did the wells in Somalia.

Some of the more cynical critics maintain that food aid disrupts normal attitudes to social well-being by apparently rewarding poverty, as a result of its being designated to help the poorest sectors of the community. An example is quoted from Guatemala where the poorest farmer who never did anything to help himself got the help, while his neighbour who had been attending agricultural classes and using soil conservation techniques and improved farming methods received nothing. It was thus claimed that food aid acted as positive reinforcement of poverty and this, in psychological terms, was the most effective means of encouraging people to remain poor.[5] The commentator omitted to state, however, that the same principles would apply to any form of social security or charity.

The Role of Voluntary Organizations

It will be found that most of the criticisms about various aspects of food aid relate to government or international programmes and little mention is made of the voluntary agencies and non-governmental organizations. Voluntary organizations are generally able to operate in small numbers much nearer to various vulnerable groups such as the rural or urban poor, children and young mothers, etc., than are the larger government agencies that are almost always based in the capital cities and are only able to make visits to outlying areas. Their perspective is therefore different from those who are able to live in the rural areas who, being closer to the affected population and generally having at their disposal more flexible and speedier methods of response to needs play an important role.

Their role is also important in providing early warning and feedback to larger official organizations about possible misadjustments in their aid packages, or in detecting signs of impending drought, crop failures, etc. This is often an important contribution to the objective of ensuring that food aid is of real help to the recipient community.

References

1. Jackson, T., with Eade, D., *Against the Grain—the Dilemma of Project Food Aid* (Oxford, 1982).

2. Hathaway, D., 'Food issues in North/South relations', *World Economy*, vol. 3(4), January 1981, Amsterdam.
3. Schwarz, W., 'Where aid produces no relief', The *Guardian*, 26 September 1984.
4. Scott, M., *Aid to Bangladesh: for Better or Worse?* (Boston, 1980).
5. Morgan, J. O., 'Problems with food distribution programs: a case in point', *World Neighbours*, (Oklahoma City, USA).

12   FOOD AID:
What next?—an overview

The preceding chapters of this book will have provided plenty of evidence that food aid remains not only a highly topical but also a highly controversial subject. This applies particularly to food aid as a developmental resource. Food aid in emergencies is less controversial, even though there remains plenty of scope for disagreement about the modalities, timing, logistics, etc. But in a normal year emergency food aid is no more than 10 to 15 per cent of total food aid, and even in the case of the African emergency in 1985 it was no more than around 20 per cent. The great bulk of food aid remains determined by developmental objectives, including the development of human resources through better nutrition of children, mothers and other vulnerable groups and also, in the coming years, rehabilitation and recovery from emergencies. It is this developmental part of food aid that is now under debate.

The chief criticisms of food aid fall under two headings.

(1)   That food aid is an inferior and less efficient form of aid compared with financial aid—an archaic throwback to barter transactions in disregard of the proved advantages of money compared with barter; and

(2)   that food aid suffers from strong counter-productive disincentive effects in two senses: (a) putting downward pressure on local food prices thus discouraging local food production; and (b) providing the recipient government of the developing country with free extra domestic financial resources from the sale of the food aid, thus reducing the government's priority for national food production, as well as the incentive to exert its own fiscal effort to mobilize money for agricultural and other development.

There are a number of other criticisms and difficulties with food aid—many of them brought out in the preceding chapters—but these two criticisms are the most widespread and fundamental.

Let us look at them one by one. Is food aid an inferior form of financial aid? This criticism of food aid has been made strongly and consistently by the British government, with the Overseas Development Administration (ODA) acting as chief spokesman. (See, for example, the memorandum by the ODA to the House of Commons Foreign Affairs Committee in the Second Report of the Committee on Famine in Africa.)[1] It is no accident that this criticism should come from that particular source. The UK has no food surpluses of any significance to give away—hence food aid for the British government involves the mobilization of financial resources in order to obtain the food and transfer it as food aid either through the World Food Programme or through the EEC or bilaterally, as the British government is now obliged to do because of Britain's obligations under the Food Aid Convention and because of its membership in the EEC and WFP. It is, therefore, quite natural that in the UK there is only one single aid budget in financial terms, and that the ODA should question whether it makes sense to earmark specific parts of this aid budget to take the form of food aid.

However, it is important to realize that the British position is exceptional among the food aid donors. Most of them, like the USA and the EEC as a whole, have food surpluses which have accumulated as a result largely of their own agricultural policies and their desire to support the standard of living of their own farmers, and for which food aid may be a convenient and low-cost outlet. The same is true, for somewhat different reasons, of Canada and Australia. For such countries the question of whether food aid is more or less efficient than financial aid is not the relevant and certainly not the only question. The fact that food aid has a lot of popular support, being considered as the friend of the donor countries' farmers, while financial aid is often very unpopular, being considered as the enemy of donor countries' taxpayers, is bound to weigh heavily in deciding to earmark part of the aid programme for food aid. (Strictly speaking, however, the taxpayer also pays indirectly for the food aid through agricultural price and export support policies. For example, in the case of the Common Agricultural Policy of the EEC, this cost absorbs the greater part of the Community's budget expenditure.) It is no accident that in the case of financial aid the UN target of 0.7 per cent of GNP of donor countries is only half fulfilled, and the degree of fulfilment has in fact fallen in recent years; whereas in the case of food aid the UN target of 10 million tonnes of cereals is satisfied to the degree of 76 per cent in the current Food Aid Convention and virtually fully satisfied in actual deliveries (in fact, currently exceeded). Moreover, the Food Aid Convention represents a multi-annual legal minimum commitment of the donor countries—something never achieved in the case of financial aid. But the achievement of the UN target of 10 million tonnes should not disguise the shortfall from minimum food aid requirements now estimated by the FAO and WFP as 18 to 20 million tonnes. So as far as the bulk of food aid is concerned the situation is not one of choosing between financial aid and the same amount of food aid out of a fixed common aid budget, but rather between food aid and nothing, or at least between food aid and a much smaller volume of financial aid. Thus, any discussion of food aid 'or' financial aid is largely academic. In the US, for example, completely separate and different legislation applies to food aid—the well-known Public Law 480 (PL 480) of 1954 with many subsequent amendments. The greater popularity and assumed smaller donor cost of food aid is also reflected in more concessional terms, usually grants in open or disguised forms.

But a more fundamental objection exists to the ODA view that food aid is at best an inferior substitute for financial aid. Can we really make such a distinction between financial aid and food aid? What we call financial aid is in fact only the first step in an aid process. What the recipient countries need for their development is not money or finance, but the necessary commodities that the aid money can buy: machinery for their development projects, raw materials for their industries, etc., and also food to feed their workers engaged on such projects. In that sense there is no such thing as financial aid. (With the exception, perhaps, of aid needed to replenish financial reserves or aid used to build up bank accounts in Switzerland. The latter type is not, however, usually considered to be among the intentional or desirable objectives of aid!) In the next round, which follows on the financial aid agreement, the aid has to be converted into developmental goods raising a whole host of new problems, such as sources of origin of the aid goods, procurement, utilization, etc. In that sense all aid is commodity aid. Food aid, in fact, could be commended for simplifying procedures by cutting out the first or financial stage of the transaction and coming directly to the substantive second stage of commodity transfer.

There is still another sense in which financial aid can be treated as food aid. If a country has a food deficit and is determined, or obliged, to import food, any financial aid which the country receives for essential developmental imports has the effect of setting free foreign exchange which can then be used for food imports. This substitution is known in economics as the principle of fungibility and it makes the distinction between financial aid and food aid much less clear-cut than it appears on the surface.

As for the alleged 'inferior' character of food aid as a throwback to the stone age by disregarding the social invention of money, we may note that a considerable proportion of world trade is also carried out in the form of barter or so-called counter trade. While in the nature of things counter trade statistics are uncertain and incomplete, the lowest present estimate (produced by the Group of 30, a non-profit organization sponsoring research on international economic problems), is that such trade accounts for between 8 and 10 per cent of the external trade of members of GATT[2] while other estimates run as high as 30 per cent; and there is agreement that there is a tendency for the share of counter trade to increase (the US Department of Commerce estimate is 20 to 30 per cent, and it reckons that this will rise to 50 per cent of world trade by the end of the 1990s).[3] The link between financial aid and direct commodity transactions is further strengthened by the wide spread of tied aid; in tied aid the financial aid is directly linked to the supply of specified commodities from the donor country. Although the accounting is done in financial terms, in practice we have here a commodity transaction very similar to food aid, and the intervention of money is purely nominal.

Just as the financial aid is in effect commodity aid (and quite often food aid), so the reverse is also true, in that food aid is often equivalent to financial aid. Leaving aside emergency aid, most food aid (over two-thirds) represents programme aid in bulk, providing balance-of-payments support. Such food aid saves the recipient government the foreign exchange which would otherwise have to be spent on importing food on commercial terms. Thus the food aid is directly equivalent to financial aid, and moreover to financial aid unconditionally available to the recipient government (except perhaps in so far as conditions attached to the disposal of counterpart funds from the food aid may refer to the import policy of the recipient government—but such a link is at most very indirect). There is, it is true, the international convention that food aid should not satisfy 'usual market requirements' (UMR). But although still formally adhered to, and administered by an international Committee on Surplus Disposal (CSD) in Washington, it is fairly widely agreed that this is of doubtful effectiveness, and that much of the bulk food aid does in fact substitute for commercial imports.

To sum up, the whole distinction between financial aid and food aid, and the alleged inferiority of food aid compared with financial aid, is a very doubtful argument. It is best to judge food aid on its own merits rather than compare it with the costs and benefits of financial aid. The increasing 'monetization' of food aid, described earlier in this book, further serves to blur the borderline between food aid and financial aid.

Turning now to the second and more serious of the main objections to food aid, namely its disincentive effects on local farmers and local food production, it must first be stated that such risks and dangers do exist and must be taken most seriously. Some qualifications, however, are in order from the very start. In the first place, the disincentive effect threatens only in the case of programme food aid, that is, food aid supplied in bulk for sale in the open market. That is where there is a risk that the extra supplies will, by reducing prices, provide a disincentive to local farmers. Even if the food is distributed free of charge to needy groups, there is still a risk that this will reduce their commercial demand for local food and so create a disincentive effect for local producers. However, where such free distribution is effectively targeted on poor and vulnerable groups which lack purchasing power for a commercial demand for food, and where food expenditure will absorb a high proportion of the income set free by subsidized or free distribution, the risk of reduction of commercial demand and hence of disincentive effects looks rather remote. The same is true of project food aid, such as food-for-work projects: where these projects are truly additional and the government could not otherwise finance them and support them with local food supplies, once again the risk of disincentive effects seems small and remote. The World Food Programme and the non-governmental organizations (NGOs) financing food-for-work projects take special care that the additionality condition of such projects is satisfied, and that disincentive effects are avoided. So the case of bulk food aid, where the food aid enters into the general system of food distribution and food trade, remains as the main area where the risk of disincentive exists. But even there, much of this bulk food aid substitutes for commercial imports, and this means that there is no additionality and hence no disincentive effect.

The second point to consider is that the disincentive risk is by no means peculiar to food aid; it also exists with financial aid, with commercial imports paid from the developing countries' own foreign exchange earnings, and for that matter even in the case of good domestic crops. This is often overlooked by the critics of food aid. Quite apart from the point previously made that there really is no such thing as 'financial' aid and that financial aid is really commodity aid at second remove, financial aid adds to the foreign exchange resources available to the recipient country and can hence be said to have a disincentive effect on local production by promoting additional imports. Such additional imports may make domestic production of the same or substitute goods less profitable or urgent; the same applies where the additional imports are financed from normal exports. This distincentive effect of financial aid is particularly important for aid recipient countries which have an industrial or production base to produce the aid goods themselves, such as India, Brazil, Egypt, and others. It also has special importance where the aid goods are relatively simple products and not beyond the technological capacity of the recipient country to produce. Multilateral donors of financial aid such as the World Bank try to avoid such disincentive effects of financial aid by allowing a preferential margin for local procurement—of 15 per cent in the case of the World Bank.

The third qualification to the disincentive effect is that a fall in domestic food prices as a result of increased food aid supplies is by no means pre-ordained. It is open to a government to distribute the additional food at low or subsidized prices to urban consumers while at the same time maintaining or even raising prices for local producers. The idea of an automatic disincentive effect due to low domestic prices is based on the assumption of a single and unified market price applying both to consumers and producers. However—just as in the case of the EEC and the US—food prices in practically all developing countries are subject to active government intervention; in many African countries, for example, the whole food trade system is controlled by governmental or parastatal organizations, such as Wheat Marketing Boards, Maize Marketing

Boards, and so on. It is quite possible for the governments of recipient countries to operate a dual price system with low prices for consumers, or selected groups of consumers, and higher prices for producers. This differential may, it is true, involve a budget deficit; but the fiscal resources to cover such a deficit should be there as a result of the increased revenue obtained by the government from the sale of food supplied as food aid.

The fourth, and perhaps most important, qualification is that any reduced demand for local food owing to the arrival of food aid from abroad could and should be offset by additional demand due to the additional incomes created by food-aid-induced accelerated development. The purpose of the food aid under review here, i.e., non-emergency programme food aid, is to promote development, both by easing the foreign exchange bottleneck and by giving the government additional resources to finance it from the sale of food aid. Such additional development would clearly benefit local food producers by creating extra demand for food and continuing to maintain or strengthen food prices. In the case of India, for instance, which all through the 1950s and 1960s was by far the largest recipient of food aid (particularly US programme food aid under Title I of PL 480) it has been pointed out that this developmental effect of increased incomes and increased demand for food has compensated or over-compensated for any possible disincentive effect on domestic prices.[4] (Defenders of food aid will argue that food aid helped India to finance the Green Revolution; critics will argue that India only increased its food production vigorously when food aid ceased to pour in. It is difficult to prove qualitatively which of these two judgements catches the relationship between food aid and domestic food production more accurately.) One may add empirically that, at least in the long run, the major recipients of food aid such as India, Korea, Israel, Greece (and for that matter the EEC countries which received such large-scale US food aid under the Marshall Plan), have in fact managed quite well to use large-scale food aid as a basis for vigorous development of local agriculture and local food production. It is, perhaps, too early to say whether Egypt and Bangladesh—presently the two largest recipients of food aid—can be added to the list, although this has been argued and there are hopeful signs for both countries.

A fifth qualification to the disincentive effect of food aid on local producers arises from the structure of food production in developing countries. To the extent that food production is subsistence production it clearly will not be affected by any possible impact of food aid on local prices. Where food is produced by small-scale producers who are partly subsistence producers but also produce a marketed surplus in order to cover fixed needs for buying seeds, fertilizer and consumption goods, or to pay rates, taxes, school fees, and so on, it is quite possible that a fall in prices may have the effect of increasing such marketed surpluses rather than reducing them. If the price falls, farmers have to market more of their production in order to cover their fixed money needs for such expenditure. This may be at the expense of their own subsistence consumption and specifically that of their children and families, and hence may not be a desirable situation—but it is not quite the disincentive effect pictured by the critics of food aid. Moreover, if farmers reduce the production of a given crop—say, wheat or maize—affected by lower prices due to food aid, this sets free land which can then be used for other crops. In the long run such crop diversification may be an advantage for the local farmers and the local economy. It can be stated generally, that the simple assumption that a lower price means less output, and a higher price more output, is an unduly simplified application of neoclassical textbook analysis (say, from Marshall's *Principles of Economics*) of a perfect capitalist market, quite likely not applicable to the much more complex case of the food market in developing countries (only partly commercial and only partly market-oriented). Incentives for farmers are governed by a spectrum of factors going well beyond price alone. 'Getting prices right' is important but not enough: the more expert advice is 'getting elasticities right'. There is no empirical evidence that the poor domestic terms of trade (prices obtained versus prices paid) of local food producers, as distinct from export crops, have been a contributory factor in the decline of food production; other types of neglect or discrimination are often more important.

In particular, the reference to bought inputs and bought consumption goods suggests still another major hole in the criticism of food aid as disincentive. The response of farmers even where it is in line with neo-classical capitalist-market forces, is determined not by the price as such but by what the farmer can buy with the price obtained. This clearly opens up further opportunities for avoiding disincentive effects. If the additional resources represented by food aid—either in terms of foreign exchange saved or in terms of revenue raised from the sale of food aid—are used for the additional import or domestic production of, say, fertilizer and its subsidized distribution to farmers, the profit margin for local food producers may be maintained or improved even if local food prices fall. The same applies to the availability of consumption goods, such as clothing, salt, soap, sugar, kerosene, etc. and their accessibility in rural areas. If the revenue from food aid is used to improve the supply of such essential consumption goods and their distribution to rural areas, this may be a more powerful incentive to farmers to increase production and marketed surpluses than a higher price. Such modifications of the simple neo-classical market model are by no means theoretical but correspond to the facts of life in most developing countries today.

All this, we repeat, is not to deny that disincentive effects are possible and must be carefully guarded against. But we are led to the conclusion that they are by no means unavoidable, and are certainly not automatic. Only careful analysis of situations in specific countries at specific periods of time can tell us whether disincentive effects have occurred and whether such effects have been compensated or over-compensated by the developmental benefits of food aid. The critics of food aid often omit to consider the potential benefits as an offset to the disincentive effects which they emphasize. Of course the advocates of food aid cannot have it both ways: just as the disincentive effects of food aid are potential rather than inevitable or automatic, the same is also true of its developmental benefits. It is quite possible for the foreign exchange saved by food aid to be wasted in the import of armaments or inessential luxury consumption goods, or in supporting capital flight, or in helping to build up bank balances in Switzerland for those in control of foreign exchange. It will be noted that the potential for avoiding disincentive, for instance, by better supply of fertilizer or consumption goods for the benefit of rural areas, depends on priority being given to agricultural and rural improvements in the use of the additional resources represented by food aid, and avoidance of 'urban bias'. Even the humanitarian and social benefits in improving the nutrition and living standards of needy and vulnerable groups are by no means automatic: project food aid can be badly targeted and programme food aid can be badly distributed, in the sense of bypassing those who need it while benefiting those who do not. It is for the governments of recipient countries, and also for the donors of food aid, to see to it that the potential developmental benefits of food aid are in fact realized and not wasted, and that the potentially harmful effects of food aid as a result of disincentives to local production are avoided.

The result of our discussions so far, therefore, serves to place a good deal of emphasis on the quality of planning and policies for development in the recipient country, whether in the sense of over-all macro-economic policy or of micro-economic efficiency in project formulation, design, and execution. This emphasis—which also underlies the current trend of linking food aid (as well as other aid) with the development of agreed 'food strategies'—links up with what we described earlier in this chapter as the second major strand of the disincentive criticism, i.e., that food aid provides an incentive for the recipient government to slacken its own efforts to promote domestic food production, and also to raise revenue and mobilize domestic resources by its own fiscal effort.

This criticism, like the one of disincentives for local food production, is subject to qualification and reply. For example, it does not seem plausible that countries, particularly smaller and recently independent countries which are otherwise so jealous of their 'national sovereignty', would easily be induced, by the mere availability of food aid, to let themselves be moved into a position of dependency on it; what could be more harmful to sovereignty than dependency on food gifts for the survival and nutrition of their people? Or again, if the result of food aid is to raise individual incomes while the government fails to 'mobilize' these resources for national development, is it not possible that the additional resources might be well used for additional development in the private sector? Is not a greater role for the private sector part of the preferred development strategy of many important food aid donors? The risk that food aid may create a state of dependency and lethargy among the recipients must be taken seriously—in food aid, as in so many other things, it is easy to slip from familiarity into acceptance as an ingrained 'right'. But it seems more an argument for constant vigilance and improvement in the delivery of food than for its termination or reduction. One of the problems with this line of criticism, for critics and advocates alike, is that it is difficult to document, let alone quantify. As one of the most perceptive of contemporary observers has put it: 'Here we are dealing with some of the most difficult areas of political economy and it would be hopeless to try and arrive at some kind of an all-things-considered synthetic judgement.'[5] But once again, there are the cases of India, Taiwan, and South Korea, quoted in earlier chapters as contradicting the 'dependency' thesis.

Part of the worry about dependency is the backwash of the food aid rhetoric which has tended to describe food aid as a 'transitional' measure. But food aid as an important development tool has been with us now for over thirty years, and is likely to be with us for another thirty. Over the last decade it has increased, and is likely to increase further over the next. So it is time to stop debating whether food aid is better or worse than other forms of aid or income transfer, to treat it as a fact of life and accept the challenge to make it more effective, maximize the potential benefits, and avoid the potential harm. For historical reasons (described in Chapter 2) food aid has tended to become a separate branch of study as well as a separate tool of development policy. But it will only have its maximum impact if it is better co-ordinated among donors, and between donors and recipients; better linked with other forms of assistance (financial, technical, health assistance, trade, etc.); and, above all, better integrated into recipient countries' development plans and policies. There is plenty of work here for the future, waiting for those concerned with food aid.

One cannot, of course, be sure exactly what the future will hold for food aid, but there are a number of developments on the horizon which could form a basis for forward planning. There is, in the first place, an almost certain concentration on the problems of Africa. As this chapter is written (May 1986) the UN General Assembly has just completed its special session on Africa—the first of its kind—and has unanimously adopted an action programme for African economic recovery and development. This programme foresees for 1986–90 the investment of 128.1 billion US dollars (approximately £80 billion). Of this total sum, African countries commit themselves to provide 82.5 billion dollars through the mobilization of domestic resources, while the international community has committed itself to making every effort to provide the remaining 45.6 billion dollars, say, £6 billion per annum, in additional resources. One can be reasonably sure that food aid will play an important part in this additional mobilization of external resources for Africa, with special emphasis on helping to finance the transition from emergency and relief in the many African countries recently affected by various kinds of emergency, to rehabilitation and development, and the prevention of future famines, specifically including the establishment of stabilization food reserves for this purpose. As a result of the recent famines and emergencies, there has already been an increased concentration of food aid on Africa; much experience has been gained in recent years, and in particular the NGOs have increasing links with Africa. Food aid is more concentrated on the poorer countries than is financial aid so there is a natural enhancement of the role of food aid in the total picture as a result of the emerging central role for Africa in the international aid picture.

There are other developments which can be confidently foreseen. Largely as a result of the work of Unicef, there has been an increasing realization of the vulnerability of children, of the importance of preserving the future human capital of poor countries in times of recession and enforced adjustment, and of building future development on the better utilization of potential human resources. This will become increasingly accepted and will enhance the importance of food aid projects and programmes directed towards children and mothers. Similarly, the increasing recognition of the crucial role of women, both as a vulnerable group and also as key agents of production, particularly agricultural production, will tend to emphasize the natural and direct relationship of the potential of food aid with the concerns of women.

The multilateral share of food aid through the UN system, chiefly the UN World Food Programme, is now firmly established at 20 to 25 per cent of total food aid. In addition, other forms of agreed multilateral action, such as the Food Aid Convention associated with the International Wheat Agreement, and European action through the EEC (described in earlier chapters of this book), have become firmly established and cover the bulk of total food aid. One may assume that this trend towards multilateral action will continue; in particular one may hope and assume that food aid will be better integrated into the discussion of aid programmes, in particular countries held as Aid Consortia or Consultative Groups under the auspices of the World Bank and the United Nations Development Programme (UNDP) as well as in the adjustment programmes propagated by the IMF. In general, a closer integration of food aid with financial aid may be expected; the monetization of food aid and the utilization of counterpart funds arising from food aid—

both discussed earlier in this book—will contribute to such closer integration.

Another development that one may hopefully look for is the increasing development of food strategies, with priorities for domestic food production, by the developing countries themselves. This would enable the food aid to be given more frequently in bulk or programme form, trusting the recipient government to make proper use of the additional resources, in line with international donor objectives as well as their own. One would also hope that the World Food Programme will play a more genuine role in controlling, through its Committee for Food Aid (CFA), not only its own corner of food aid but the total global food aid programme: even the role of food aid in the total global aid effort. There is a clear need for such a forum and co-ordinating body. When the governing body of the World Food Programme, the Inter-governmental Committee (IGC) was converted into the CFA, that was precisely the intention. But it cannot be said that this intention has been entirely fulfilled. This also still remains one of our hopes for the future.

References

1. Committee on Famine in Africa, *Second Report*, House of Commons Paper 56 (HMSO, 1985).
2. Group of 30, *Counter Trade in the World Economy* (New York, 1986).
3. Strange, S., 'Protectionism—why not?', *The World Today*, vol. 41, Nos. 8–9 (August (1986)).
4. Isenman, P. J., and Singer, H. W., 'Food aid: disincentive effects and their policy implications', *Economic Development and Cultural Change*, vol. 25, No. 2 (1977).
5. Sen, A. K., *Food Entitlement and Food Aid Programmes*, in WFP/Government of the Netherlands Seminar on Food Aid, The Hague, 1983.

APPENDICES

APPENDICES

Appendix 1 Agricultural Trade Development and Assistance Act 1954 (Public Law 480)

1. Title I authorized the President to use, with the agreement of the recipient government, foreign currencies earned from the sale of US agricultural commodities for eight different purposes: less developed countries (LDC) economic development, US agricultural market development, payment of US obligations, international education exchange, procurement of military supplies, carrying out programmes of US government agencies, purchase of goods and services from other countries, and purchase of strategic materials. Ten per cent of the local currencies were to be subject to congressional appropriation.

2. Title II provided for use of food commodities on a strictly grant basis for famine relief and/or other foreign emergency purposes.

3. Title III authorized the Commodity Credit Corporation to make commodities available to private voluntary organizations (e.g., CARE, etc.) for distribution in the US and abroad. It also permitted the President to barter food commodities for strategic material and goods not produced in the US.

Appendix 2 General Guidelines for the Establishment of WFP Rations

1. The WFP food basket is generally composed of cereals, dairy products, fats, canned meat, canned and dry fish, sugar, dried fruits, and special foods and food mixtures (blended foods, fish protein concentrate, biscuits). This composition is however subject to fluctuations, and may vary considerably from year to year. The average nutritive value of WFP commodities is reported in the attached table.

2. Because of the nature of the foods available, WFP rations cannot provide all the nutrients necessary to cover the daily requirements of beneficiaries; therefore they always have to be complemented with local foods, particularly local staple foods and fresh fruits and vegetables. It is also advisable, in order to facilitate logistics, to limit the number of commodities in individual projects to a maximum of six items, preferably less.

3. The composition of WFP rations is influenced by the following factors:
    (i)   the nutritional requirements of beneficiaries;
    (ii)   the availability of commodities and their relative price on the international market;
    (iii)   the specific objectives of food assistance in each type of project;
    (iv)   the average composition of the local diet, and the pattern of food habits;
    (v)   the acceptability of WFP foods;
    (vi)   logistics, i.e. facilities for and conditions of transport, storage, preparation (where applicable), and distribution of commodities within the recipient country;
    (vii)   government preferences and policies;
    (viii) possibility of market displacement;
    (ix)   WFP budget allocation for individual countries and projects.

4. Within the limitations determined by the mentioned factors, the rations provided by WFP in different types of projects should aim so far as possible at covering the requirements of beneficiaries as described below.
    (i)   *Supplementary feeding projects*
            These projects include pregnant and nursing women, and pre-school children from 6 months to 5 years of age. The daily rations for these groups should aim at supplying foods providing energy and protein in a concentrated form, to facilitate their distribution through the health channels, whose capacity for food transport, storage and handling is almost always very limited. It is recommended to provide on average for children 50 per cent of the daily energy, and most of the daily protein requirements; and for preg-

nant and nursing women at least the additional energy and protein requirements for the latter half of pregnancy (350 calories and 6 g of protein) and the first six months of lactation (500 calories and 17 g of protein).

In practice, the average provision of 600 calories and 20 g of protein (the latter preferably of high biological value) would satisfy the above recommendations. It is advisable, when the foods are distributed in dry form for home consumption, to provide the same rations for both types of beneficiaries, since this facilitates distribution procedures. Dry skim milk for these beneficiaries should be enriched with Vitamin A.

The average duration (or entitlement) of food distribution recommended is: for women, 4–5 months of pregnancy and first 6 months of lactation; and for each pre-school child, 1 to 2 years or until the weight/age has been maintained at the normal range for at least two months. Selection of beneficiaries on the basis of nutritional, health or economic needs is advisable. Infants below 6 months of age should normally be breastfed, and for this reason also, the supplement is given to the mothers, so as to avoid displacement of breast-feeding. Distribution should be as often as possible, ideally once per week or twice per month to individuals, whenever the ideal system of 'on-the-spot' feeding proves to be impractical.

Similar criteria should be followed in establishing rations for another group of beneficiaries, namely hospital outpatients (tuberculosis patients and lepers), who receive the foods through the health channels with the above-mentioned limitations. The food entitlement for those patients is recommended to be on average 2 years.

(ii) *Institutional feeding projects*
These projects include primary and secondary school children (in day or boarding schools), adults in training institutions, patients in hospitals, and displaced people in camps. In these projects food is prepared, distributed and consumed on the spot; and the WFP rations should be established on the basis of full information on facilities, equipment, and personnel available for food handling, as well as on local food supply. The table in Annex I summarizes the average recommended supplies of energy and protein for each group.

(iii) *Food-for-work projects*
These projects include workers in various types of activities (agriculture and rural development, building of infrastructures, resettlement). WFP rations are provided either as part-payment of wages or as incentive to participate in voluntary work; or as the main source of sustenance in resettlement projects, until the new land

starts producing food for the families. Except for the last type of project, the nutritional objective in these projects is secondary; economic considerations prevail, and the value of the ration in monetary or incentive terms has priority.

The average ration recommended should provide about 2000 calories and 30 g protein, for each member of the worker's family; each worker is usually allowed to receive 5 rations (which constitutes a 'family ration') for each working day. The energy and protein value of the ration is calculated to cover 80 per cent of the average family energy and protein requirements.

In the case of settlers, it may be necessary to provide almost 100 per cent of these requirements in the first year, gradually decreasing in the subsequent years. Distribution of rations should be, if possible, once every fortnight, or at least once every month.

(iv) *Emergency situations*

In emergency situations, WFP is usually not the only donor; many others participate in providing food and other necessities. WFP rations are therefore limited both in terms of number of commodities (to expedite delivery) and in quantities. The main commodity is the staple food, a cereal; associated if possible and if necessary, with a source of protein (DSM) and a concentrated source of energy (a fat). An average ration providing about 1400 calories and 40 g of protein is recommended. Special provision for food supplies on an *ad hoc* basis would have to be made, however, in case WFP should be the only donor, and in cases where nutrition rehabilitation of severely malnourished children has to be established.

5.   Annex I summarizes the average recommended supplies of energy and protein as described under 4 above.

Annex II gives the maximum amount recommended for each commodity, or group of commodities, in different types of projects.

November 1980

Annex I. Average recommended supplies of energy and protein

	Pre-school children (approx. 6 months–5yrs)	Primary school children including kindergartens (day students) (approx. 5–12 yrs)	Boarders in training institutions	Hospital inpatients	Displaced persons in camps	Food-for-work
MEAL per day		1 snack / 1 meal	2–3 meals	2–3 meals	2–3 meals	2–3 meals
ENERGY per day	600 calories Pre-school (10–50% of requirement) Pregnant and nursing (>100% of additional requirement)	1 snack 400 calories (20% of requirement) 1 meal 800 calories (40% of requirement)	1800 calories (70/75% of requirement)	1500 calories (75% of requirement)	2000 calories (80% of requirement)	2000 calories (80% or requirement)
PROTEIN per day	20g Pre-school (100% of requirement) Pregnant and nursing (>100% of additional requirement)	15g (50% of requirement) 30g (100% of requirement)	40g (100% of requirement)	40g (80% of requirement)	40g (100% of requirement)	30g (80% of requirement)
DURATION	Pre-school (1–2 years) Pregnancy (from 4–5 months) Lactation (first 6 months)	School days/year	Training days/year	365 days/year taking into account average bed-occupancy rate	As required	Number of man/days

Annex II. Maximum quantities* of WFP commodities for individual rations in different projects (grammes/day)

Commodity	Projects			
	Supplementary feeding	Institutional feeding	Food-for-work	Emergencies
Cereals	150	400	500	400
Dairy products	40	40	40	40
Canned meat	20	40	40	20
Canned fish	20	40	40	20
Pulses	20	40	40	20
Dried fish	10	30	30	10
Fats/oils	20	40	40	40
Sugar	10	20	20	20
CSM/WSB	100	100	100	100
Soy fortified cereals	100	100	200	

* As stated under item 2 in establishing the rations it is recommended to select not more than 6 commodities, preferably less, from the above list, in quantities not to exceed those indicated.

Appendix 3. Low-income food deficit countries (FAO and IBRD Formulae)

A. Agriculture and food

	Value added in agriculture (millions of 1980 dollars)		Cereal imports (thousands of metric tons)		Food aid in cereals (thousands of metric tons)		Fertilizer consumption (hundreds of grams of plant nutrient per hectare of arable land)		Average index of food production per capita (1974–76 = 100) 1982–84
	1970	1984[a]	1974	1984	1974/75	1983/84	1970[b]	1983	
Low-income economies			24,017 *t*	26,430 *t*	5,651 *t*	4,878 *t*	178 *w*	661 *w*	116 *w*
China and India			15,101 *t*	17,355 *t*	1,582 *t*	580 *t*	230 *w*	923 *w*	121 *w*
Other low-income			8,916 *t*	9,075 *t*	4,069 *t*	4,298 *t*	78 *w*	195 *w*	102 *w*
Sub-Saharan Africa			2,560 *t*	5,195 *t*	796 *t*	2,087 *t*	23 *w*	49 *w*	92 *w*
1 Ethiopia	1,663	1,971	118	506	54	172	4	35	100
2 Bangladesh	5,427	6,703	1,866	2,136	2,076	1,163	142	596	99
3 Mali	403	606	281	367	107	111	29	75	101
4 Zaire	1,503	1,866	343	246	1	53	8	14	92
5 Burkina Faso	444	521	99	89	28	57	3	50	94
6 Nepal	1,102	1,364	18	27	0	30	30	137	91
7 Burma	1,705	3,403	26	7	9	6	34	158	124
8 Malawi	257	427	17	20	(.)	3	52	164	100
9 Niger	851	649	155	45	73	13	1	5	113

	Value added in agriculture (millions of 1980 dollars)		Cereal imports (thousands of metric tons)		Food aid in cereals (thousands of metric tons)		Fertilizer consumption (hundreds of grams of plant nutrient per hectare of arable land)		Average index of food production per capita (1974–76 = 100) 1982–84
	1970	1984[a]	1974	1984	1974/75	1983/84	1970[b]	1983	
10 Tanzania	1,583	..	431	364	148	136	30	42	100
11 Burundi	468	585	7	14	6	11	5	21	106
12 Uganda	2,388	2,682	37	20	0	10	13	..	98
13 Togo	212	238	6	95	11	9	3	21	92
14 Central African Rep.	256	324	7	30	1	8	11	7	94
15 India	45,772	59,681	5,261	2,170	1,582	371	114	394	110
16 Madagascar	1,111	1,269	114	172	7	74	56	46	89
17 Somalia	434	..	42	330	111	177	31	23	69
18 Benin	..	463	8	65	9	6	33	30	97
19 Rwanda	..	..	3	20	19	25	3	3	112
20 China	69,147	134,877	9,840	15,185	0	209	418	1,806	128
21 Kenya	1,198	2,183	15	560	2	122	224	376	82
22 Sierra Leone	261	330	72	61	10	16	13	11	95
23 Haiti	..	..	83	205	25	72	4	36	90
24 Guinea	..	794	63	186	49	43	18	6	93
25 Ghana	3,360	2,522	177	311	33	74	9	77	73
26 Sri Lanka	812	1,224	951	685	271	391	496	740	125
27 Sudan	1,610	2,203	125	530	46	450	31	67	93

28 Pakistan	5,007	6,581	1,274	291	584	395	168	586	104
29 Senegal	603	567	341	698	27	151	20	48	66
30 *Afghanistan*	..	..	5	20	10	100	24	63	102
31 *Bhutan*	..	..	3	11	0	7	(.)	10	104
32 *Chad*	339	..	37	74	20	69	7	17	95
33 *Kampuchea, Dem.*	..	..	223	25	226	43	13	16	107
34 *Lao PDR*	..	..	53	37	8	2	4	6	129
35 *Mozambique*	..	..	62	392	34	297	27	77	73
36 *Viet Nam*	..	..	1,854	436	64	2	512	471	123
Middle-income economies			41,135 t	84,988 t	2,329 t	4,719 t	214 w	443 w	104 w
Oil exporters			18,022 t	45,487 t	1,135 t	2,712 t	140 w	466 w	102 w
Oil importers			23,113 t	39,501 t	1,194 t	2,007 t	258 w	431 w	105 w
Sub-Saharan Africa			1,361 t	4,849 t	114 t	503 t	46 w	109 w	92 w
Lower middle-income			17,128 t	32,838 t	1,624 t	4,685 t	76 w	431 w	104 w
37 Mauritania	200	215	115	277	48	129	6	..	95
38 Liberia	235	334	42	109	3	47	55	75	91
39 Zambia	473	627	93	236	5	76	71	130	74
40 Lesotho	94	..	49	141	14	50	17	151	78
41 Bolivia	541	723	209	320	22	284	13	18	84
42 Indonesia	12,097	21,229	1,919	1,926	301	466	119	745	120
43 Yemen Arab Rep.	..	..	158	612	33	5	1	57	84
44 Yemen, PDR	..	..	149	291	(.)	16	(.)	103	83
45 Cote d'Ivoire	1,733	2,542	172	545	4	0	71	107	110
46 Philippines	5,115	8,694	817	964	89	54	214	320	107
47 Morocco	2,784	2,905	891	2,610	75	448	130	293	91
48 Honduras	475	687	52	130	31	97	160	159	99

| | Value added in agriculture (millions of 1980 dollars) | | Cereal imports (thousands of metric tons) | | Food aid in cereals (thousands of metric tons) | | Fertilizer consumption (hundreds of grams of plant nutrient per hectare of arable land) | | Average index of food production per capita (1974–76 = 100) 1982–84 |
	1970	1984[a]	1974	1984	1974/75	1983/84	1970[b]	1983	
49 El Salvador	740	868	75	221	4	263	1,048	1,132	88
50 Papua New Guinea	655	926	71	174	..	..	76	182	95
51 Egypt, Arab Rep.	3,282	4,795	3,877	8,616	610	1,783	1,282	3,605	91
52 Nigeria	17,943	19,062	389	2,351	7	0	3	87	96
53 Zimbabwe	556	823	56	334	0	76	466	576	69
54 Cameroon	1,492	1,991	81	121	4	1	28	48	83
55 Nicaragua	410	606	44	135	3	56	184	483	78
56 Thailand	5,631	9,829	97	150	0	13	76	240	115
57 Botswana	20	74	21	59	5	32	14	10	61
58 Dominican Rep.	953	1,235	252	436	16	148	354	288	99
59 Peru	1,716	1,893	637	1,205	37	207	297	224	84
60 Mauritius	178	152	160	188	22	22	2,081	2,538	88
61 Congo, People's Rep.	147	178	34	113	2	1	112	24	96
62 Ecuador	1,054	1,413	152	369	13	14	123	283	89
63 Jamaica	205	235	340	432	1	54	886	628	89
64 Guatemala	..	..	138	142	9	19	224	474	101
65 Turkey	8,701	13,400	1,276	1,627	16	0	166	581	103

Note: For data comparability and coverage, see the technical notes.
Source: World Development Report 1986: World Bank, Washington, 1986.

Definitions and data notes

The principal country groups used in the text of this Report and in the World Development Indicators are defined as follows:

- *Developing countries* are divided into: *low-income economies*, with 1984 gross national product (GNP) per person of less than $400; and *middle-income economies*, with 1984 GNP per person of $400 or more. Middle-income countries are also divided into *oil exporters* and *oil importers*, identified below.

- *Middle-income oil exporters* comprise Algeria, Angola, Cameroon, People's Republic of the Congo, Ecuador, Arab Republic of Egypt, Gabon, Indonesia, Islamic Republic of Iran, Iraq, Malaysia, Mexico, Nigeria, Peru, Syrian Arab Republic, Trinidad and Tobago, Tunisia, and Venezuela.

- *Middle-income oil importers* comprise all other middle-income developing countries not classified as oil exporters, A subset, *major exporters of manufactures*, comprises Argentina, Brazil, Greece, Hong Kong, Israel, Republic of Korea, Philippines, Portugal, Singapore, South Africa, Thailand, and Yugoslavia.

- *High-income oil exporters* (not included in developing countries) comprise Bahrain, Brunei, Kuwait, Libya, Oman, Qatar, Saudi Arabia, and United Arab Emirates.

- *Industrial market economies* are the members of the Organisation for Economic Co-operation and Development, apart from Greece, Portugal, and Turkey, which are included among the middle-income developing economies. This group is commonly referred to in the text as industrial economies or industrial countries.

- *East European nonmarket economies* include the following countries: Albania, Bulgaria, Czechoslovakia, German Democratic Republic, Hungary, Poland, Romania, and U.S.S.R. This group is sometimes referred to as nonmarket economies.

- *Sub-Saharan Africa* comprises all thirty-nine developing African countries south of the Sahara, excluding South Africa, as given in *Toward Sustained Development in Sub-Saharan Africa: A joint Program of Action* (World Bank 1984).

- *Middle East and North Africa* includes Afghanistan, Algeria, Arab Republic of Egypt, Iran, Iraq, Israel, Jordan, Kuwait, Lebanon, Libya, Morocco, Oman, Saudi Arabia, Syrian Arab Republic, Tunisia, Turkey, United Arab Emirates, Yemen Arab Republic, and People's Democratic Republic of Yemen.

- *East Asia* comprises all low- and middle-income countries of East and Southeast Asia and the Pacific, east of, and including, Burma, China, and Mongolia.

- *South Asia* includes Bangladesh, Bhutan, India, Nepal, Pakistan, and Sri Lanka.

- *Latin America and the Caribbean* comprises all American and Caribbean countries south of the United States.
- *Major borrowers* are countries with disbursed and outstanding debt estimated at more than $15 billion at the end of 1984 and comprise Argentina, Brazil, Chile, Egypt, India, Indonesia, Israel, Republic of Korea, Mexico, Turkey, Venezuela, and Yugoslavia.

Economic and demographic terms are defined in the technical notes to the World Development Indicators. The Indicators use the country groupings given above but include only countries with a population of 1 million or more.

Billion is 1,000 million.

Tons are metric tons, equal to 1,000 kilograms, or 2,204.6 pounds.

Growth rates are in real terms unless otherwise stated. Growth rates for spans of years in tables cover the period from the beginning of the base year to the end of the last year given.

Dollars are current U.S. dollars unless otherwise specified.

The symbol .. in tables means 'not available'.

The symbol — in tables means 'not applicable'.

All tables and figures are based on World Bank data unless otherwise specified.

Data from secondary sources are not always available through 1984. The numbers in this *World Development Report* shown for historical data may differ from those shown in previous Reports because of continuous updating as better data become available and because of recompilation of certain data for a ninety-country sample. The recompilation was necessary to permit greater flexibility in regrouping countries for the purpose of making projections.

Appendix 3. B. IDA Commitments by Country ($ million)

	1961–65	1966–70	1971–76	1977	1978	1979	1980	1981[a]	1982	Cumulative 1961–82[ab]
I. Current IDA recipients										
A. Pure IDA countries	63.3 t	235.4 t	2,485 t	522.5 t	750.6 t	1,007.3 t	1,221.9 t	1,256.2 t	1,275.0 t	8,818.4 t
Sub-Saharan Africa	59.5 t	223.7 t	1,361.9 t	297.5 t	418.7 t	446.8 t	683.8 t	715.3 t	649.5 t	4,857.1 t
South Asia	—	1.7 t	853.6 t	176.0 t	211.7 t	353.0 t	460.0 t	451.2 t	521.0 t	3,028.3 t
Others	3.8 t	10.0 t	270.0 t	49.0 t	120.2 t	207.5 t	78.1 t	89.7 t	104.5 t	933.0 t
Lao PDR	—	—	—	—	8.2	10.4	13.4	—	15.0	47.0
Chad	—	5.9	23.3	20.0	21.7	7.6	—	—	—	78.5
Bangladesh	—	—	655.1	122.0	139.0	271.0	267.0	334.0	391.0	2,179.2
Ethiopia	13.5	21.5	252.1	57.0	24.0	—	—	75.0	30.0	473.1
Nepal	—	1.7	66.0	28.0	67.2	39.8	33.0	62.2	30.0	327.9
Somalia	6.2	2.9	67.0	12.0	17.0	24.0	18.0	10.2	15.0	172.4
Guinea-Bissau	—	—	—	—	—	9.0	—	6.8	—	15.8
Burma	—	—	132.5	26.0	5.5	39.0	160.0	55.0	100.0	518.0
Afghanistan	3.5	10.0	87.0	18.0	40.0	71.6	—	—	—	230.1
Viet Nam	—	—	—	—	—	60.0	—	—	—	60.0
Mali	—	16.8	76.4	26.0	25.0	21.0	8.0	20.7	20.0	213.9
Burundi	—	3.3	17.7	10.0	17.4	6.8	30.0	56.0	21.2	162.4
Rwanda	—	9.3	30.6	19.8	15.0	14.0	21.0	22.5	40.9	173.1
Upper Volta	—	0.8	55.8	23.6	17.4	—	35.0	62.0	33.0	227.7
Zaire	—	11.0	155.5	26.0	9.0	46.0	29.5	29.3	100.8	407.1
Gambia	—	2.1	11.8	—	8.5	5.0	—	—	8.0	35.4
Maldives	—	—	—	—	—	3.2	—	—	—	3.2

	1961–65	1966–70	1971–76	1977	1978	1979	1980	1981[a]	1982	Cumulative 1961–82[ab]
Haiti	0.3	—	51.5	10.0	31.6	16.5	—	21.2	18.0	149.2
Sierra Leone	—	3.0	20.1	—	8.2	—	2.5	30.5	5.0	69.3
Tanzania	18.6	29.8	164.6	39.2	100.5	76.5	109.5	92.8	75.0	706.5
Guinea	—	—	21.0	—	—	21.6	23.4	46.0	19.0	131.0
Central African Rep.	—	8.5	3.9	—	—	18.0	—	9.4	18.0	57.8
Comoros	—	—	—	—	—	5.0	5.2	—	12.3	22.5
Equatorial Guinea	—	—	2.0	—	—	—	—	—	—	2.0
Western Samoa	—	—	4.4	—	—	—	8.0	2.0	—	14.4
Uganda	—	33.0	11.3	—	—	—	72.5	17.0	109.0	242.8
Benin	—	4.6	35.0	7.2	21.0	8.3	10.0	43.3	23.8	153.2
Niger	1.5	6.7	45.4	—	9.5	37.0	36.7	21.5	26.1	184.5
Madagascar	—	24.1	87.1	14.0	33.0	49.0	48.0	45.3	20.7	321.2
Sudan	13.0	8.5	172.0	25.0	78.0	56.0	170.0	73.0	56.0	651.5
Ghana	—	24.8	71.7	9.0	—	19.0	54.5	29.0	—	208.0
Lesotho	—	4.1	15.1	2.5	13.5	15.0	10.0	10.0	—	70.2
Yemen, PDR	—	—	38.4	—	11.4	14.0	22.2	24.0	19.5	129.5
Yemen Arab Rep.	—	—	88.7	21.0	29.0	35.0	34.5	41.0	42.0	291.3
Mauritania	6.7	3.0	22.5	6.2	—	8.0	—	15.0	12.7	74.2
Solomon Islands	—	—	—	—	—	—	—	1.5	5.0	6.5
Djibouti	—	—	—	—	—	—	—	—	3.0	3.0
Dominica	—	—	—	—	—	—	—	—	5.0	5.0

Appendix 3. B. IDA Commitments by Country ($ million)—cont.

B. IDA/IBRD blend

countries	765.1t	1,363.3	3,445.0t	689.2t	1,259.2t	1,591.2t	2,068.6t	2,000.8t	1,394.3	14,350.5t
Sub-Saharan Africa	10.3t	92.4t	282.2t	72.0t	142.6t	142.2t	204.1t	215.8t	173.3t	1,335.1t
South Asia	754.8t	1,030.0t	3,138.0t	594.2t	1,107.2t	1,424.0t	1,851.5t	1,650.0t	1,157.0t	12,706.7t
Others	—	13.9t	24.8t	23.0t	10.0t	25.0t	135.0t	13.0t	64.0t	308.7t
Malawi	—	33.2	64.0	15.0	21.2	36.5	13.8	74.0	11.3	269.1
India	485.0	786.0	2,854.7	481.0	951.5	1,192.0	1,535.0	1,281.0	900.0	10,466.2
Sri Lanka	—	23.9	59.5	33.2	33.5	68.0	151.5	167.0	86.0	622.6
China	—	—	—	—	—	—	—	100.0	60.0	160.0
Pakistan[c]	269.8	220.1	223.8	80.0	122.2	164.0	165.0	202.0	171.0	1,617.9
Togo	—	3.7	24.2	10.0	19.8	16.2	11.0	25.7	5.5	116.1
Kenya	10.3	38.4	99.6	40.0	58.0	40.0	122.0	50.0	61.0	519.3
Senegal	—	17.1	77.4	—	26.3	24.5	42.3	47.1	19.5	254.3
Liberia	—	—	17.0	7.0	6.0	14.0	—	4.0	25.5	73.5
Zambia	—	—	—	—	11.3	11.0	15.0	—	50.5	87.8
Zimbabwe	—	—	—	—	—	—	—	15.0	—	15.0
Guyana	—	2.9	10.6	—	10.0	5.0	—	8.0	2.0	38.5
Papua New Guinea	—	11.0	14.2	23.0	—	20.0	13.0	27.0	2.0	110.2

Source: IDA in Retrospect: The first two decades of the IDA, July 1982.

Appendix 3. C. Shipments of Food Aid in Cereals by Recipients* – July/June

Recipient Countries	TOTAL					Average
	1979/80	1980/81	1981/82	1982/83	1983/84	
	(...................... thousand tons, grain equivalent ....)					
AFRICA – Total	3 662.3	4 511.7	4 937.6	4 635.2	5 138.7	4 577.1
Of which: Low-Income, Food Deficit						
Countries	3 426.9	4 320.5	4 773.9	4 429.9	4 844.8	4 359.2
Of which: Sub-Sahara	1 549.8	2 335.3	2 339.8	2 471.9	2 609.2	2 261.2
Algeria	18.9	28.5	5.4	2.3	6.5	12.3
*Angola	10.9	24.8	74.5	59.8	68.9	47.8
*Benin	5.0	11.1	8.3	14.0	5.6	8.8
Botswana	20.0	11.3	6.5	11.9	31.9	16.3
*Burkina Faso	36.5	51.1	80.9	45.4	57.3	54.2
*Burundi	8.2	11.6	9.0	6.6	11.4	9.4
Cameroon	3.6	10.2	10.5	5.6	1.1	6.2
*Cape Verde	34.1	31.1	53.6	34.8	62.5	43.2
*Central African Republic	3.0	2.6	2.0	4.5	7.6	3.9
*Chad	16.2	14.1	28.6	36.0	73.8	33.7
*Comoros	2.6	2.2	7.9	6.9	5.3	5.0
Congo	4.2	1.7	0.4	8.8	0.7	3.2
*Djibouti	4.9	13.7	11.3	8.4	10.7	9.8
*Egypt	1 758.0	1 865.0	1 956.6	1 816.0	1 782.9	1 835.7
*Equatorial Guinea	0.3	2.1	7.9	11.8	9.8	6.4
*Ethiopia	111.5	227.9	189.7	344.0	179.9	210.6
*Gambia	6.8	16.2	21.0	12.8	16.9	14.7

*Ghana	110.0	94.3	43.1	58.4	73.8	75.9
*Guinea	24.2	33.9	38.6	25.0	42.6	32.9
*Guinea Bissau	17.6	26.2	30.3	34.9	19.4	25.7
*Ivory Coast	2.0	—	0.9	—	—	0.6
*Kenya	86.4	172.9	127.2	164.5	121.8	134.6
*Lesotho	28.6	44.1	34.2	27.5	50.2	36.9
*Liberia	3.2	26.3	42.4	57.4	47.0	35.3
*Madagascar	13.6	26.8	87.1	141.1	74.0	68.5
*Malawi	4.7	16.7	2.0	2.6	3.1	5.8
*Mali	21.8	50.3	66.4	88.1	108.4	67.0
*Mauritania	26.2	106.2	86.4	71.3	128.8	83.8
Mauritius	21.5	20.8	42.5	12.9	21.9	23.9
*Morocco	119.2	120.3	477.5	141.9	452.7	262.3
*Mozambique	151.0	154.6	148.5	167.0	304.8	185.2
*Niger	9.1	10.9	71.4	11.8	12.7	23.2
*Nigeria	—	—	1.4	—	—	0.3
*Rwanda	14.3	14.9	12.6	11.9	25.3	15.8
*Sao Tomé and Principe	1.6	1.5	3.1	1.6	9.4	3.4
*Senegal	60.8	152.6	82.7	91.0	146.3	106.7
Seychelles	2.1	1.3	1.3	0.2	1.5	1.3
*Sierra Leone	36.4	11.7	28.9	29.0	15.9	24.4
*Somalia	136.8	329.9	185.9	188.5	180.5	204.3
*Sudan	212.3	194.5	194.1	330.0	451.6	276.5
Swaziland	0.5	0.9	1.0	3.6	8.4	2.9
*Tanzania	89.3	235.8	307.5	171.4	135.5	187.9
*Togo	7.4	4.2	4.6	6.7	8.8	6.3

Recipient Countries	TOTAL					Average
	1979/80	1980/81	1981/82	1982/83	1983/84	
	(........................ thousand tons, grain equivalent ....)					
Tunisia	164.5	98.7	96.0	153.5	146.0	131.7
*Uganda	16.7	57.0	48.5	14.3	10.4	29.4
*Zaire	69.3	77.0	97.5	109.6	53.1	81.3
*Zambia	166.5	84.5	100.0	83.4	76.1	102.1
Zimbabwe	—	17.7	—	6.4	75.9	20.0
LATIN AMERICA – Total	721.0	583.3	711.9	1 264.4	1 294.7	915.1
Of which: Low-Income, Food Deficit						
Countries	232.9	223.5	297.0	568.7	711.2	406.7
Antigua	—	—	0.1	0.1	0.2	0.1
Barbados	0.4	0.3	0.2	0.4	0.1	0.3
Belize	—	—	—	0.5	—	0.1
*Bolivia	150.2	54.6	44.2	173.9	279.9	140.6
Brazil	3.4	3.0	3.0	—	2.5	2.4
Chile	22.1	21.3	18.3	1.9	20.8	16.9
Colombia	2.8	5.4	2.6	1.2	3.4	3.1
Costa Rica	0.8	0.9	45.2	194.4	38.9	56.0
Cuba	—	—	—	2.1	—	0.4
Dominica	2.2	0.3	0.5	—	0.5	0.7
Dominican Republic	120.3	73.1	57.1	167.1	147.6	113.0
Ecuador	8.2	9.1	8.3	8.1	16.0	9.9
*El Salvador	3.2	49.4	129.1	210.6	262.4	130.9

Grenada	—	1.0	0.2	—	0.2	0.3
Guatemala	9.7	13.9	10.6	19.1	18.8	14.4
Guyana	1.6	4.5	1.3	3.2	0.3	2.2
*Haiti	52.7	83.7	89.9	89.7	71.6	77.5
*Honduras	26.8	35.8	33.8	94.5	97.3	57.6
Jamaica	116.9	37.1	82.8	126.5	52.5	83.2
Martinique	—	—	—	—	1.5	0.3
Mexico	—	—	—	—	1.3	0.3
Nicaragua	69.6	58.3	103.6	56.5	56.2	68.8
Panama	2.0	2.3	3.1	2.8	1.9	2.4
Paraguay	11.4	10.9	1.1	0.5	8.2	6.4
Peru	109.2	116.0	76.2	110.8	211.9	124.8
St. Cristopher and Nevis	—	—	0.1	0.2	0.2	0.1
St. Lucia	0.5	2.2	0.5	0.4	0.5	0.8
St. Vincent	—	0.3	—	—	—	0.1
Uruguay	7.0	—	—	—	—	1.4
ASIA – Total	4 097.6	3 559.7	2 916.9	2 967.5	3 315.3	3 371.4
Of which: Low-Income, Food Deficit Countries	3 670.2	2 618.6	2 378.6	2 742.4	3 227.6	2 927.5
*Afghanistan	175.6	75.0	81.8	66.0	100.0	99.7
*Bangladesh	1 479.5	736.9	1 005.5	1 252.3	1 162.7	1 127.4
*Bhutan	0.8	1.2	1.1	2.5	6.5	2.4
Burma	11.1	7.0	5.0	10.0	6.0	7.8
*China	11.5	37.0	78.4	44.5	209.1	76.1
Cyprus	5.3	5.3	4.4	5.5	2.8	4.7

Recipient Countries	TOTAL					Average
	1979/80	1980/81	1981/82	1982/83	1983/84	
	(........	....	thousand tons, grain equivalent	....	....	........)
*Democratic Kampuchea	187.6	133.0	49.9	45.8	36.7	90.6
East Timor	1.3	—	—	—	—	0.3
Gaza Strip	15.8	24.1	5.9	10.8	6.1	12.5
*India	242.9	435.4	337.6	281.6	371.3	354.0
*Indonesia	831.2	381.7	106.6	155.3	461.3	387.2
Iraq	—	—	—	0.1	—	—
Israel	30.9	9.9	0.2	—	—	8.2
Jordan	72.0	95.4	72.5	39.9	24.3	60.8
Korea, Rep. of	184.3	678.2	429.2	52.9	—	268.9
*Laos	2.9	2.0	1.3	0.4	2.0	1.7
Lebanon	13.4	42.9	9.0	69.2	18.4	30.6
*Maldives	1.0	—	7.0	—	0.6	1.7
*Nepal	21.3	45.2	23.2	43.6	29.2	32.5
*Pakistan	146.3	276.8	347.4	368.6	380.3	303.9
*Philippines	95.1	84.5	54.5	48.6	53.5	67.2
*Sri Lanka	170.2	226.2	202.5	369.0	391.2	271.8
Syria	74.4	43.5	9.3	27.6	17.3	34.4
Thailand	3.2	25.5	2.3	9.2	12.8	10.6
Turkey	15.8	9.1	0.3	—	—	5.0
*Viet Nam	184.1	150.4	43.8	27.2	1.9	81.5
*Yemen, A.R.	6.2	4.2	12.9	27.9	5.4	11.3
*Yemen, P.D.R.	12.9	29.3	25.3	9.2	15.9	18.5

OCEANIA – Total	13.5	7.4	2.8	0.1	2.2	5.2
Of which: Low-Income, Food Deficit Countries	4.0	0.9	2.7	0.1	0.6	1.7
Fiji	9.5	6.5	0.1	—	1.6	3.5
*Kiribati	1.0	0.4	0.5	—	0.6	0.5
*Samoa	1.6	0.5	—	—	—	0.4
*Tonga	1.4	—	2.2	0.1	—	0.7
EUROPE – Total	267.9	259.8	425.9	83.2	42.0	215.8
Malta	1.1	4.5	8.5	—	—	2.8
Poland	—	—	417.4	83.2	42.0	108.5
Portugal	266.8	255.3	—	—	—	104.4
UNSPECIFIED†	124.7	20.1	145.2	247.6	34.3	114.4
WORLD – Total	8 887.0	8 941.6	9 140.2	9 198.0	9 827.2	9 198.8
Total Low-Income, Food Deficit Countries	7 334.0	7 163.7	7 452.1	7 741.0	8 784.2	7 695.0
Total Low-Income, Food Deficit Countries as Percentage of Total	82.5	80.1	81.5	84.2	89.4	83.7

* Recipients indicated by an asterisk are low-income, food deficit countries with per caput income below the level used by the World Bank to determine eligibility for IDA assistance (i.e. US$ 790 and below in 1983) which in accordance with the guidelines and criteria agreed by the CFA should be given priority in the allocation of food aid.

† Refers mainly to cereals channelled through multilateral organisations for which no country-breakdown is available. Includes also minor shipments to some other countries and territories.

Source: FAO Food Aid Bulletin, January, 1985.

Appendix 4. Cereals Equivalents under 1986 Food Aid Convention (figures in tonnes)

Product	Net weight of cereal	Base figure	Yield
Common wheat	1000	1000	1000
Durum (hard) wheat	1000	1000	1000
Maize (corn)	1000	1000	1000
Sorghum	1000	1000	1000
Common wheat flour	1370	1000	730
Maize (corn) flour	1695	1000	590
Maize (corn) meal (grits)	1923	1000	520
Rolled oats (oat flakes)	1724	1000	580
Spaghetti*	2000	1000	500
White rice (milled)	2900	1000	345
Broken rice	2000	1000	2000

* Including macaroni and other pasta, made from durum wheat and having an ash content (by weight) referred to dry matter of 0.95% or less. Other equivalents apply for other qualities.

Appendix 5. Disbursements of food aid by DAC member countries in $US million[1]

	1971	1972	1973	1974	1975	1976	1977	1978	1979	1980	1981	1982
Australia	12.5	18.5	19.6	75.2	61.0	35.8	24.2	40.6	80.5	64.0	102.7	101.0
Austria	0.8	0.8	0.9	0.3	1.1	1.1	1.9	4.3	2.9	2.6	11.0	8.0
Belgium	2.8	11.2	15.9	36.4	28.7	18.5	23.4	28.0	33.9	39.3	44.8	39.0
Canada	88.5	87.8	96.4	139.2	263.3	189.3	184.9	224.9	156.5	164.8	162.7	214.0
Denmark	7.3	8.0	13.9	21.0	19.9	22.5	28.6	25.7	33.8	45.0	37.8	31.0
Finland	—	0.8	2.8	4.5	7.8	10.0	7.5	1.1	5.6	4.2	6.7	8.0
France	13.8	32.6	67.4	105.2	83.7	50.2	51.8	78.8	84.2	122.8	168.1	136.0
Germany	17.3	44.5	91.9	144.4	131.4	90.6	132.2	163.9	171.9	213.7	275.5	233.0
Italy	8.9	20.1	29.3	47.6	45.1	20.0	45.6	49.8	47.2	75.8	143.6	119.0
Japan	134.2	34.2	105.8	74.0	15.3	8.1	15.1	21.8	113.0	261.3	346.2	140.0
Netherlands	9.3	20.3	33.0	47.8	44.6	45.2	64.8	118.7	85.7	103.2	107.1	80.0
New Zealand	—	0.9	1.2	1.6	6.0	2.7	1.3	0.5	0.1	0.9	[2]	1.0
Norway	4.1	2.5	3.7	7.8	7.6	14.0	19.5	18.6	18.5	22.3	23.5	28.0
Sweden	5.6	6.5	11.2	35.2	75.4	31.9	38.6	49.5	45.3	47.2	22.5	36.0
Switzerland	4.1	7.9	8.5	10.0	12.5	13.7	16.6	23.1	25.1	27.9	22.3	23.0
United Kingdom	17.5	2.7	12.5	43.8	60.2	33.3	46.7	80.6	85.2	116.7	178.1	154.0
United States	805.0	978.0	618.0	728.0	1 266.0	1 210.0	1 210.0	1 118.0	1 302.0	1 307.0	1 262.0	1 000.0
Total DAC Countries	1 131.7	1 277.1	1 132.2	1 521.6	2 129.6	1 796.9	1 912.7	2 048.0	2 291.5	2 618.6	2 934.7	2 351.0

Source: Compiled from data provided by OECD.
[1] Includes contributions by EEC countries channelled through the EEC, but not actual amounts disbursed by the EEC.
[2] New Zealand supplied 440 tons of dried skim milk in 1981, the value of which was not reflected in the data provided by OECD.

Appendix 6. International Emergency Food Reserve 1984 and 1985 – Position as of 22 November 1985

Commodity/Donor	Channelled through UN/FAO WFP			Bilateral	Total contributions
	Sub-Total	Donated specifically for:			
		African emergency	Afghan refugees		
				tons	
YEAR 1984 Cereals[1]	546 751	120 088	170 000	73 640	620 391
Non cereals	43 129	1 605	7 157	1 700	44 829
YEAR 1985 Cereals[1]	688 123	207 786	160 000	77 464	765 587
Australia	—	—	—	50 000	50 000
Austria	5 000	—	—	—	5 000
Belgium	5 000	—	—	—	5 000
Burma	—	—	—	500	500
Canada	72 738	45 298	—	—	72 738
Denmark	27 171	20 000	—	5 000	32 171
EEC	40 000	—	—	—	40 000
Egypt	50	50	—	—	50
France	23 000	7 000	10 000	4 000	27 000
Germany, Fed. R.	38 638	18 638	—	—	38 638
India	100 000	100 000	—	—	100 000
Italy	21 992	—	—	—	21 992
Japan	2 000	2 000	—	4 464	6 464

Mauritius	4	—	—	—	4
Netherlands	8 250	—	—	—	8 250
New Zealand	472	—	—	—	472
Norway	9 740	—	—	—	9 740
Spain	6 500	6 500	—	3 500	10 000
Sweden	35 000	—	—	10 000	45 000
Switzerland	22 702	—	—	—	22 702
United Kingdom	20 000	—	—	—	20 000
United States	249 866	8 300	150 000	—	249 866
Pulses	4 391	1 772	—	—	4 391
Canada	603	—	—	—	603
Denmark	960	—	—	—	960
Germany, Fed. R.	1 772	1 772	—	—	1 772
Greece	258	—	—	—	258
Iceland	24	—	—	—	24
Lesotho	11	—	—	—	11
Malta	3	—	—	—	3
Norway	90	—	—	—	90
Togo	1	—	—	—	1
United States	669	—	—	—	669
Vegetable oils/Edible fat	21 699	2 700	1 598	800	22 499
Canada	484	—	—	—	484
EEC	2 000	—	—	—	2 000
Finland	1 527	—	—	—	1 527
Norway	1 668	—	1 598	—	1 668
Sweden	2 500	—	—	—	2 500

Commodity/Donor	Channelled through UN/FAO WFP			Bilateral	Total contributions
	Sub-Total	Donated specifically for:			
		African emergency	Afghan refugees		
	(............................. tons ....)				
YEAR 1984 Cereals[1]	546 751	120 088	170 000	73 640	620 391
Non cereals	43 129	1 605	7 157	1 700	44 829
United States	13 520	2 700	—	800	14 320
Dried skim milk/Dried whole milk	8 456	225	1 800	42	8 498
Canada	488	—	—	—	488
Finland	200	—	—	—	200
Switzerland	375	225	—	42	417
United States	7 393	—	1 800	—	7 393
Wheat soy milk/Corn soy milk	20 060	9 000	—	—	20 060
United States	20 060	9 000	—	—	20 060
Comp. F. Biscuits	216	166	—	—	216
Switzerland	216	166	—	—	216
Tea	—	—	—	20	20
Sri Lanka	—	—	—	20	20
Sugar	500	—	—	—	500
EEC	500	—	—	—	500
Total non cereals	55 322	13 863	3 398	862	56 184

Source: Compiled from WFP records.
[1] Includes wheat, coarse grains and rice.
Food Outlook, December 1985.

Select Bibliography

Adams, J. M., and Shulter, G. G. M., 'Losses Caused by Insects and Micro-organisms' in Harris, K. L., and Lindblad, C. J., (eds), *Post-harvest Grain Loss Assessment Methods* 1978

Africa Bureau, Cologne/IDS, *An Evaluation of the EEC Food Aid Programme* (Brighton)

Agricultural Development Council, 1979, 'Implementation of United States Food Aid—Title III', 'Seminar Report No. 20, August (New York)

Agricultural Development Council, 1981, *Food Aid and Development*, Report to conference, Colombo, 18–20 August 1980 (New York)

Basu, K., 1981, 'Food for Work Programmes: Beyond Roads that get Washed Away', *Economic and Political Weekly*, vol. 16(1), January

Berridge, G., and Jennings, A., (eds), 1985, *Diplomacy at the UN* (London)

Bryson, J. *et al.*, 1984, *Assessment/Redesign of the CRS PL 480 Title II Programme in Indonesia*, International Science and Technology Institute (Washington)

Canadian International Development Agency, 1984, *A Review of CIDA's Counterpart Fund Policy and Practice*, executive summary and approved policy decisions (Ottawa)

Christensen, C. and E. Hogan, 1982, 'Food Aid as an Instrument of Development: A Seminar Report', *The Developmental Effectiveness of Food Aid in Africa*, Agricultural Development Council (New York)

CIDA, 1983, *Evaluation Assessment of the Canadian Food Aid Programme*, pp. 16–17

Clay, E., *Review of Food Aid Policy Changes since 1978*, World Food Programme, Occasional Paper No. 1

Clay, E. J., 1982, 'Food Aid and Food Security in Sub-Saharan Africa', *The Developmental Effectiveness of Food Aid in Africa*, Agricultural Development Council (New York)

Clay, E. J., and Mitchell, M., 1983. Is European Community Food Aid in Dairy Products Cost Effective? *European Review of Agricultural Economics*, vol. 10

Clay, E. J., and J. Pryer, 1982, 'Food Aid: Issues and Policies', *Discussion Paper* No. 183, IDS, University of Sussex (Brighton)

Clay E. J. and Shaw J. (eds), 1987, *Poverty, Food and Development*, Festschrift for Hans Singer (London)

Clay E. J., and H. W. Singer, 1982, *Food Aid and Development: The Impact and Effectiveness of Bilateral PL 480 Title I Type Assistance* IDS, University of Sussex (Brighton)

Clay, E. J., and Singer, H. W., 1985, *Food Aid and Development: Issues and Evidence*, World Food Programme, Occasional Paper No. 3

Committee on Famine in Africa, *Second Report*, House of Commons Paper, 56, 1985 (HMSO)

Dawson, A., 1981, *Promoting Success in WFP-Aided Projects*, paper for WFP Field Officers' Seminar, December (New Delhi)

Development Assistance Committee, OECD, 1985, *Aid Agency Co-operation with Non-Governmental Organizations* (Paris)

Ending Hunger, 1986, World Hunger Project

European Communities Commission, 1983, *Food Aid for Development*, Commission communication to the Council, COM(83)141 final, 6 April (Brussels)

Ezekiel, M., 1985, 'Issues of Agricultural Surpluses to Finance Economic Development in Underdeveloped Countries: A Pilot Study in India', in *FAO: Food for Development* (Rome)

FAO, 1952, *Report of Working Party on Emergency Famine Reserve*, Council Document 16/14 (Rome)

Food Aid Convention, 1967 Cmnd. 3840 (London)

Food and Agricultural Organization, 1984, *Food and Nutrition*, vol. 10, no. 1, pp. 91 ff. (Rome)

Fryer, J., 1981, *Food for Thought: The Use and Abuse of Food Aid in the Fight Against World Hunger*, report prepared for the World Council of Churches, June

Geldof, Bob, 1986, *Is That It?* (London)

Government of Canada, 1981, *Official Development Assistance Strategic Overview* (Ottawa)

Group of 30, 1986, *Counter Trade in the World Economy* (New York)

Hathaway, D., 1981, '*Food Issues in North/South Relations*', World Economy, vol. 3(4), January (Amsterdam)

Hopkins, R., 1986, 'Food Aid and Development: The Evolution of the Food Aid Regime', in *WFP/Government of the Netherlands Seminar on Food Aid* (The Hague)

Huddleston, B., 1983, 'The Case for Increasing Food Aid: How much and to Whom?' *IDS Bulletin*, vol. 14(2), University of Sussex (Brighton)

Isenman, P. J., and Singer, H. W., 1977, 'Food Aid: Disincentive Effects and their Policy Implications', *Economic Development and Cultural Change*, vol. 25, no. 2, January

Jackson, T., and Eade, D., 1982, *Against the Grain: The Dilema of Project Food Aid*, (Oxford)

Jolly, R., and Cornia, G. A., (eds), 1984, *The Impact of World Recession on Children: A Study prepared for Unicef* (Oxford)

Lappe, F. M., and Collins, J., 1977, *Food First: Beyond the Myth of Scarcity*, p. 328 (Boston)

Lipton, M., 'Post-harvest Technology and the Reduction of Hunger', *IDS Bulletin*, vol. 13, no. 3 (Brighton)

Matzke, O., 1984, 'Food Aid: Pros and Cons', *Aussenpolitik*, vol. 35(1) (Hamburg)

Maxwell, S. J., 1978, 'Food Aid, Food for Work and Public Works', *IDS Discussion Paper* No. 127, IDS, University of Sussex, (Brighton)

Maxwell, S. J. and Singer, H. W. 1979, 'Food Aid to Developing Countries: A Survey', *World Development*, vol. 7, pp. 225–47

Meier, G. M., and Seers, D., (eds), 1984, *Pioneers in Development* (New York and Oxford)

Minear, L., 1985, 'The Role of NGOs in Development', in Clay E. J. and Shaw J. (eds) *Poverty, Development and Food*, Festschrift for Hans Singer (London, 1987)

Morgan, J. O., 'Problems with Food Distribution Programs: A Case in Point', *World Neighbours*

New York Times, 30 January 1979

OECD, 1984, *Development Co-operation*, Review 1, p. 22

Potter, G. A., 1979, *PL 480 Foreign Assistance Food Aid: Dependency or Development?*, Testimony to the House Subcommittee on Foreign Operations, 4 April (Washington DC)

Pym, F., 1983, *Speech to the Royal Commonwealth Society on Britain's Contribution to Development*, December

Reuters Glossary of International Economic and Financial Terms, 1982 (London)

Reutlinger, S., 1983, *Project Aid and Equitable Growth: Income Transfer Efficiency First*, WFP/Government of the Netherlands Seminar on Food Aid (The Hague)

Reutlinger, S. and Pelckson, J. van Holst, 1986, *Poverty and Hunger: Issues and Options for Food Security in Developing Countries*, World Bank Policy Study

Sahn, D. E., 1984, *Methods for Evaluating the Nutritional Impact of Food Aid Projects: Lessons Learned from Past Experience*, paper for the UN ACC Subcommittee on Nutrition, Doc. No. SCN 84/6D

Schultz, T. W., 1980, 'Effects of the International Donor Community on Farm People', *American Journal of Agricultural Economics*, vol. 62(5), December, pp. 873–8

Schwarz, W., 1984, 'Where Aid Produces no Relief', *The Guardian*, 26 September

Scott, M., 1980, *Aid to Bangladesh: For Better or Worse?* (Boston)

Sen, A. K., 1981, *Poverty and Famines: An Essay on Entitlement and Deprivation* (Oxford)

Sen, A. K., 1983, *Food Entitlement and Food Aid Programmes*, in WFP/ Government of the Netherlands Seminar on Food Aid (The Hague)

Shaw, D. J., 1983, 'Triangular Transactions in Food Aid: Concept and Practice—the Example of the Zimbabwe Operations', *IDS Bulletin*, vol. 14(2), IDS, University of Sussex (Brighton)

Smith, C. W., 1975, *The Great Hunger* (London)

Singer, H. W., 1978, *Food Aid Policies and Programmes: A Survey of Studies of Food Aid*, WFP/CFA 5/5–C, FAO (Rome)

Strange, Susan, 1986, 'Protectionism—Why Not?', in *The World Today*, August/September, vol. 41, nos. 8–9

UN ECOSOC, 1952, *Food and Famine: Procedures for International Action in the Event of Emergency Famines from Natural Causes*, Document E/2220, 14 May (New York)

Vengroff, R., 1982, 'Food Aid Dependency: PL 480 to Black Africa', *Journal of Modern African Studies*, vol. 20(1), March, pp. 27–44

Weiss, T. G., and Jordan, R. S., 1976, *The World Food Conference and Global Problem Solving* (New York)

WFP/CPA 15/5, 1983, *Review of Food Aid Policies and Programmes*, World Food Programme, April (Rome)

WFP/CPA 15/8, 1983, *Sales of Grain to Help Meet the Internal Costs in Least Developed Countries*, World Food Programme (Rome)

Whitaker, B., 1983, *A Bridge of People. A Personal View of Oxfam's First Forty Years*, p. 17

Wightman, D., 1968, *Food Aid and Economic Development* (New York)

Wood, J. B., 1982, 'Uncharted Territory between Relief and Development: A Comment on the Somalia emergencies', *Studies in Humanities and Natural Sciences*, vol. 4 (Hamburg)

Wood, J. B., 1984, 'Openendedness', paper produced for the World Food Programme, IDS, University of Sussex (Brighton)

INDEX